D0349677

THE BOOK OF BOYS' NAMES

Uniform with this volume

THE BOOK OF
GIRLS' NAMES

THE BOOK OF BOYS' NAMES

by

LINWOOD SLEIGH

and

CHARLES JOHNSON

THOMAS Y. CROWELL COMPANY

NEW YORK · ESTABLISHED 1834

Printed in Great Britain

Library of Congress Catalog Card No. 63-8047

How to use this Book

The first part of this book, after the Introduction and Calendar of Saints, is devoted to the boys' names principally used in English-speaking countries. Their origins and meanings are fully given, together with many intriguing facts that have affected their popularity in different periods.

The Main Index, containing over 1700 names, is an index to this first part; you will find listed there all the main names and the varying forms they have taken.

The Supplementary List contains 1150 more names—the rarer, the fanciful, the recent—with an indication of their sources and meanings.

Thus by using both lists you have a choice of 2850 boys' names. Whatever is not in one list should be in the other. Remember, though, that new variants of old names and newly invented names are appearing every day. Omissions are inevitable, but we believe these lists are as comprehensive as any such lists can be at any given moment.

Each name, with its related details, is like a small piece of jigsaw, but the introduction gives you the complete picture which emerges when all these names are surveyed together. The interlocking elements of history, fashion, law, and language then become visible. When you have seen your name in close-up, as it were, read the Introduction, for this shows you it in perspective.

CONTENTS

INTRODUCTION

THE name most used in English-speaking countries is John. There are millions of Johns in the world to-day, thousands of them known as Jack. If every reader of this page stopped for a moment to recall every John and Jack he has heard or read about, the combined total would add up to three or four figures—perhaps even more.

Then there are the foreign forms: the French Jean, the German Johann and Hans, the Spanish Juan, the Italian Giovanni. In Europe alone there are over eighty ways of spelling or pronouncing this single name. John and Jack look different enough; the Swiss Hasli to us is unrecognizable. How, then, do we know that they are the same name at all?

We know because every one of these versions, however much it differs from the rest, is a member of an ancient family, spreading across the world and through the centuries, from one single ancestor: the name given to some long-forgotten baby in Palestine. For though the first historic John was the one we know as John the Baptist, countless other bearers lived and died before him unrecorded. And as names were given thousands of years before writing was invented, and spelling has only become standardized in Europe during the past three hundred years or so, it is not surprising that nearly every name has more than one form.

Every name has a meaning, or once had a meaning that is now forgotten. A name is more than a label or a mere arrangement of sounds and letters. Bound up with each there is history, legend, fact and fancy, poetry and prose; even geography and grammar. This book delves into the treasure hoard.

Some names have been given far more space than others. The commoner a name is the more there is to be known about it. A name that is thought of as 'ordinary' has only become so because of its distinguished bearers. Readers who are interested in less common names will realize that these, just because they are uncommon, lend themselves less to discussion; but their very uncommonness is itself a distinction.

The chief reason for the giving of names is to distinguish their bearers from one another. There is a gentleman in Lewis Carroll's *Hunting of the Snark* who had wholly forgotten his name:

> He would answer to "Hi!" or to any loud cry,
> Such as "Fry me!" or "Fritter my wig!"
>
> While for those who preferred a more forcible word,
> He had different names from these;
> His intimate friends called him "Candle-ends,"
> And his enemies "Toasted-cheese."

While the last four methods of calling him may have been effective, "Hi!" can hardly have proved satisfactory in a crowd. But such nicknames as "Fatty" or "Chimp" are often excellent descriptions. Some of the most ancient names were similarly derived from personal appearance. Edom in Hebrew, Rufus in Latin, Roy in Gaelic, all mean 'red.' The Celts of Great Britain and Ireland appear to have been particularly fond of such names. The Israelites, on the whole, at least in early times, preferred those that indicated the parents' feelings at the time of the birth of their child: Isaac means 'laughter,' Jabez 'sorrow.' The Greeks as a rule chose 'lucky' names, containing such notions as 'glory' ('cle-'), 'lover of' ('phil-'), or 'best' ('aristo-'). Latin names were generally simple. Though, like the Celts, the Romans often used descriptive names, they did not trouble to confine themselves to those with pleasing associations; Caius, it is true, may mean 'gay'; but Plautus, meaning 'flat-foot,' and Ravilius, 'bleary-eyed,' are hardly inspiring, and unlikely to be used to-day.

Anglo-Saxon and Viking names, practically all of which go back to the time when the ancestors of the English, Dutch, Germans, and Scandinavians were a single group of tribes, generally have a special characteristic: each is made up from two 'elements.' It looks as though the forefathers of the Germanic peoples—to use a common term—hit on the idea of compiling a list of words (a *word-hoard*, as they would have called it), each item of which had a general feeling of luck, strength, or power about it; they would combine these in couples, and so produce an almost infinite variety.

Presumably such double-word names had at first a grammatical meaning; Bernard, which is 'bear-strength,' gives an example. But as the population increased any pair might be used together to make up a new name. William, for instance, a combination of 'will' and 'helmet,' makes little sense to us. Anyone with a two-part name, like Egbert—'sword-bright'—is free to interpret the two parts just as he wishes: 'bright sword,' 'sword-brightness,' 'bright as a sword,' and so on.

In many languages names were taken from objects—precious possessions, birds, and animals—things which were noted for certain real or imaginary characteristics; in most cases they were the symbols, even the earthly forms, of gods. The raven was the bird of Odin, the 'All-father' and sky god of the Scandinavians; the bear, largest and most intelligent of northern wild beasts, was looked upon as a semi-divine creature in itself, as it was among the Red Indians. Objects such as the spear, the helmet, and the cauldron were associated with gods and heroes in the ancient myths.

Divine beings form parts of names in several languages. Denys is derived from the wine-god Dionysus; Thurstan is 'stone of Thor,' the Norse thunder-god; the Phoenician divine-name Baal occurs in the last syllable of Hannibal. The majority, perhaps, of the names we inherit from the Bible contain the syllable 'iah,' 'ias,' 'jo,' or 'je,' all standing for Jehovah ('the Lord'), or the syllable 'el' that means 'god' in a general sense.

Just as in pre-Christian times divine-names were taken, so among Christians saints' names were used; like the gods before them, the saints were looked upon not only as earthly models for their namesakes, but as heavenly protectors. Gregory the Great insisted that saints' names only should be taken at baptism; even to-day a clergyman is entitled to refuse to christen a child under a name he considers unsuitable; in this he is luckier than the Civil Registrar, who must record any name the parents insist upon. Not long ago a father called his son Cheyenne after a Red Indian tribe he had met with in a Western—for a bet! And it was duly registered; so, once, was Mogador. It is unlikely that many rejoice in either of these names, but should any bearers become famous it may spread, as Winston has since 1940. Most European countries do not allow such freedom, but restrict parents to choosing from an approved list.

The Church's insistence on limiting names to saints' names greatly restricted the possible choices. A popular name (such as Thomas became after St Thomas à Becket's martyrdom) would be given to so large a number of children that it was soon scarcely more useful than "Hi!" If a villager called out "Tom!" twenty or thirty boys might answer. This led to the adoption of surnames, by which the many bearers of one Christian name could be distinguished from one another.

The second consequence of using saints' names was the introduction of names from other countries and other ages. A saint may have been Jewish, Greek, or Roman, and lived as early as the time of Christ; he may have been French, German, or Spanish, but once he had been canonized (that is, listed in the official catalogue of saints) his name had the approval of the Church; the effect of this was to make many names international. The Calendar of Saints included in this book shows both the frequent use of certain names and their international character. It also suggests suitable dates for celebrations when a birthday falls on a date unsuitable for a party: in France the saint's name-day, or *fête*, is kept with more festivity than the anniversary of birth.

After the Reformation non-biblical saints' names became unpopular among Protestants; but the custom of giving religious names led to the giving of Old Testament names instead, particularly among Puritans. It was they who made so many Hebrew names popular in America, where to-day they are still in use—more so than in England.

The adoption of surnames not only preserved old forms of Christian names (Hodges, for instance, comes from an old pet form of Roger) but also provided an almost infinite store of new personal names. The practice of using surnames as Christian names generally began with a child's receiving his mother's maiden name, or the name of some related family. As a rule surnames were given as a *second* personal name; but after a few generations the family name began to sound normal, and would become a first name, which would be used by admirers of some famous bearer, and so spread everywhere. We find the English Midland place-name Dudley becoming a surname, and ultimately the personal name of the Ceylon statesman Dudley Senanayaka.

Among the famous characters from past and present history mentioned in this book will be found a number of characters from fiction. The great figures of literature are to most people as real as historical characters. Londoners have often been asked by visitors to show the way to Sherlock Holmes's apartments in Baker Street; children have written to boys in the Billy Bunter stories asking for a reply, even suggesting a meeting. Literature is also a guide to fashion. The writer in search of a name for one of his creations must choose one appropriate to the period of his story.

But the bulk of the characters given as examples of the use of a name have really existed, and have been selected from a wide variety of types and callings. There is a tendency to imagine that a particular name must always be associated with a particular sort of character. But this is not so; no Desmond need be dismal; every name has had a surprisingly varied range of bearers.

One disadvantage of personal names is that they have been chosen not by, but for, their bearers, generally even before they were born. It may often happen that when the child has grown and developed a character of his own his name may seem, particularly to himself, woefully inappropriate. But its history and its significance will often reconcile him to his lot; for when its meaning and importance are known every Tom, Dick, and Harry—every man Jack, in fact—should be convinced that his name is not one to be uttered in a shamefaced whisper, but proudly proclaimed to all the world.

In every name there is much food for reflection, and the compilers hope that each reader, when he has read all that concerns himself in these pages, will be found, like T. S. Eliot's cat,

> . . . Absorbed in the rapt contemplation
> of the thought, of the thought, of the thought of his name:
> His ineffable, effable,
> Effanineffable,
> Deep and inscrutable, singular name.

B.L.S.
C.B.J.

ACKNOWLEDGMENTS

THE authors are indebted to Mr Trefor Rendall Davies for his valuable help with the Welsh names in this book; to Dr Tomás de Bhaldraithe for useful advice on Irish names; to the Rev. Paul Browne, O.S.B., for checking the derivations of Hebrew names; and to the High Commissioners for Australia, Canada, and New Zealand for regional information.

CALENDAR OF SAINTS

As the introduction to this book explains, the names of saints are among the most popular in past and present use. Though their use was generally discouraged in England at the Reformation, many were too familiar to be abandoned and remain popular to-day. John, Andrew, Peter, Antony, and Christopher are a few examples.

Each saint is particularly commemorated on a certain day: as a rule the day of his death, regarded as his 'heavenly birthday.' Some are associated with more than one day: John the Baptist's birth and beheading were given each a separate date for celebration. Sometimes, to avoid a 'clash,' the day varied in different places where a popular local saint displaced one less popular. The transfer of a saint's remains to a new shrine (his 'translation') also gave rise to a new feast-day, And feast-days were originally real days of feasting: the early Christians used to hold banquets round the tombs of the martyrs, after fasting on the 'vigil' or 'eve.' And to-day, if it happens that a birthday falls on an inconvenient date, the feast of a saintly namesake may provide a more suitable occasion for enjoyment.

Hence it will be found that such popular names as John occur on several dates in the Calendar that follows. Yet even so, not every saint of this name has been included. For reasons of space not more than three are noted for each day, but as far as possible every name with a saintly bearer has been given once. Some of the saints with more familiar names have therefore been omitted to allow others to take their place; but none of the more important have been left out. Where several have the same name, the better-known have been given their special titles, such as 'Apostle' or 'à Becket.' In certain cases a name is followed by another version in brackets, such as Evertius, which is our Everard.

The Calendar names have been chosen from three sources. Butler's *Lives of the Saints*, though published in 1756, has been recently revised and is the most reliable; it gives a short biography of each saint, and may be found in any public library. The names taken from it have no letters in brackets after them in our list. Butler was a Roman Catholic, but the Reverend Sabine Baring-Gould was a clergyman of the Church of England. His *Lives of the Saints* (1897) contains acccounts of many British saints not found in Butler's book, and has a special appendix of these: he also lists Old Testament Prophets. Names taken from his fifteen volumes have the letters *BG* after them. But though his list is larger than Butler's, it is not so up to date or so easy to lay hands on, except in the larger libraries. The letters *BCP* after a name show that it occurs in the Calendar of the Book of Common Prayer. There are comparatively few of these, because the Reformers wished to cut down the number of feast-days, considering that they interfered too much with time needed for work, and so encouraged idleness. After all, if every saint's day were a holiday no work could be done at all!

Two names have been printed in square brackets. "King Charles the Martyr" is Charles I. He was regarded as a saint by his partisans, and two or three English churches are dedicated to him. Alfred the Great, though never universally accepted as a saint, has been noted on October 26, because there is no canonized (officially listed) saint of his name, and because he is given this day in the Calendar of the unofficial 'revised' Prayer Book (the "Deposited Book"), published in 1928 but never officially authorized; and, lastly, because if any man has earned saintly commemoration it is "England's darling."

JANUARY

1. William; Clair; Felix
2. Caspar (Jasper); Isidore; Maximus *BG*
3. Peter; Florence; Primus *BG*
4. Roger; Gregory; Titus *BG*
5. Edward *BG*; Simeon
6. Melchior *BG*; Peter *BG*
7. Canute *BG*; Cedd *BG*; Valentine
8. Baldwin *BG*; Lucian *BCP*; Laurence *BG*
9. Adrian; Julian
10. John; William; Peter
11. Egwin *BG*; Balthasar *BG*
12. Benet Biscop; Victorian; John *BG*
13. Mungo *BG*; Hilary *BCP*; Godfrey
14. Felix; Roger; Antony
15. Paul; Maurus; Alexander
16. Henry; James; Marcellus *BG*
17. Antony; Julian; Sabine *BG*
18. Peter Apostle; Paul
19. Wulfstan; Albert; Marius
20. Sebastian; Fabian *BCP*; Benedict *BG*
21. Patroclus
22. Walter; Vincent *BCP*; Dominic
23. Raymond; Clement; Bernard
24. Timothy; Cadoc *BG*
25. Artemas; Paul Apostle *BCP*; Henry *BG*
26. Alberic (Aubrey); Conan; Xenophon
27. Theodoric (Derek); John Chrysostom; Julian
28. Cyril *BG*; Peter Nolasco; Charlemagne
29. Francis of Sales; Gildas; Valerius
30. Felix; Sebastian; ["King Charles the Martyr"]
31. Madoc; John Bosco; Cyrus *BG*

FEBRUARY

1. Ignatius (Inigo); John; Raymond
2. Cornelius; Laurence *BG*; Peter
3. Blaise *BCP*; Laurence; Meirion *BG*
4. Andrew; Theophilus; Abraham
5. Bertulf *BG*; Ronan *BG*
6. Titus; Amand; Sylvanus *BG*
7. Richard; Theodore; Moses
8. Cuthman; Stephen; Paul
9. Teilo; Cyril; Victor *BG*
10. Arnold *BG*; William; Zeno
11. Paschal; Martin *BG*; Lucius
12. Ethelwold; Julian; Antony
13. Martian; Stephen; Castor
14. Valentine *BCP*; Adolf; Bruno *BG*
15. Barry *BG*; Jordan; Siegfried
16. Samuel *BG*; Elias; Jeremy
17. Donat *BG*; Julian
18. Flavian; Simeon; Colman
19. Conrad; Boniface
20. Wulfric; Leo *BG*
21. George; Zachary; Maurice *BG*
22. Peter; Maximian; Allen *BG* (Elwyn)
23. Boswell (Boisil); Jermyn *BG*; Peter
24. Matthias *BCP*; Ethelbert *BG*; Lucius
25. Ethelbert; Victor; Felix *BG*
26. Alexander; Victor; Nestor *BG*
27. Leander; Gabriel; John
28. Oswald; Romanus; Hilary

MARCH

1. David; Albin *BG*; Siward *BG*
2. Chad; Basil *BG*; Paul *BG*
3. Aelred; Felix *BG*; Florian *BG*
4. Adrian; Casimir; Owen *BG*
5. Peter; Keverne; John-Joseph
6. Cyril; Victor; Marcian *BG*
7. Thomas Aquinas; Paul
8. Humphrey; Felix; Stephen
9. Cyril *BG*; Dominic; Gregory
10. Alexander *BG*; Denys *BG*; Cyprian *BG*
11. Angus; Constantine; Vincent *BG*
12. Maximilian; Alphege; Gregory the Great *BCP*
13. Roderick; Gerald; Solomon
14. Eustace; Boniface; Lubin
15. Zachary; Nicander *BG*; Clement
16. Herbert; Julian; Abraham
17. Patrick; Joseph of Arimathea; Paul
18. Edward the Martyr; Cyril; Alexander
19. Joseph of Nazareth; Quintus *BG*; Adrian *BG*
20. Cuthbert; Martin; Herbert
21. Benedict; Elias *BG*
22. Nicholas; Basil; Paul
23. Joseph; Alphonso; Ethelwald
24. Gabriel the Archangel; Mark *BG*; Timothy *BG*
25. Humbert *BG*; Richard *BG*; William *BG*
26. Basil; Felix
27. Rupert; Matthew; William
28. John; Alexander *BG*
29. Jonas; Mark; Cyril
30. Secundus *BG*; John; Regulus
31. Benjamin; Guy; Daniel *BG*

APRIL

1. Gilbert; Hugh; Victor *BG*
2. Francis
3. Richard *BCP*; Pancras; Joseph *BG*
4. Ambrose *BCP*; George; Isidore
5. Gerald; Albert; Vincent
6. Elstan *BG*; William; Sixtus
7. Llewellyn *BG*; George
8. Walter; Denys
9. Hugh; Marcel *BG*
10. Terence *BG*; Michael
11. Isaac; Leo the Great; Philip
12. Julius; Constantine; Guthlac
13. Martius; Caradoc *BG*
14. Caradoc; Justin; Lambert
15. Sylvester; Padarn
16. Magnus; Drogo; Benedict-Joseph
17. Stephen Harding; Robert
18.
19. Alphege *BCP*; Leo; Gerold
20. Caedwalla; Victor *BG*; Theodore *BG*
21. Conrad; Beuno; Anselm
22. Theodore; Alexander; Clement *BG*
23. George *BCP*; Felix; Albert
24. Ives; Egbert; William
25. Mark the Evangelist *BCP*; Ermin
26. Peter; Basil *BG*; Stephen
27. Peter; Stephen
28. Paul; Cyril; Mark *BG*
29. Robert; Wilfrid; Hugh
30. Archibald (Erconwald); James *BG*; Laurence *BG*

MAY

1. Philip the Apostle *BCP*; James the Apostle *BCP*; Asaph
2. Peregrine; German *BG*; Antony *BG*
3. Timothy; Alexander; Philip
4. Cyriac; Florian
5. Hilary; Angelo; Maximus *BG*
6. John the Evangelist *BCP*; Edbert; Lucius *BG*
7. John of Beverley; Stanislaus
8. Michael the Archangel; Victor; Peter
9. Gregory; Andrew *BG*; Goronwy (Gerontius)
10. Job *BG*; Antoninus; Gordian
11. Walter; Francis; Fremund *BG*
12. Dominic; German; Pancras
13. Robert; Peter; Andrew
14. Victor; Boniface; Paschal
15. Rupert; Isidore; Nicholas
16. Brendan; Simon Stock; John
17. Bruno; Paschal; Madern
18. Eric; Felix; Theodotus
19. Dunstan; Ivo; Peter
20. Bernardine; Ethelbert
21. Theobald; Godric; Silas *BG*
22. Peter; Romanus; Marcian *BG*
23. Yvo; John-Baptist; William *BG*
24. Vincent; David of Scotland
25. Denys; Aldhelm; Leo
26. Philip; Lambert; Augustine of Canterbury *BCP*
27. Bede; Julius; Frederick *BG*
28. Augustine of Canterbury; William; Bernard
29. Cyril; Stephen; Raymond
30. Ferdinand; Isaac; Felix
31.

JUNE

1. Inigo; Wystan; Theobald
2. Erasmus; Nicholas; Stephen
3. Claude *BG*; Kevin; Cecilius
4. Walter *BG*; Petroc; Francis
5. Ferdinand *BG*; Boniface *BG*
6. Bertrand; Philip; Claude
7. Meriadec; Paul; Robert
8. William of York; Godard; Maximin
9. Columba; Vincent; Richard
10. Yvo *BG*; Felix *BG*
11. Barnabas Apostle *BCP*; Felix; Fortunatus
12. Humphrey; John; Peter
13. Antony of Padua; Peregrine
14. Basil the Great; Mark *BG*; Elias *BG*
15. Guy (Vitus); Bernard *BG*
16. John-Francis; Aurelian; Berthald
17. Alban *BCP*; Hervé; Adolf
18. Marcus; Felix *BG*; Amand
19. Gervase; Bruno; Odo
20. Edward the Martyr *BCP*; John; Adalbert
21. Ralph; Aloysius; Albin
22. Everard; Alban; Paulinus
23. Jacob *BG*; Zeno *BG*; Joseph
24. John the Baptist *BCP*; Bartholomew of Farne; Ivan *BG*
25. Prosper; Solomon; William
26. John; Paul; David *BG*
27. Ladislas; Sampson; Ferdinand
28. Paul; Leo *BG*; Plutarch
29. Peter the Apostle *BCP*; Paul the Apostle; Cyrus *BG*
30. Paul the Apostle; Bertrand; Theobald *BG*

JULY

1. Thierry (Derek); Simeon; Martin
2. Swithun; Otto
3. Julius; Aaron; German *BG*
4. Ulric; Martin *BCP*; Andrew
5. Antony; Stephen *BG*
6. Gervase *BG*; Isaiah the Prophet *BG*
7. Thomas *BG*; Claudius *BG*; Cyril
8. Edgar *BG*; Adrian; Kilian *BG*
9. John Fisher; Thomas More; Nicholas
10. Canute; Antony; Felix
11. Drostan (Tristram); John
12. Luke *BG*; Andrew *BG*; Jason
13. Eugene; Joel *BG*; Ezra *BG*
14. Cyrus; Silas; Francis
15. Donald; Swithun *BCP*; Henry
16. Helier; Eustace
17. Kenelm; Clement; Alexis
18. Frederick; Arnold *BG*; Bruno
19. Vincent de Paul; Martin *BG*; Ambrose
20. Jerome; Joseph; Elias the Prophet
21. Victor; Claudius *BG*; Daniel the Prophet *BG*
22. Theophilus *BG*; Joseph
23. Caspar (Jasper); Melchior; Balthasar
24. Boris; Francis
25. James the Apostle *BCP*; Christopher
26. Erastus *BG*; Simeon *BG*; Peregrine *BG*
27. Theobald; Hugh *BG*; Laurence
28. Samson; Eustace *BG*; Raymond
29. Olaf (Oliver); William; Felix *BG*
30.
31. German; Peter; Ignatius (Inigo)

AUGUST

1. Kenneth *BG*; Peter the Apostle *BCP*; Ethelwold *BG*
2. Alphonsus; Stephen
3. Walthew *BG*; German; Stephen
4. Dominic; Walthew
5. Abel *BG*; Oswald *BG*
6. Sixtus
7. Albert; Donat *BG*
8. Cyriac
9. Oswald; John; Julian *BG*
10. Laurence *BCP*; Geraint *BG*; Hugh *BG*
11. Gerard; Alexander
12. Murtach (Murdoch)
13. Cassian; Maximus; John *BG*
14. Marcellus
15. Arnolf; Cormac *BG*
16. Joachim; Armel; Theodore *BG*
17. Hyacinth; Paul *BG*
18. Florus; "Little" St Hugh
19. Louis; Timothy; Magnus *BG*
20. Bernard; Ronald *BG*; Samuel the Prophet *BG*
21. Abraham; Julian *BG*
22. Siegfried; Timothy; Andrew
23. Philip; Eugene (Eoghan); Claudius
24. Bartholomew the Apostle *BCP*; Theodore *BG*; Peter *BG*
25. Louis of France; Gregory
26. Secundus; Adrian *BG*; Alexander
27. Joseph; Gerard *BG*; Marcellus
28. Austin *BCP*; Vivian *BG*; Moses
29. John Baptist *BCP*
30. Felix
31. Aidan; Raymond; Paulinus

SEPTEMBER

1. Giles *BCP*; Joshua *BG*; Gideon *BG*
2. Stephen; William; Antonine
3. Simeon; Zeno
4. Cuthbert *BG*; Valerian; Marcellus
5. Laurence; David *BG*; Raymond
6. Zachary *BG*
7. Evertius (Everard) *BCP*; Gilbert *BG*; John
8. Adrian
9. Bertram; Peter; Isaac
10. Nicholas; John
11. Deiniol (Daniel); Hyacinth; Peter
12. Guy
13. Cyprian *BCP*; Philip *BG*; Austin *BG*
14. Cornelius *BG*; Cyprian *BG*; Victor *BG*
15. Albin; Mirin
16. Ninian; Cornelius
17. Lambert *BCP*; Francis of Assisi; Stephen
18. Joseph; Thomas *BG*
19. Constantine; David; John
20. Eustace; Vincent; Theodore
21. Matthew the Apostle *BCP*; Michael; Theodore
22. Thomas; Maurice
23. Adamnan; Constantius *BG*
24. Robert; Gerard
25. Cadoc; Albert; Vincent
26. Noel; René (Renatus); Cyprian *BCP*
27. Cosmas (Cosmo); Adulf *BG*
28. Wenceslas
29. Michael the Archangel *BCP*; Richard; Cyriac
30. Jerome *BCP*; Simon; Gregory

OCTOBER

1. Remi *BCP*; Michael *BG*
2. Thomas of Hereford *BG*; Theophilus *BG*
3. Edmund *BG*; Denys *BG*; Maximian *BG*
4. Francis of Assisi; Peter *BG*; Boniface *BG*
5. Murdach *BG*; Simon *BG*; Placid
6. Bruno; Magnus *BG*; René *BG*
7. Mark; Augustus; Marcellus
8. Hugh *BG*; Simeon; Felix *BG*
9. Cadwallader *BG*; Denys *BCP*; Louis-Bertrand
10. John of Bridlington *BG*; Paulinus; Francis
11. Kenneth (Canice); Alexander; Bruno
12. Edwin; Maximilian; Wilfrid of York
13. Edward the Confessor *BCP*; Maurice; Luke *BG*
14. Dominic; Cosmas *BG*
15. Leonard; Sabine *BG*
16. Silvanus *BG*; Bertrand; Gerard
17. Ethelred *BG*; Ethelbert *BG*; John
18. Luke *BCP*; James *BG*; Justus
19. Peter; Lucius; Maximus *BG*
20. John; Andrew
21. John of Bridlington
22. Philip; Mark *BG*; Alexander *BG*
23. Inigo (Ignatius); John *BG*; Theodore *BG*
24. Martin; Antony; Felix
25. Crispin *BCP*; Crispian (Crispinian); George
26. Aneurin *BG*; Cedd; [Alfred the Great]
27. Vincent *BG*; Lucian *BG*
28. Simon the Apostle *BCP*; Jude the Apostle *BCP*; Ingram *BG*
29. Terence *BG*; Abraham; James *BG*
30. Claude *BG*; Gerard; Marcellus
31. Quentin *BG*; Alphonso *BG*; Urban *BG*

NOVEMBER

1. Harold *BG*; Julian; Marcellus
2. George *BG*; Ambrose *BG*
3. Hubert; Malachy; Valentine *BG*
4. Charles; Clair; Thomas *BG*
5. Zachary; Gerald *BG*; Martin
6. Illtyd; Leonard *BCP*; Felix *BG*
7. Rufus *BG*; Antony *BG*
8. Godfrey; Maurus *BG*; Claude *BG*
9. George *BG*; Alexander *BG*; Theodore
10. Quintin *BG*; Justus; Tertius *BG*
11. Martin *BCP*; Valentine *BG*; Bartholomew
12. Matthew *BG*; Benedict; Martin
13. Stanislas; Nicholas; Eugene
14. Dyfrig (Dubricius); Laurence; Clement
15. Leopold; Albert the Great; Eugene *BG*
16. Edmund; Mark *BG*; Paul *BG*
17. Fergus *BG*; Hugh *BCP*; Denys
18. Odo; Romanus
19. Crispin *BG*; James *BG*; Egbert *BG*
20. Edmund the Martyr *BCP*; Octavius *BG*; Sylvester *BG*
21. Albert; Rufus *BG*; Clement *BG*
22. Philemon; Marcus *BG*; Stephen *BG*
23. Clement *BCP*; Alexander *BG*
24. John; Alexander *BG*; Marinus *BG*
25. Moses; Mercury; Erasmus *BG*
26. Conrad; Leonard; Sylvester
27. Virgil; Fergus; James
28. Philip *BG*; Joseph; James
29. Blaise *BG*; Demetrius; Saturnin
30. Andrew the Apostle *BCP*; Isaac; Tudwal *BG*

DECEMBER

1. Tudwal; Richard; Hugh
2. Victorin *BG*; Peter *BG*; Marcel *BG*
3. Francis Xavier; Jason *BG*; Lucius
4. Osmund; Barnard; Clement *BG*
5. Julius *BG*; John *BG*; Gerald *BG*
6. Nicolas *BCP*; Abraham; Peter-Paschal *BG*
7. Urban *BG*; Ambrose; Martin *BG*
8.
9. Peter; Cyprian *BG*
10. Daniel (Deiniol) *BG*; Gregory
11. Daniel (Deiniol); Sabine *BG*
12. Constant; Alexander
13. Judoc (Jocelyn); Aubert (Aubrey)
14. Fulk *BG*; John *BG*; Justus *BG*
15. Drostan (Tristram) *BG*; Paul; Valerian
16. Valentine *BG*
17. Lazarus; William
18. Quintus *BG*; Rufus; Moses *BG*
19. Darius *BG*; Secundus *BG*; Anastasius (Anstice)
20. Dominic; Eugene *BG*; Zeno *BG*
21. Thomas the Apostle *BCP*
22. Felix *BG*; Zeno *BG*
23. Ivo *BG*; Thorlac
24. Gregory
25. Christmas (Noel); Peter *BG*; Fulk *BG*
26. Stephen *BCP*; Denys
27. John the Evangelist *BCP*; Theodore; Maximus *BG*
28. Antony; Theodore
29. Thomas à Becket; David the King *BG*; Marcellus
30. Egwin; Eugene *BG*; Sabine
31. Sylvester *BCP*; Marius *BG*; John *BG*

ABEL The name of Adam's second son, killed in jealousy by his brother Cain, was in Hebrew *Hebel*, meaning 'breath,' and so 'fleeting.' It was the translators of the Old Testament into its first Greek version, in the third century B.C., who wrote it as Abel. His story may be read in the fourth chapter of Genesis.

Abel, taken as a name by monks in Anglo-Saxon England, was still popular after the Norman Conquest, when it sometimes came to be written *Able*.

In Ben Jonson's play *The Alchemist*, written early in the seventeenth century, Abel Drugger is a tobacconist—the first known to English literature. Drugger is addressed by his friends as *Nab*, showing that the name was common enough to have a pet form; it also explains the origin of the surname Nabbs.

The Puritans took the name with them to the New World, and though never fashionable, it continued in use both in America and in this country. In *Great Expectations* Dickens calls the escaped convict who plays so important a part in the story Abel Magwitch. The leading character in W. H. Hudson's forest romance *Green Mansions*, published in 1904, is a 'Mr' Abel.

Abe and *Abie*, the present-day short forms of Abel, are also used for *Abraham*.

ABRAHAM *Abram*, 'high father,' the original name of the biblical patriarch, was changed to Abraham, 'father of a multitude,' when he left his home in Chaldea to settle in Palestine, for he was to be the ancestor of all the Israelites. It was a frequent custom among the Jews to adopt a new name when some great change occurred in their lives: Simon Bar Jonah, for instance, in the New Testament, became Peter.

Though the syllable 'ab-,' from the Hebrew 'abba,' meaning

'father,' occurs at the beginning of many biblical names, such as *Absalom*, 'father of peace,' and *Abner*, 'father of light,' Abraham's descendants, from respect, avoided the use of his name for many centuries. It seems to have been first revived among Eastern Christians: a fifth-century Syrian hermit of the name was taken prisoner by brigands during a pilgrimage. He escaped, but was shipwrecked on the French coast near Clermont, where he settled, to become revered as St Abraham of Auvergne. The name then spread north, and in the Netherlands reverted to its original form of Abram, and it is still used there, as it is in Wales.

Though it occurs as the name of an eleventh-century Welsh bishop of St Davids and in that treasury of names, Domesday Book, Abraham seems to have been practically confined to Jews until the Reformation, when names of saints came to be replaced by those of characters from the Old Testament. The poet Abraham Cowley, for instance, lived in the seventeenth century. His contemporary, the French admiral Abraham Duquesne, was the only Huguenot whom Louis XIV expressly allowed to remain in France: this was in recognition of his defeating the combined Dutch and Spanish fleets in 1676. In the eighteenth century Abraham Darby, of Coalbrookdale, discovered how to smelt with coke.

But it was in the United States, in more modern times, that the name became most popular, with the shortened form *Abe*, by which the great President Lincoln was affectionately known. Another present-day short form is *Ham*. A less common short form is *Bram*, used by Abraham Stoker, author of *Dracula*, the greatest of Vampire horror stories.

'Abraham's Bosom' is an expression for Heaven; it is used by Jesus in his parable of the rich man and the beggar (Luke, chapter xvi).

'Abraham Men' were inmates of Bedlam, the old London hospital for the insane, who were allowed out to beg for alms: they were quartered in the 'Abraham' ward. Later, sham beggars were given the same general nickname.

It was at the storming of the Heights of Abraham, outside Quebec, so named from their former Scottish owner, Abraham Martin, that General Wolfe met his death, but won Canada for Britain from the French.

ADAM—the first man, according to the book of Genesis—took his name from the 'red earth' of which God formed him.

Never used by the Jews, Adam was taken as a Christian name by the Irish, at least as early as the seventh century A.D., when St *Adamnan*, 'Adam the Little,' was Abbot of Iona; he wrote a classic among biographies, the Life of St Columba, his master.

Adam occurs in Domesday Book. In the thirteenth century, Chaucer gave the name to the scrivener, or notary, in his *Canterbury Tales*. But during the Middle Ages it was most prevalent in the North. The outlaw Adam Bell was a ballad hero of the North Country much resembling Robin Hood, and most surnames derived from the name seem to have originated above the Humber. In the South the surnames Adcock and Atkins suggest that the pet form *Ade*, probably introduced by Flemish wool-dealers, was not uncommon.

Adam continued in use up to the seventeenth century, but seems to have been confined to the humbler classes. Shakespeare, in *As You like It*, gives the name to Orlando's faithful retainer; one of the few small parts the busy dramatist could find time to play himself.

After the Elizabethan age Adam seems to have been neglected until the eighteenth century, when Adam Smith wrote

The Wealth of Nations, a pioneer work on economics. In the nineteenth century lived the horse-loving Australian poet, Adam Lindsay Gordon. *Adam Bede* is the title of George Eliot's story of a young carpenter, largely based on the life of the author's father.

A variation of the name is *Edom*, alternative name of Esau, elder son of Isaac and brother of Jacob. Edom, as well as Adam, was revived by the Scots. The ballad *Edom o' Gordon* shows that this version was used by the Gordon clan; its pet forms were *Edie* and *Yiddie*. *Adda* is a Welsh form, but everywhere to-day Adam is the favourite form, with the diminutive *Ad*.

In Germany Adam was regarded as a name promising a long life, and given particularly to a second son born after the death of his elder brother. It was naturally often used, with Eve, for twins.

The expression 'the old Adam' is used to symbolize the weakness of human nature; Jesus was the 'second Adam,' who restored man to God's favour. Adam's ale is water; the Adam's apple is the protruding end of the thyroid cartilage, so named from the superstition that a piece of the forbidden fruit stuck in the first man's throat. Adam's Peak is a mountain in Ceylon, believed by Moslems to be the spot where the First Man did penance after his banishment from the Garden of Eden, by standing on one foot for a thousand years; the footprint is still visible, some five feet long!

ADRIAN It seems that, at some early date in the history of Rome, an immigrant from the seaport of Adria—which gave its name to the Adriatic Sea—settled in Rome and became known as 'the man from Adria'—in Latin, *Adrianus*. Going back further, we find that Adria means 'black town,' from its black sands: the Latin adjective for coal-black being 'ater.'

The Romans were never too sure of their h's, and the name was also spelt as *Hadrian*, particularly among the Aelian clan, from a branch of which came Publius Aelius *Hadrianus*, the emperor who built the wall across Northern England to keep out the marauding Picts. But the city of Adrianople, also named after him, shows that he was known too by the older and more correct form.

Though there were other Adrians in antiquity, the survival of the name is chiefly due to the soldier-saint Adrian, who was put to death, together with his wife, under the Emperor Galerius in the fourth century. He is represented in Roman military dress, with the anvil beside him on which his limbs were severed.

Adrian came to England as a Christian name in the seventh century with a North African monk, St Adrian, who helped Theodore of Tarsus, Archbishop of Canterbury, in reorganizing the English Church. Another St Adrian was a Bishop of St Andrews put to death by the Danes on the Isle of May, in the Forth Estuary. And it was in the north that the name became most popular, giving the variation *Arrian* and the shortened form *Arne*—which was, incidentally, the surname of the composer of *Rule, Britannia*, the eighteenth-century Dr Thomas Arne.

In the South the name never found much favour, though Nicholas Breakspeare, of St Albans, chose it as his official name on becoming pope in the mid twelfth century—the only Englishman so far to have been elected Supreme Pontiff.

Adrian is most popular in the Low Countries, where the Roman martyr's relics came eventually to lie. The only Dutch pope, elected in the early sixteenth century, was Adrian VI;

a notable Dutch painter of the seventeenth century was *Adriaen* van Ostade. Of Flemish extraction was Sir Adrian Carton de Wiart, the British general who won more awards (V.C., K.B.E., C.B., C.M.G., D.S.O., etc.), survived more serious injuries, and enjoyed more adventures than did any other British officer of modern times, as his autobiography, *Happy Odyssey* (1950), records.

Sir Adrian Boult was among our leading orchestral conductors of recent date. The name is becoming increasingly popular.

ALAN The first recorded bearer of this name was *Alawn*, a legendary British poet of the first century A.D.—appropriately enough, for the name means 'harmony': he was reputed to be one of the "three excellent musicians of Britain." But from early times the name had been spelt in various ways: St *Eilian*, for instance, is the patron saint of Llaneilian, in Anglesey; another saint gave his name to St *Allan*'s church at Powder, in Cornwall. Other forms are *Ailin*, *Alun* and *Alon*.

The Bretons, originally British settlers in France, shared most Welsh names, and when many of them returned in the train of William the Conqueror to the land of their ancestors the old British names came back with them. *Alain* le Roux was one; he was granted the earldom of Richmond, in Yorkshire, and built the castle there. Allan-a-Dale was the minstrel whose betrothed Robin Hood helped to rescue from a curmudgeonly old knight about to marry her by force. In the late fourteenth century Chaucer, in his *Reeve's Tale*, mentions two North Country men:

> One was called John, and Alan was the other;
> Both born in the same village, name of Strother.

But by this time the name had become general all over England.

Alan of Walsingham, for instance, an East Anglian, was the architectural genius who constructed the great octagonal tower of Ely Cathedral. Alan is also found surviving, or revived, in Scotland, where Alan the Royal Steward helped to found the fortunes, and misfortunes, of the Stuart family. The spread of the name was probably helped by its similarity in sound to the Saxon *Aylwyn*, or *Alwyn* ('famous friend'): one of the several saints of the name is also recorded as St *Elwyn*, a form occasionally found to-day.

In later times the name persisted. Allan Ramsay, born in 1686, was a poet and wig-maker who inaugurated circulating libraries in Scotland; his son, of the same name, became Court painter to George III. Stevenson, in *Kidnapped*, calls his Jacobite adventurer Alan Breck Stewart. To-day Alan Brooke, Chief of the Imperial General Staff during the Second World War, has the appropriate title of Lord Alanbrooke. A. A. Milne, creator of Winnie the Pooh and Christopher Robin, was Alan Alexander Milne; A. P. Herbert, sailor and author, is Sir Alan Patrick Herbert; Alan Rawsthorne is a composer, best known for his piano concertos; Commander Alan Shepard is the pioneer American space-man.

Alan is undoubtedly the usual written form of the name to-day: Allan seems to have been most used in the nineteenth century, when Allan Cunningham wrote the song *A Wet Sheet and a Flowing Sea*, and Rider Haggard created the tough elephant-hunter, Allan Quatermain, whose extraordinary adventures are told in the novel that bears his name, and in *King Solomon's Mines*. *Allen* is the usual surname spelling, but, like other surnames, such as *Allin*, *Alleyn*, and *Alleyne*, is, so to speak, a petrified spelling of the personal name, showing a slight difference in pronunciation.

Al and *Ally* are possible pet forms.

ALBAN, in the original Latin *Albanus*, means 'man from Alba,' capital of the earliest Roman kings, which was situated on a white hill. 'Albus'—'alba' is the feminine—means 'white.'

It was probably during the persecution of Christians by the Emperor Decius in the mid third century that Alban, presumably a Roman inhabitant of the Roman-British city of Verulamium, tried to save a Christian priest from arrest by exchanging clothes with him, but was himself arrested for 'aiding and abetting' a criminal, and executed with the man he had tried to help. Thus he became the first British martyr, and it was in his honour that Verulamium was renamed St Albans. Nevertheless, his name has rarely been taken in England, though it occurs in the Middle Ages. The last bearer of any note for some centuries was a physician, Dr Alban Hill, who died in 1565; but it continued to be used still later in the St Albans district.

Even among Catholics, Alban has no great popularity, though it is to the learned Dr Alban Butler, an eighteenth-century scholar, that we owe nearly all the information on the lives of the saints mentioned in this book.

In recent times the Austrian Alban Berg composed the opera *Wozzeck*.

Albany, a name still sometimes used, has been claimed as a variant of Alban; but as it is practically confined to Scottish bearers, it is more likely to come from the old territorial name Albainn, meaning Northern Scotland, which provided the title of the Dukes of Albany. *Albin* and *Albyn* are also found.

ALBERT was earlier *Adalbert*, a combination of 'athal' and 'berhta,' 'noble' and 'illustrious.' The Anglo-Saxon form was *Aethelbeorht*, better recognized as *Ethelbert*, the name of the sixth-century Kentish king who invited St Augustine to Christianize his kingdom: for this he came to be regarded as a saint. Another St Ethelbert was a King of Wessex murdered at Hereford a century later. A third royal Ethelbert was an elder brother of Alfred the Great.

After the Norman Conquest, like most other old English names, Ethelbert to all intents disappeared in England, to be replaced by Albert—*Albertus*, as Domesday Book records it—and the French *Aubert*; though the surname Allbright and the rare personal name *Aylbricht* show that there was another form much resembling the German *Albrecht*.

It is to Germany that we must go to find the two greatest bearers of the name. Albertus Magnus (Albert the Great), a thirteenth-century scholar, wrote thirty-eight books treating of every branch of knowledge, and insisted that no theory was valid unless it could be proved by experiment. In 1941 he was appropriately proclaimed patron saint of scientists. Albrecht Dürer of Nuremberg, in the sixteenth century, was the greatest German painter, and is regarded as the inventor of etching.

Though it seems that Albert, like Ethelbert, died out in Southern England, as *Halbert* it survived in the North, and in Scotland, where it was given the pet forms *Hab* and *Hobbie*.

It was through the marriage of Queen Victoria to Prince Albert of Saxe-Coburg-Gotha that the name came back to this country; it became popular, and so did the girls' name Alberta. The Prince Consort was regarded as the ideal husband and father; to his enthusiasm for art and science we owe the museums in Kensington, endowed from the profits of the Great Exhibition of 1851 organized under his patronage. The Royal Albert Hall and the Albert Memorial also commemorate him. The Albert Medal for life-saving was instituted as a civilian parallel to the Victoria Cross in 1866. A watch-chain worn across the waistcoat was also given the Prince Consort's name.

Though by the end of the Victorian age Albert had become chiefly a working-class name, the male members of our Royal Family until recently nearly all included it among their several Christian names: Edward VII and George VI were both known to their family as *Bertie*, and it is the second name of the Duke of Windsor, and the fourth name of his brother the Duke of Gloucester. *Bert* is a less aristocratic form, but like Bertie may be used for *Bertram* and *Bertrand*. *Al* and *Albe* are also used, particularly in America.

Bearers of the name to-day may well owe it either to King Albert of the Belgians, who in 1914 led his people in their gallant resistance to the German invasion, or to Dr Albert Schweitzer, the musician and African missionary, one of the most revered religious leaders of our time.

ALDOUS This name, pronounced 'All-dus,' is probably the old German *Aldo* with the added Latin ending '-us,' derived from the Germanic 'ald,' meaning 'old.' 'Ald-' was used as the first syllable of several Anglo-Saxon names, such as *Aldred* ('old-counsel'), still occasionally used.

It has been claimed that Aldous was originally a surname meaning 'old house'; but since there have been three saints Aldo—one Scottish, one Belgian, and one Italian—all of the eighth century, before surnames were known, this origin seems unlikely: they were known in Latin as *Aldus*.

Aldous has been used in England at least since the thirteenth century, though only with East Anglian connexions. But its most distinguished bearer in the past was Aldo Manuzzi (Aldus Manutius), the Venetian Renaissance printer who popularized the 'octavo' size book pages (one large sheet folded to make eight small sheets); he also first used italic type. Spenser, the Elizabethan poet, introduces a knight, Sir Aldo, in his *Faërie Queene*. Aldous is best known to-day as the name of that gloomy prophet of a 'Brave New World,' Aldous Huxley.

ALEXANDER, 'protector of men,' was a title of honour given, it is said, to Paris of Troy (later the abductor of the beautiful Helen and cause of the Trojan War), for saving his father's herdsmen from a gang of cattle-rustlers. But this seems to have been a fanciful explanation; for even earlier, in 1300 B.C., an historical King *Alaksandus* is named on a Hittite clay tablet recently discovered.

Alexander, alternating with Philip, became hereditary among the Macedonian kings, and world-famous with Alexander the Great, who extended his dominions from Greece to the Punjab. Indian Moslems claim that every boy born after Alexander's eastern conquests was given his name. He certainly gave it to several cities—notably to Alexandria, in Egypt—and has become a legendary figure among Mohammedans, as *Iskander*.

Throughout Eastern Europe Alexander has remained a favourite name, particularly among royal families. Eight Popes have chosen the name: the first was a martyr in the second century. The sixth—Alexander Borgia—was, to say the best of him, hardly a saintly figure. The popular Italian form became *Sandro*, the Christian name of the artist nicknamed Botticelli, painter of the famous *Primavera* ('Spring') and *The Birth of Venus*.

The masculine form was helped to its popularity in the Middle Ages in Western Europe by the French *Romance of*

Alisaundre, that bade fair to rival even the stories of King Arthur's knights in both popularity and extravagance; its long lines of twelve syllables have probably named the 'Alexandrine' metre in verse. *Alysandyr* was a medieval Scottish version.

Alexander was introduced into Scotland earlier than into England. Queen Margaret, in the eleventh century, christened her third son by the name, which she brought from Hungary, where she had spent her youth. He became King Alexander I, and two further kings of the name reigned successively from 1214 to 1285. This spread it throughout the kingdom, often as *Alisander*, while *Sandy* has become a national name in the Lowlands; the northern English call a Scotsman a *Sawnie*. In the Highlands the forms *Alistair*, *Alastair* and *Alasdair*, also *Alister*, *Aleister* and *Allister*, have survived to the present day. Scott, in *Peveril of the Peak*, gives another old Northern form to the dwarf *Elshender*. *Ellick* is another Northern shortened version, with pet forms *Eck* and *Eckie*. A *Saunder* is a special Scottish type of meat pie, and shows yet another short form. But the normal Alexander is equally popular everywhere north of the Border.

Alexander Selkirk was the Scottish sailor whose experiences as a castaway gave Defoe the inspiration for *Robinson Crusoe*, and to the poet Cowper the subject of his poem beginning, "I am monarch of all I survey."

Famous bearers of more recent times can be found in many countries. In the nineteenth century the two Frenchmen, father and son, both named *Alexandre* Dumas, produced a record number of best-selling novels, the best-known being *The Three Musketeers*. In America Alexander Graham Bell invented the telephone. The Russian Alexander Alekhine was three times world chess champion, and died in 1946. The most aptly named Alexander of modern names is undoubtedly the late Sir Alexander Fleming, discoverer of penicillin and there-fore truly a 'protector of men.'

The English short form *Alec* has become practically an independent name. Nobody would think of calling the great actor, or the author of the first 'modern' school story, or the former England and Surrey cricketer, anything but Alec Guinness, Alec Waugh, and Alec Bedser. *Alex* and *Alick* do not seem quite to have reached this distinction.

A closely related name, probably an abbreviation, is *Alexis*, with its Latin form *Alexius*.

ALFRED Aelfraed, the earliest known form of Alfred, means in Anglo-Saxon 'elf-counsel'; though it has absorbed another ancient name, *Ealdfrith* ('old-peace').

But there were several Old English 'elf' names: *Aelfric* ('elf-rule'), for instance, was the first English writer of a Latin Grammar, in the eleventh century; St *Alphege* or *Aelfheah* ('elf-high') was an Archbishop of Canterbury captured and killed by the Danes at Greenwich; he is also known as St *Elphege*. Though now thought of as the 'little people,' or fairies, elves were regarded by the Anglo-Saxons as powerful nature-spirits.

Alfred the Great, 'England's Darling,' deeply religious as well as being a soldier, a scholar, and a statesman of the first rank, has never been granted official canonization, though he has been inserted, on October 26, in the Calendar of the revised Book of Common Prayer (1928). There is no universally recognized St Alfred.

From Domesday Book onward the name only survived in a latinized form, *Alured*, a spelling due to the medieval habit of writing the letter f as a v or a u. From Alured came several other variations, such as *Auveray* and *Avery*; even an *Avere,* found in 1608, is claimed as a late form.

With this doubtful version the name appears to have died out until the eighteenth century, when historians gradually began to realize that the Saxons were something more than barbarians without interest or importance. In fact, by the 1800's the name had spread to the Continent; Alfred de Vigny and Alfred de Musset, in the early nineteenth century, were two of the foremost French poets. Later Alfred Nobel, the Swedish millionaire inventor of dynamite, left a vast sum to provide prizes annually for work in physics, chemistry, medicine, literature, and the promotion of peace. Nearer to our time, another Frenchman, Alfred Binet, with his colleague Dr Simon, was the first psychologist to devise intelligence tests, and the Austrian Alfred Adler, who died in 1937, shares the honours of psychoanalysis with Jung and Freud. To him we owe the discovery of the 'inferiority complex.'

In England Alfred, Lord Tennyson, was Queen Victoria's melodious Poet Laureate; later Alfred Harmsworth, better known as Lord Northcliffe, introduced the modern illustrated daily paper.

Alf and *Alfie* are obvious pet forms; *Fred* is another, shared with *Frederick*. *Alf's Button* was a best-selling story in the years between the World Wars, in which the last remnant of Aladdin's Lamp is made into a button, with unexpected results when the owner tries to polish it. Relatives of H. G. Wells's Mr Polly called him *Elfrid*—almost the Anglo-Saxon pronunciation.

ALGERNON Two eleventh-century Counts of Boulogne, both christened *Eustace*, their traditional family name, came to be distinguished by their respective nicknames: the father was

Eustace à l'œil ('with the eye'), the son was Eustace aux gernons ('with the whiskers'), on account of his 'handlebar' moustaches.

But it was only when the meaning of the descriptive term had been practically forgotten that William's sixteenth-century descendant, the fifth Earl of Northumberland, was given Algernon as a second font-name. This Henry Algernon Percy's sumptuous habits, shown to full effect at the Field of the Cloth of Gold—where he accompanied Henry VIII—made him known as 'Algernon the Magnificent.'

Through the marriage of Algernon Percy's daughter to a Sidney, the name came to Sir Algernon Sidney, one of the commissioners for the trial of Charles I, and a convinced republican. It then passed through intermarriages to both the Howard and the Swinburne families, and accounts for the naming of Algernon Charles Swinburne, whose *Atalanta in Calydon* contains some of the most musical lines in English poetry.

But by the end of the nineteenth century Algernon had come into general use, and was common enough to have the pet forms *Algy* and *Algie*, which occurs in the shortest tragic tale in our language:

Algy met a bear.
The bear was bulgy.
The bulge was Algy.

Algernon Moncrieff, the character who shares with John Worthing the leading rôle in Oscar Wilde's *The Importance of Being Earnest*, again suggests that the name by the 1890's had taken on a somewhat humorous flavour. The late Algernon Blackwood, the writer and broadcast story-teller, wrote, notably in his "Doctor Silence" series, stories of unequalled eeriness.

AMBROSE, from the Greek 'ambrosios,' means 'immortal.' It was on ambrosia that the gods of Olympus fed: nectar was their drink.

In the fourth century St Ambrose (*Ambrosius*), the first distinguished bearer of the name, was so greatly respected as provincial governor of Northern Italy that his fellow-townsmen of Milan forced him against his will to become their bishop. He is generally represented in pictures holding a beehive, symbol of both sweetness and eloquence, and a scourge, instrument of punishment for wrongdoers: he rebuked even an Emperor for cruelty.

In Britain, during the Dark Ages, the name won glory through Ambrosius Aurelianus, an historical character, sometimes supposed to be the real King Arthur, who organized resistance to the Saxon invader. The magician Merlin was also given the title Ambrosius, from the legend that he never died, but was imprisoned by the sorceress Vivien for ever in a tree. Though some Celtic names formerly supposed to be derived from Latin originals have a doubtful claim, *Emrys* is universally agreed to be the Welsh version of Ambrose.

Ambrosius is found in Domesday Book. Odd pet forms, such as *Brush* and *Nam*, are met with at different periods. Ambrose Philips, a minor poet of the eighteenth century, was nicknamed Namby-Pamby by his rival Henry Carey.

Nobody, however, could describe as 'namby-pamby' the full-blooded stories written by the nineteenth-century American Ambrose Bierce. Earlier in this century lived Ambrose McEvoy, the portrait-painter. The former Bishop of Johannesburg, Dr Ambrose Reeves, is a champion of the equality of races in South Africa to-day. Sir Ambrose Heal, the modern furniture-designer, was given the proud designation 'Royal Designer for Industry.'

Though the older pet forms of Ambrose have to-day fallen out of use, both *Ambie* and *Rosie*—regrettably, as some people think—sometimes take their place.

ANDREW The brother of Simon Peter is called in the Gospels by the Greek name *Andreas*, meaning 'manly'—probably a new name given him after he became an Apostle. St Andrew preached the Christian faith in the Balkans and in Southern Russia, but returned to Greece, where he was put to death at Patras on an X-shaped cross; hence the term 'St Andrew's Cross' for the design on the Scottish flag.

The Apostle's close identification with Scotland came about after some of his relics had been brought to the city now known as St Andrews, which was made chief bishopric of the country where his name has ever since been universally popular. The short forms *Andy*, *Dandie*, and *Tandy* are all Scottish in origin.

Though three kings of Hungary bore the name, it was not till 1960 that it became the official first name of any member of the British Royal Family, with the christening of Prince Andrew, second son of Queen Elizabeth II. This has made the name more of a favourite than ever, though it was already sixth in popularity in 1958, and third in 1959.

Scandinavian connexions with Scotland have made *Anders* popular in Denmark. There Andersen is as common a surname as Anderson among the Scots: Hans Christian Andersen is its best-known bearer. In Russia also St Andrew was regarded as the national patron, from the tradition that he preached there.

In England the name was not used before the Norman Conquest; its first recorded appearance is in Domesday Book in its original Greek form. There is, however, an Anglo-Saxon poem, *Andreas*, describing the journeys of the Apostle, and containing a vivid description of a storm at sea.

In the Middle Ages many churches were dedicated to St Andrew, including the cathedrals of Rochester and Wells. The name is often recorded in documents, with spellings that show that it had approximately the same pronunciation as early as the thirteenth century as it has to-day.

Shakespeare's comic Sir Andrew Aguecheek in *Twelfth Night*, and the term Merry Andrew, used for a quack doctor's attendant who attracted fairground visitors with his 'gags,' both suggest that at the time of James I the name had taken on a generally humorous flavour in England.

At the time of the Commonwealth lived Andrew Marvell, the poet remembered by his *Song of the Emigrants to Bermuda* and his masterly ode on the death of Charles I.

In more recent times, Andrew Jackson was seventh President of the United States: he paid off his country's National Debt in full. Andrew Johnson was the seventeenth President. Andrew Carnegie is the best-known Scottish bearer of recent date. A poor boy from Dunfermline, he became a millionaire, and founded the Carnegie Trust, providing funds for all manner of educational and cultural purposes; he died in 1919.

Andrea is the Italian version, though in England it is only used as a feminine name. The French *André*, however, is occasionally given to English boys. André Ampère (1775–1864) gave us the common electrical term 'amps.'

Andy is now the commonest short form of the name. Samuel Lover's nineteenth-century novel *Handy Andy* tells of the ridiculous situations produced by its principal character, the boy who always misinterprets his orders. The Scottish *Dandy* has given the common word for a well-dressed man.

ANEURIN This well-known Welsh name, also written and pronounced *Aneirin*, is usually said to be derived from the Latin *Honorius*, connected with 'honour.' It may equally well, however, be a compound of the Welsh 'an' and 'eur,' 'all' and 'gold,' with '-in' used as a diminutive ending. The Cornish surname Annear looks as if it has the same origin.

The seventh-century Aneurin of the Flowing Muse (Aneurin ap Caw) is celebrated in ancient tradition as one of the three premier bards of Britain.

The modern short form, *Nye*, by which the Socialist M.P. Aneurin Bevan was familiarly known, shows that the name should be spoken with the accent on the second syllable.

ANGUS One of the most popular of exclusively Scottish names to-day, Angus was originally *Aonghus*, meaning in Gaelic 'unique choice.' Its first known bearer was Aonghus Turimleach in the third century B.C. He was, it is said, one of the three brothers from Ireland who invaded and ruled Scotland, bequeathing his name to the county and to its famous black cattle. But the name also continued in Ireland; a King Aonghus of Munster gave St Patrick half his family of twenty-four children, to become monks and nuns—literally six of one and half a dozen of the other. St Angus was an Irish bishop in the ninth century. Shakespeare has an eleventh-century Thane of Angus, a loyal subject of King Duncan, whom Macbeth cannot seduce from his allegiance.

Apparently never used outside the Celtic areas, Angus took odd forms in the Middle Ages. In the Arthurian romances there is a King *Anguish* of Orkney, and classically-minded scholars regarded it as identical with *Aeneas*. Possibly the visit of Aeneas Silvius Piccolomini to Scotland as papal legate in the fifteenth century encouraged this amalgamation. Aeneas, or *Eneas*, has remained in use there to this day, and is supposed to have given the surname MacNeice.

The original Aeneas, hero of Virgil's epic *The Aeneid*, led the remnant of Trojans who escaped the sack of their city, eventually landing in Italy, to found the greatness of Rome.

ANTONY The Latin name *Antonius*, a Roman clan name, is claimed to mean 'praiseworthy' or 'priceless.' Marcus Antonius, Caesar's friend, and lover of Egyptian Cleopatra, was the most notable early bearer. His career may be traced in two of Shakespeare's plays—*Julius Caesar* and *Antony and Cleopatra*. A later connexion of the clan was the Emperor Antoninus Pius, builder of the Antonine Wall from the Clyde to the Forth, who died in A.D. 161, leaving a line of unusually respectable successors, the Antonines, from whom we get the rare Christian name *Antoninus*.

The present popularity of the name, however, can be traced to two saints. The earlier was St Antony of Egypt. Disgusted with the vices of fourth-century Alexandria, he fled to the solitude of the desert. There, in spite of his solitary life, he was sought after by emperors for advice, and so many imitators settled round his hermitage that he is looked upon as the first abbot of a community of monks. He can be recognized in pictures by a 'T'-topped staff and his pet pig at his feet. These became his emblems, and gave rise to the term St Antony's cross, and the now unused 'tantony pig,' meaning the youngest of a litter.

The second important St Antony, though known as St Antony of Padua, was born in Lisbon, and became a favoured disciple of St Francis of Assisi. His learning and eloquence were so great that he is said to have drawn a congregation of fishes to raise their heads out of the sea and listen to him breathlessly. He is regarded as the saint to appeal to for finding lost property, and is represented as a friar with the Child Jesus resting on his book—an allusion to a vision in which Mary entrusted her Son to his care.

Antonio, the Italian version of the name, is almost a national nickname. Shakespeare appropriately gives it to the not very important name-part of *The Merchant of Venice*. The Italians were also fond of the classical flavour of the combined form *Marcantonio*.

The spelling *Anthony*, now more usual, was invented at the Renaissance, under the mistaken impression that the name had some connexion with the Greek 'anthos,' meaning 'flower.' This spelling has not affected the pronunciation in England so much as in America, where the 'th' is often sounded as in 'thorn.' The Irish have their own form, *Anthin*.

The name has been used in England at least since the twelfth century. In Scotland it was common enough to have a short form, *Nanty*. The English diminutive *Tony* is as old as the seventeenth century. Goldsmith's rustic Tony Lumpkin, in *She Stoops to Conquer*, is an eighteenth-century example, and still a favourite rôle of many comic actors.

Anthony came into regular use in England in Stuart times; the Flemish immigrant who was Charles I's Court painter was knighted as Sir Anthony Vandyke. Anthony Ashley-Cooper was the personal name of the great nineteenth-century anti-slavery campaigner, Lord Shaftesbury. Antony Armstrong-Jones, now Lord Snowdon, is the first commoner to have married a Royal Princess in Westminster Abbey.

ARCHIBALD This old Germanic name began in England as *Eorconbald*, meaning 'truly bold,' and seems to have come into use among the East Anglian royal family. One of this kingly line and name, St *Erkenwald*, was Bishop of London in the seventh century. He built the original 'Bishop's Gate,' now surviving only as a street name.

But the chief home of Archibald—as it gradually became—is in Scotland. James I brought a jester of the name with him to England, *Archie* Armstrong, who was a real character, and who figures in Scott's *Legend of Montrose*.

Archibald remains predominantly a Scottish name. Archibald (A. J.) Cronin, the author, and Sir Archibald MacIndoe, the great R.A.F. plastic surgeon, are instances. Field Marshal Lord Wavell, another example, was distinguished for his services in the East during the Second World War. Archie Jackson, who played cricket for Australia at eighteen, and the American Archie Moore, light-heavyweight boxing champion in his forties, show its general popularity.

Americans prefer the short form *Archy*, as given by Don Marquis in his wise-cracking verses *Archy and Mehitabel* to a cockroach and a cat. But *Arch* and *Baldie* are short forms found on both sides of the Atlantic.

ARNOLD The old German *Arinwald* is a combination of 'eagle' and 'power.' There was a similar name, *Arinwulf*, meaning 'eagle-wolf,' still used as *Arnolf* and *Arnolphe* in Germany and France. But the two were sometimes confused. The patron saint of Metz, in Alsace, now known as St *Arnauld*, was actually called Arinwulf, though Arnauld is a French version of Arnold.

Ernald, in Domesday Book, seems to have been brought over by the Normans. But though it is written there as *Ernaldus*, it is probable that the general pronunciation was more like the French Arnauld, which has given the surname Arnott. Eventually, after widespread use in various forms, it became

Arnold; but by the seventeenth century it was falling out of favour, and in the nineteenth seemed almost forgotten. To-day, however, it has unaccountably become almost a common choice. The suggested explanation for this revival is that Dr Arnold, the headmaster of Rugby who reformed the public-school system (he appears in *Tom Brown's Schooldays*), and his son, the poet Matthew Arnold, brought the name back into public notice through their combined distinction. The novelist Arnold Bennett (his first name was Enoch), who wrote especially about life in the Potteries, was born in 1867, some twenty years earlier than the death of Arnold the poet.

There were famous bearers on the Continent in the Middle Ages. Arnold of Brescia in the twelfth century led a revolution in Rome against Church control of civil affairs. Arnold von Winkelried, a Swiss national hero, during the struggle against Austrian domination in the fourteenth century made it possible for his countrymen to penetrate the enemy ranks by clasping to his breast the spears of the opposing soldiery.

Modern bearers of prominence are the American chess champion Arnold Denker, the musician Arnold Bax, and the historian Arnold Toynbee.

Arn and *Arny*, and in America *Arno*, are present-day short forms.

ARTHUR There has been as much controversy over the origin of the name Arthur as over the existence of the British chieftain who made it famous. However, the quarrel seems pointless; for, whether derived from the Roman family name *Artorius*, or from the Celtic *Art* or *Arth*, the name is connected with 'bear.' The most obvious interpretation is that Arthur is a compound of the Old Welsh 'arth,' 'bear,' and 'gwr,' 'hero.'

Present-day historians mostly claim Arthur as an historical personage, even though he is not mentioned before the eighth century. Probably there was a semi-divine character in old Celtic legends whose fabulous exploits were ascribed to a real fifth-century organizer of resistance to the Anglo-Saxon invaders.

There was, however, an undoubtedly historical Irish chieftain of the name in the sixth century, and some hundred years later lived a Scottish King *Art* of Dalriada. The name occurs in both Ireland and Scotland in the ninth century as *Artuir* and *Arth*. *Arthen* ('little bear') was a King of Cardigan at the same time, and there is another old Welsh name, *Arthgen*, meaning 'son of the bear.'

In Domesday Book the forms *Artor* and *Artur* are numerous; but in spite of the tales of the Round Table and its champions, the name had fallen out of grace before the fourteenth century. This may have been on account of the untimely fate of Prince Arthur of Brittany, so movingly described by Shakespeare in *King John*. In fact, the boy who melted the heart of Hubert de Burgh, sent to put out his eyes, was sixteen when he died, and had already led an army to besiege his grandmother, Eleanor of Aquitaine. In Ireland, during the reign of Richard II, Art McMurrough of Leinster held out successfully against costly English expeditions for forty years.

Though the Welsh-born Henry VII christened his eldest son Arthur, the name did not regain prestige in England; the young man died when he was sixteen, apparently a dangerous age for royal Arthurs. Only the country form, *Arter*, survived. But in Scotland, where King Arthur was also looked upon as a national hero, his name persisted, particularly in the Galbraith and Hamilton families. It was from a Scottish grandmother's family that the Duke of Wellington inherited it. And so it passed back to England, its glory fully restored.

Queen Victoria named her youngest son Arthur, Wellington being his godfather, and the name spread throughout her reign, popular in both life and literature. Thackeray's Arthur Pendennis is a self-portrait of the author. Tennyson's greatest poem, *In Memoriam*, was written to lament the early death of his friend Arthur Hallam. Sir Arthur Sullivan wrote the music both of the Gilbert and Sullivan operas and of *Onward, Christian Soldiers*. Later Sir Arthur Evans discovered the lost civilization of Ancient Crete. H. G. Wells's *Arty* Kipps shows the short form of the name in the novel *Kipps*, a vivid picture of English social life at the turn of the century. Other short forms are *Artie* and *Arth*. Kipling's Arthur Corkran, the 'Corky' of *Stalky & Co.*, is a leading member of the 'gang' whose exploits changed the whole pattern of school stories.

In 1919 Arthur Whitten Brown made the first Atlantic flight from east to west. Sir Arthur Eddington, the great modern British astronomer, died in 1944.

AUBREY The Anglo-Saxon *Aelfric*, meaning 'elf-rule,' was in Old German *Alberic*. Alberic, king of the dwarfs, and guardian of the treasure of the Niebelungs, wrested from him by Siegfried, seems to have been the original bearer. Among the Franks the name became *Aubert*: St Aubert, Bishop of Arras, died in 669.

By the thirteenth century Aubert had developed a diminutive, *Auberon*, in romance King of the Fairies, "a dwarf with an angelic visage." He befriends Sir Huon of Bordeaux, giving him a magic horn with which to summon him at need. It was this name that Shakespeare took and spelt phonetically for his jealous elfin King *Oberon*, in *A Midsummer Night's Dream*.

Long before this, however, an English Alberic is recorded

in Domesday Book as living in the time of Edward the Confessor; possibly he was an early Norman settler. The same name was borne by Alberic de Vere, who came to England in 1066, perpetuating his name in the form *Albery*—later to become *Aubrey*, as we know it—among the de Vere family, from which came the poet Aubrey de Vere, who died in 1902. But the name spread beyond a single family. Aubrey Beardsley, the artist of the 1890's, best known for his illustrations to Oscar Wilde's play *Salome*, was born in 1872. A well-known later example was Sir Aubrey Smith, the cricketer known from his peculiar style of bowling as "Round-the-Corner Smith," and later knighted for his acting in films.

AUGUSTUS Julius Caesar's adopted son—actually his great-nephew—Octavius, having disposed of his enemies and his rivals, became undisputed master of the Roman world. The Senate decreed him the title "Augustus," virtually corresponding to 'Majesty.'

Augustus became the official designation of every Roman Emperor. But it was never given as a personal name—though the last Roman Emperor of the West, Romulus Augustus, was nicknamed *Augustulus*, 'little Augustus,' on account of his ineffectiveness. The French king who reigned from 1180 till 1223, and made himself first real ruler of the whole country, was acclaimed as Philippe *Auguste*, "Philip the Majestic," again as a title of honour.

It was only in 1526 that this name was given at the font, to Augustus of Saxony who, like his son Augustus the Strong, shows the tendency among German princelings of the time to match their Roman-style palaces and their statues, oddly dressed up in flowing classical draperies and great curly periwigs, by taking imposing Roman names. As *August*, pronounced 'ow-goost,' the name then became general, and spread through Germany and the neighbouring countries, and to France as *Auguste*.

The name came to England with the Hanoverians in the eighteenth century. Augustus Frederick, Duke of Sussex, was a son of George III. In the nineteenth century Augustus Toplady wrote the hymn *Rock of Ages*, and Augustus Welby Pugin, the Gothic-revival enthusiast, designed all the architectural and ornamental details of the Houses of Parliament, down to umbrella-stands and ink-pots. Augustus John, who died in 1961, was the 'grand old man' of English art. And everyone should know Belloc's Charles Augustus Fortescue, "who always did what was Right, and so accumulated an Immense Fortune." He is to be found in *Cautionary Tales for Children*.

In the circus August(e) is the stock name for the Second Clown. Pet forms are *Gus*, *Gussie*, *Gustus*; even *Augie* has been noted.

AUSTIN Though for centuries the imperial title Augustus was never taken as a personal name, the derived form *Augustinus*, meaning something like 'His Majesty's subject,' was in fairly general use, at any rate by the time of the later Roman Empire.

St *Augustine* of Hippo, in North Africa, foremost churchman of his day, was born in the mid fourth century; his *Confessions* is still widely read to-day, as one of the world's greatest autobiographies.

The other St Augustine is now more familiar to English people, as he was sent by Pope Gregory the Great to Christianize England. Landing in Thanet in 597, he became the first Archbishop of Canterbury.

The Anglo-Saxons, however, never cared for foreign names, and even that of the virtual founder of their Church found no namesakes, it seems, before 1187, when it appears as *Austin*, which became the usual English form, with the variant *Austen*; it was common in the Middle Ages.

Though the name lost favour at the Reformation, it never died out. Austin Dobson was a Victorian poet, expert in the study and imitation of eighteenth-century verse; Austen Chamberlain was Foreign Secretary in the 1920's.

Augustine was revived by the Victorians. Augustine Birrell was a Liberal statesman and writer at the turn of this century. *Augustin* is an old alternative spelling. The Welsh spell the name *Awstin*.

BALDWIN This name was the Old German *Baldavin*, made up of 'balda,' 'bold,' and 'vini,' 'friend.' Its earliest discoverable bearer was the nephew of Roland, one of Charlemagne's paladins, or champions. It was a popular Norman name, particularly during the early Crusading period. In the second half of the twelfth century, for instance, there were a King Baldwin of Jerusalem, a Baldwin, Count of Edessa, and an Archbishop of Caesarea, all flourishing at the same time. After the Crusaders had conquered Constantinople two 'Latin' Emperors also bore the name.

In England a *Baldewyne* was abbot of Bury St Edmund's and Royal Physician to both Edward the Confessor and William I. Baldwin of Maeles was Sheriff of Devon in 1100. The last prominent English bearer was the rebel Baldwin of Redvers, the Sheriff's grandson, a leading opponent of King Stephen.

But gradually the popularity of Baldwin declined, at least after the thirteenth century; though it is found as late as 1694 in the degenerate form *Bodwine*, and provided us with such surnames as Bowden and Bodkin (from the diminutive *Baudkin*, of Flemish origin) as well as the normal form, Baldwin. Its revival dates from the last century.

The King of the Belgians is the first modern royal bearer, thus reviving the favourite name of the old Counts of Flanders. He is known to his Flemish subjects as *Boudewyn*, to the French-speaking Walloons as *Baudouin*.

BARNABY As Dickens's novel *Barnaby Rudge* shows, the usual English form of this name was Barnaby. It was never common in this country, though occurring as early as the thirteenth century in the original form of *Barnabas*.

The first known bearer was the Apostle, companion of St Paul on his first missionary journeys, as we can find in the Acts of the Apostles. His name in Aramaic, the late Hebrew dialect used in Palestine in his time, means 'son of exhortation,' rather than 'son of consolation,' as it is often interpreted. He was a Cypriot by origin, and, returning to his native island after his travels, was stoned to death. June 11, the date of his church festival, was the longest day in the year until the calendar was reformed in 1752. The poet Spenser, in his *Epithalamium*, refers to this in the lines:

> This day the sun is in his chiefest height
> With Barnaby the Bright.

"Barnaby Bright" was the popular name for this day.

The affected gait of professional jesters was known as the 'Barnaby Dance,' from a famous droll. The later familiar form *Barney* gave the slang term 'to barney,' meaning to humbug; *a* barney was used of a prize-fight.

Barn and *Barney* are modern short forms that show the name to be sufficiently common, both in England and the United States, to need them.

BARRY The Old Celtic *Bearrach* means something like 'good marksman.' An Irish St *Bearach*, or *Barry*, lived in the sixth century, and as a Christian name it generally indicates Irish connexions. Thackeray's *Barry Lyndon* is the story of an Irish scoundrel, self-deceiving narrator of his own misfortunes.

During the nineteenth century the name lost its exclusively Irish character. Barry Pain, besides being a well-known comic writer at the turn of this century, particularly in his parodies of serious authors of the day, also wrote effective ghost stories. Sir Barry Jackson, born in 1879, owed his title to his life-work for the Repertory Theatre movement.

It is often claimed that most families surnamed Barry derive it from the old French province of Berri. This may occasionally be true. Others, however, may have taken it from Barry Island, which owes its name to a Celtic hermit who built his cell there. But with some Welsh bearers the name may equally well have originally been Ap Harry, 'son of Harry,' and so identical with the surname Parry.

BARTHOLOMEW The Apostle Bartholomew was, in fact, called *Bar Talmai*, meaning 'son of the furrow.' St Bartholomew is generally supposed to have been *Nathanael* (see p. 202), the Galilean of whom Jesus said, "Behold an Israelite without guile."

Never used in England before the Norman Conquest, except when assumed by monks, Bartholomew came into normal use in the twelfth century. This was possibly due to the foundation of St Bartholomew's Hospital in London by

Rahere, said to have been Court Jester to Henry I. On a visit to Rome he fell ill, but was cured after a vision of St Bartholomew, whose relics were enshrined on an island in the Tiber. Converted by this miracle, he became a cleric, and was not only helped by his royal master to found the hospital but given the right to hold an annual fair to assist its upkeep. The fair continued until suppressed in the nineteenth century on account of its rowdiness, a picture of which is given in Ben Jonson's comedy *Bartholomew Fayre*.

The usual medieval form of the name in England became *Bartlemey*, derived from the Old French *Bartelemieu*; but it acquired numerous shortened versions such as *Bart* (the hospital is known to-day as Bart's), *Bartley*, *Tolly*, *Batty* and *Bate*. In the North the accepted form was *Bartle*.

The name is chiefly remembered because of the notorious Massacre of St Bartholomew's Eve, August 24, 1572, when an attempt was made by the Catholic royalist party in France to suppress the growing Protestant influence of the Huguenots by a general 'purge.'

But both before and after this tragic event there were famous bearers of the name. *Bartolomeu* Diaz was the Portuguese navigator who first rounded the Cape of Good Hope, in 1486. The Florentine *Bartolommeo* Cristofori, in the early eighteenth century, constructed the first piano; the Frenchman *Barthelémy* Thimonnier, about a hundred years later, invented the sewing-machine.

A "Bartholomew doll" (sold at the London fair) came to be applied to an overdressed woman; a Bartholomew pig was a term once used for any fat person—again from the fair, where fat pigs were a great attraction, roasted whole. In Westmorland a bartle was the name given to the king-pin of a set of skittles.

BASIL This name, in the original Greek 'basileios,' means 'kingly,' but owes its use to three Eastern saints. Basil of Caesarea, a fourth-century preacher and writer, who organized monastic life in the East, is known as St Basil the Great. Several Emperors of Constantinople bore the name, which spread to Russia as *Vassily* (*Vaslav* in Poland). St Basil's Cathedral in Moscow's Red Square is one of the most extraordinary buildings in Europe.

The Crusaders introduced the name into the West after their contacts with the Empire of the East; but it never became popular in England until the nineteenth century. In Scotland, however, the name occurs in the eighteenth century. The frequency of Basil with a Scottish surname suggests strongly that it has been taken as a substitute for the Gaelic *Boisil* (*Boswell*). Basildon, Essex, is actually Baestel's dene (wooded valley of Baestel).

In the present century *Vaslav* Nijinski, a Pole, was a phenomenal ballet dancer. He was able to make ten entrechats in one leap, so that he appeared to his audience to be literally poised in mid-air. To-day Basil Spence has earned a knighthood by his designs for the new Coventry Cathedral; Basil Cameron is a great orchestral conductor.

The plant called basil, the 'sovereign' herb, was formerly used in embalming. An Italian story by Boccaccio, concerning a lady whose murdered lover's head was concealed in a pot of basil, is retold by the poet Keats in *Isabella, or the Pot of Basil.*

Baz and *Basie* are used as short forms of the name.

BENEDICT 'Benedictus' in Latin means 'blessed.' St Benedict of Nursia, born in 480, founded the historic abbey at Monte Cassino, in Italy. To-day the name *Benedictine* is best-known from the liqueur originally made at the French abbey of Fécamp. Between 575 and 1922 fifteen Popes were named Benedict.

The first recorded bearer of the name in England is St Benedict Biscop (Benedict the Bishop). He founded the monasteries of Monkwearmouth and Jarrow in Northumbria in the seventh century, beautifying the churches there with the first glass windows seen in Britain. It was at Jarrow that the Venerable Bede, our first great historian, received his education.

Benedict appears in the thirteenth century with the variant *Benett*, an adaptation of the French form *Benoît*. Corpus Christi College at Cambridge was formerly called *Benet* College. *Bennet* and *Bennett* are also found. Shakespeare uses the almost Latin form *Benedick* for the reluctant wooer of Beatrice in *Much Ado about Nothing*, and this form is now used for any bachelor unwillingly persuaded into marriage. From Benedick we have the surname Bendix.

Benedict, except among Catholics, is rare as a personal name in England to-day. The pet form *Ben* is shared by Benjamin (see below). In Latin countries the name has flourished in several versions. *Benedetto* Croce was the greatest Italian philosopher of modern times; *Benito* Mussolini was the Italian Fascist dictator.

BENJAMIN Rachel on her deathbed named her last-born son *Ben Oni*, 'son of sorrow'; Jacob, in his delight at this unexpected child of his old age, changed the baby's name to *Benjamin*, 'son of the right hand'—the right hand implying strength and good fortune. The full story may be read in the thirty-fifth chapter of Genesis. The later history of Benjamin led to his being regarded as the type of a favourite son.

The name was used by Jews in the Middle Ages; Benjamin of Tudela was a Spanish rabbi of the twelfth century, the earliest European traveller to give first-hand accounts of the Far East—even earlier than Marco Polo.

It was not until after the change of religion in the sixteenth century that Benjamin became popular, as one of the many Scriptural names from the Old Testament not previously used. *Ben* Jonson, a bricklayer's stepson and apprentice who turned playwright, was a scholar as well, and was regarded by his contemporaries as superior to Shakespeare. On his grave in Westminster Abbey is inscribed one of the shortest and most flattering of epitaphs: 'O rare Ben Jonson.'

Since then every century has produced a notable example of British or American origin. Benjamin West, American by birth, was appointed second President of the Royal Academy by George III; Benjamin Franklin, one of the 'Founding Fathers' of the United States, became their first envoy to France, and also invented the lightning-conductor; Benjamin Jesty, a Dorset farmer, forestalled Jenner: as his tombstone declares, he "introduced the Cow Pox by Inoculation" in 1774. Benjamin Disraeli was Queen Victoria's most picturesque Prime Minister and virtual 'godfather' of the modern Conservative Party; Benjamin Waugh was part-founder of the N.S.P.C.C. For a musician we have had to wait till our own century, with Benjamin Britten.

The original short form was *Ben.* Big Ben, the great bell of the Houses of Parliament, was named after Sir Benjamin Hall, First Commissioner of Works at the time of its installation. Ben Gunn is the name given by Stevenson to the marooned pirate in *Treasure Island. Benjy* and *Benjie* are modern. Contemporary examples are the Americans Ben Cailin, who crossed the Atlantic by amphibious jeep in 1955, and Benny Goodman the clarinettist; *Benny* is a specially Jewish choice. The Indian *Bannerjee* is an unexpected eastern version.

Ben is often used before other names by Jews, as in *Ben Oni* (see *Benjamin*, p. 65) and *Ben Hur*, 'Son of Hur,' Lew Wallace's story of the early Christian age. Mr Ben Gurion, the modern Israelite statesman, is 'son of the young lion.'

BERNARD *Beornheard* in Anglo-Saxon means 'bear-hard.' The bear, largest and strongest animal of the North, was regarded as sacred. In France, right up to the Middle Ages, he was known as "the great father." Like *Arth* (see *Arthur*, p. 55), *Bjorn*, the Scandinavian word for a bear, has been used as a name from time immemorial. But except for the rare *Berno*, sometimes used in Germany, Bernard is the only 'bear' name that has everywhere prevailed.

Bernardo del Carpio was a legendary Spanish champion of the ninth century, who lived up to his 'bear' name by hugging Roland the Paladin to death at Roncesvalles. A century later St Bernard of Menthon, after whom the St Bernard dog is named, founded the Alpine hospice for travellers. Greatest of all was St Bernard of Clairvaux, the twelfth-century monk who became the adviser of kings, and roused all Europe for the Second Crusade. The Latin original of the hymn *How Sweet the Name of Jesus Sounds* is his composition.

The name landed in England with the Normans, and came to be pronounced *Barnard*, as shown by the place-name Barnard Castle.

After the sixteenth century Bernard went out of favour until the time of Queen Victoria. Of modern bearers, George Bernard Shaw, the playwright, is always known by his second name. Bernard Bosanquet, early in our own century, was known as "the cricket conjuror" for perfecting the googly. Bernard Miles is the founder of the London Mermaid Theatre in the City.

Bernard Braden, the Canadian comedian, uses the common short form *Bernie*; other modern short forms are *Berney*, *Barney* (shared with Barnaby), and *Nardie*.

BERTRAM and *Bertrand* were originally separate names with separate meanings. Bertram being in Old German *Berahtraben*, 'bright raven'; the raven was the bird of Odin, 'All-father' god of the North. Bertrand was 'bright shield.' But owing to the tendency in France—where both Bertram and Bertrand were early in fashion—to omit final consonants in pronunciation, the two names merged into one in common use. A celebrated medieval Bertrand was Bertrand du Guesclin, Constable of France and gallant adversary of the English in the Hundred Years War.

The greatest English philosopher of the present century is Bertrand Russell. Bertram Mills gives his name to a famous circus, and careful readers of P. G. Wodehouse's books will know that the *Bertie* Wooster of the 'Jeeves' series is a Bertram too.

BORIS is the only Russian masculine name that has become generally used in England. It is said to mean 'fight,' from an old Slav word 'borotj.'

Boris Godunov was son-in-law to Ivan the Terrible, the Tsar who proposed to Queen Elizabeth I. Becoming Regent, and later Tsar of Russia, he died in 1605. The opera *Boris Godunov*, by Moussorgsky, tells his story.

Boris Karloff is well known for his horrific rôles in many films. Best known, however, is Boris Pasternak, the Russian author of *Dr Zhivago*, the greatest contemporary Russian novel; he died in 1960.

BRENDAN St *Brendan* or *Brandan*, as Charles Kingsley calls him in *The Water Babies*, founded the monastery of Clonfert, in Ireland, in the sixth century. The Irish spelling, however, is *Brenainn*, claimed to mean 'dweller by the beacon.'

Legend has it that the saint sailed far out into the Atlantic, where he encountered many wonders before reaching a delightful island—one of those many islands of the West that may have been mere myths of an earthly paradise which lay towards the setting sun, or possibly indications that the dauntless Celtic seafarers of the Dark Ages had actually discovered America. In some medieval maps St Brendan's Isle is marked, west of the Cape Verde Islands.

The Irish form gave a surname, *Brennan*. Brennan of the Moor was a generous highwayman who is said to have given all his loot to the poor, and when condemned to death, held the court at bay with a blunderbuss smuggled in by his wife.

A notable modern example is Brendan Behan, the contemporary playwright.

Though hardly complimentary, it should be mentioned that a recent interpretation of the name links it with the Old Irish 'bren' and 'find,' meaning 'stinking hair'! This seems most improbable, as Celts were not in the habit of giving their children unpleasant names.

BRIAN, a Celtic name, has no certain meaning, though it has been connected both with 'bre,' 'hill,' and with 'brigh,' 'strength.'

Brian Boru, King of Munster and Leinster, the first recorded bearer, is also known as *Brien*, as in the surname O'Brien. Boru means 'of the tribute,' and refers to the enormous sum of money he exacted from the conquered men of Ulster. He was found dead in his tent after the battle of Clontarf in 1014.

Equally popular, it seems, in Ireland and Brittany, the name came to England with the many Breton followers of the Norman William. Its first written English form was *Brienus*, in Domesday Book; but this great census was all in Latin, and the -us endings of names in it were added to the spoken forms by the scribes, not really used. Sir Walter Scott appropriately chose this name for the Norman Sir Brian de Bois-Guilbert in *Ivanhoe*. It was popular throughout the country, as can be seen from such surnames as Briant and Bryanson, at least till the time of Henry VIII, when Sir Brian Tuke—whose portrait as a young man by Holbein can still be seen—was a prominent civil servant. But it went out of fashion, except in the old Celtic areas of the north-west and among the Irish.

It was probably through bearers of Irish origin living in England that the name came back in the late eighteenth century. Bryan Proctor, who wrote under the name of Barry Cornwall, and is remembered by his poem *To a Fountain*, was born in Leeds in 1787.

The spelling Brian seems most favoured to-day, though *Bryan* is not uncommon. Brian Colquhoun, a Scottish bearer, designed the Mersey tunnel at the age of twenty-eight; Bryan Donkin was the English inventor of preserving food in tins. Brian Statham, the England fast bowler, is another example.

BRUCE Bruis, or Braose, now known as Brieuse, is a village with a castle near Cherbourg, giving its name to the family who were once its feudal lords. The first member of the line who arrived in Britain accompanied William the Conqueror; his descendants split into two branches, English and Scottish.

It was the Scottish branch that produced, in the eighth

recorded Robert of the name, Scotland's national hero, Robert Bruce, who secured the independence of his country in the fourteenth century. The story goes that, after six vain attempts to defeat the English, he took refuge on a remote island. There one day, as he lay on his bed, almost despairing, he noticed a spider try six times unsuccessfully to hang its web from a beam; with the seventh effort it succeeded. Inspired by its persistence, Bruce too decided on a seventh attempt; in two years he was master of Scotland and crowned King.

As a Christian name, however, even north of the Tweed, Bruce does not seem to occur before the end of the nineteenth century. To-day it is common, generally still with Scottish connexions; Bruce Marshall, for instance, the novelist, is a Scotsman, and so too was Bruce Bairnsfather, the most successful cartoonist of the First World War.

CECIL The Caecilian clan of Rome appears to have come by its name through an ancestor who was blind, 'caecus,' though its members preferred to derive it from 'caeculus,' 'hearthstone,' name of a mythical son of the smith-god Vulcan. The most noteworthy Christian of the name was, of course, St Cecilia; though there was a third-century St *Caecilius*, and St *Kilian*, a seventh-century Irishman who evangelized Bavaria, had his name latinized into *Cecilianus*.

Cecil was used in medieval England for both sexes; but its present popularity as a boys' name only began during the last century, and is due to the famous family, of which the head is the Marquess of Salisbury, descended from Lord Burleigh, Queen Elizabeth's great Minister. This family originated in Monmouthshire, and was originally named *Seissylt*, which is a Welsh corruption of the Latin *Sextilius* (from *Sextilis*, a name derived from 'sextus,' 'sixth'). But the name had been borne long before as a Christian name by *Sysyllt*, Lord of Gwennydd in the tenth century, and *Seissyllt* ap Dyfnwal, a chieftain murdered at Abergavenny in 1175. Another old Welsh form is *Sitsyllt*.

Nineteenth-century examples were Cecil Rhodes, founder of Rhodesia, and Cecil Sharp, who revived folk-dancing. To-day Cecil Day Lewis, the poet, also writes under the pen-name of Nicholas Blake.

Though the name scarcely needs a short form, *Cec*, *Cis*, and *Ceese* are used both in England and America to-day. *Sissy* is hardly a popular version.

CEDRIC In naming his Saxon thane in *Ivanhoe* Cedric, Sir Walter Scott has been accused of misspelling the Old English name *Cerdic*. But as he gives the thane's daughter the unquestionably Celtic name of Rowena, and his other Saxon characters have remarkably Celtic-looking names, his Cedric is probably *Cedrych*, from the Welsh 'ced,' 'bounty,' and 'drych,' 'pattern,' and so meaning 'pattern of bounty.'

The usual explanation of Cedric, however, is that it should be Cerdic. This is the name given to the chieftain who founded the kingdom of Wessex, and was the progenitor of our present Royal Family. He seems to have been of British, not Saxon, origin, and in all probability was named *Ceredig*, meaning 'amiable.' There was a Scottish king of the Dumbarton region of this name who lived in the mid sixth century.

A closely related name is *Caradog*, or *Caradoc* (originally *Caratacos*), with much the same meaning. This name was latinized by the Roman historian Tacitus into *Caractacus*, in his account of the British resistance led by the chieftain, whose bravery, even as a prisoner, moved the Emperor Claudius to spare his life. Caer Caradoc in Shropshire is traditionally the site of his capital; Cardigan (in Welsh, Ceredigion) is also said to bear his name.

From its patriotic associations, Caradoc became particularly popular in Wales, giving the surname Craddock, which shows that the accent should correctly be on the second syllable. Its continuing use is shown in the name of Caradoc Evans, the Welsh novelist of the present century, a stern critic of his people.

CHAD can only come from the Celtic 'cad,' meaning 'battle,' a word occurring in many Welsh names, such as *Cadog*, 'warlike,' *Cadwaladr*, 'battle-arranger,' and *Cadwallon*, 'battle-scatterer,' but never appearing in Wales as a name in itself.

According to the Venerable Bede, St Chad, whom he calls *Ceadda*, was an "Angle by race," born in Northumbria. But his elder brother, St *Cedd*, has a name that is almost the Welsh 'ced,' meaning 'bounty,' and the two remaining brothers were *Celyn* and *Cynebil*, which latter must be a version of *Cunobelin* (*Cymbeline*); Chad's family were clearly of British extraction.

Chad eventually became Bishop of Lichfield, and though he travelled up and down the country—the London district of Shadwell is named after him—his name seems to have been used at the font only in the Lichfield area.

Some Staffordshire namesake of the saint, as yet untraced, must have emigrated to New England, and it is only in America that the name is familiar in modern times.

Walter Edmonds, in the present century, wrote his boys' story of circus life, *Chad Hanna*. It was an episode in this book, and the film made from it, which made the name familiar in England during the Second World War. Chad Hanna, looking longingly over a fence at the circus, was drawn on innumerable walls, and scribbled on Forces memoranda, as a much simplified pair of eyes and a nose, with the caption "Wot, no . . .?" filled in with the name of any commodity in short supply; this drawing was universally known as 'a Chad.'

The only well-known Chad to-day is the Rev. Chad Varah, founder of the Samaritans, an organization which offers help to would-be suicides.

CHARLES and 'churl' are in origin identical. Even to-day in the Cotswolds the name is pronounced 'Charrel,' almost in its Anglo-Saxon form *Ceorl*, meaning 'a man.' In German, 'Kerl' ('chap, fellow') has more or less kept its ancient meaning. Churl, from its old use for 'a countryman,' has with us come to mean a rough-spoken individual.

By the eighth century the personal name had become *Karel*, latinized by scholars into *Karolus* or *Carolus*, whence the Rumanian *Carol*. But its later form, Charles, used in both England and France, is now the most familiar.

Charles Martel, Charles 'the Hammer,' was virtual ruler of France in the early eighth century, leading the Franks to victory against the Saracens at Poitiers in A.D. 732, and so saving Christianity from extinction in the West. His son Pépin was the father of Charles the Great, whom the French called *Charlemagne* (from the Latin Carolus Magnus), founder, in 800, of the Holy Roman Empire.

Ten French kings and fifteen rulers of Sweden have been named Charles; the greatest Duke of Burgundy was the fifteenth-century Charles the Bold. In fact, so common was the name in the Middle Ages on the Continent that most historical bearers were distinguished by individual nicknames, such as Charles the Bald, Charles the Fat, Charles the Lame.

In England, though there was a Mercian King Ceorl, the

name seems to have died out before the Norman invasion. Place-names beginning Charl- or Carl- seem to have been derived from the normal meaning of the word, not from a personal name.

James Stuart, convinced that his own name was unlucky, on account of the misfortunes of his five namesakes who had ruled Scotland before him, brought back the name to Britain by christening his eventual successor Charles, as a name of good omen. This caused it to spread, particularly among those of Cavalier sympathies—though it did not save Charles I from an unlucky end.

Among Continental Catholics at the same time, the reputation of of St Charles (*Carlo*) Borromeo, Archbishop of Milan and reformer of Church abuses, won his name a popularity that persists to this day. In the United States, owing to German and Scandinavian immigration, *Karl*, or *Carl*, was thirty-eighth in popularity among American boys' names, at least up to 1950, and *Carlo* is also sometimes used. In Welsh, which has no 'ch' sound, *Siarl* is used. The Gaelic form is *Tearlach*.

Even after the accession of George I, Charles remained in favour in England, often as a sign of sympathy with the exiled House of Stuart. In the Townshend family, for instance, Charles was used continuously between 1674 and 1810. Charles Darwin, who propounded the Origin of Species, was born in 1809, Charles Dickens, the novelist, in 1812. Charles Wordsworth initiated the annual Oxford and Cambridge boat race in 1829. In the same year was born Charles Arnold of Liverpool; he died in 1941, reaching the greatest age officially registered in this country—112 years. The American Charles Lindbergh was the first to fly the Atlantic from east to west, in 1927.

Strictly speaking, *Charlie* is the Scottish pet form, as with

'Bonnie Prince Charlie.' The correct English equivalent is *Charley*, as in *Charley's Aunt*. The London-born Charles Chaplin is, however, generally known as Charlie Chaplin, except in France, where he has been given the native diminutive *Charlot*. Other short forms are *Charly*, *Chollie*, *Chuck*, and—in Australia—*Chilla*. The written abbreviation is *Chas*.

Charles's Wain is the English traditional name for the constellation of Great Bear, originally Carles waegn. The expression 'a proper Charlie' seems to derive from the earliest night-watchmen, the predecessors of the Metropolitan Police; instituted by Charles I, and selected from among aged military pensioners, who were regarded as particularly stupid.

CHRISTIAN Exceptionally, the feminine Christina or Christiana is older as a name than the masculine Christian; there is more than one St Christina and no St Christian. The masculine form has, however, been used by ten Danish kings, beginning with *Christiern* of Oldenburg in the fifteenth century. *Chrétien* de Troyes, the greatest writer of romances in the twelfth century, shows that the name was used also in medieval France.

In England the name seems not to occur before the fifteenth century, when, in John of Gaunt's register of retainers, we find one *Christian*, and one *Payn* (*i.e.*, 'pagan'). But the name has never been popular, in spite of the Christian who is the hero of Bunyan's allegory *Pilgrim's Progress*.

Chris and *Christy* are the short forms, shared with Christopher. The English form has superseded *Chrétien* in France to-day.

CHRISTOPHER St Christopher was a Lycian martyred under the Roman Emperor Decius in A.D. 250. According to legend, he was first named *Offeros*, and lived by a river. One night he heard a child calling for help to cross to the other side. Offeros, a man of gigantic stature, took pity on it. He waded into the stream with the child on his shoulder; but as the stream grew deeper his burden seemed to grow heavier than the largest man, and the child explained that He was Christ, laden with the sins of the world, and gave him the new name *Christopheros,* 'Christ-bearer.' Hence St Christopher is regarded as patron of wayfarers, and his figure is familiar everywhere to-day.

The name is found recorded in England as early as 1201, but hardly seems to have become popular here until nearly three hundred years later. In 1500, in Durham alone there were at least fifteen bearers, and, unlike most non-scriptural saintly names, it survived the Reformation.

The greatest Elizabethan dramatist, next to Shakespeare and Ben Jonson, was Christopher Marlowe; Shakespeare introduces the tinker Christopher Sly into the prologue of *The Taming of the Shrew*; Sir Christopher Hatton was Lord Chancellor towards the end of Queen Elizabeth's reign. Sir Christopher Wren, builder of St Paul's and most of the London City churches, was born in 1632 and died in 1723. Christopher continued to be used extensively, and in the 1900's it became one of the most fashionable boys' names, as A. A. Milne's childhood classics of the 'twenties show with their hero, Christopher Robin—a typical combination of the period.

In Scotland the Gaelic *Gillecriosd*, meaning 'servant of Christ,' and giving the surname Gilchrist, was used as a Highland equivalent; *Chrystal* and *Crystal* were Lowland versions. *Christie* is used in Ireland: Christie Mahon is the playboy in J. M. Synge's play *The Playboy of the Western World*.

Xit, the dwarf in Harrison Ainsworth's *Tower of London*, shows an odd pet form used in the sixteenth century, the more usual being *Kit*, which was used for Marlowe by his friends. It has named the island of St Kitts, was taken by Dickens for Little Nell's faithful Kit Nubbles, in *The Old Curiosity Shop*, and is still in use to-day. *Chris* is, however, the most popular short form at present. Other short forms are *Kester*, the written version *Kris.*, and occasionally *Chippy*.

No account of this name would be complete without mention of the discoverer of the New World. *Cristoforo* Colombo was born in Genoa. In Spain he was called *Cristobal* Colon. We give him the English form of his Christian name, but have changed his surname into Latin, and so speak of *Christopher* Columbus.

CLARENCE A hermit named *Clarus*, in Latin 'famous,' was murdered near Rouen in the ninth century and acclaimed as a martyr. Three villages in the neighbourhood of his cell came to be called Saint-*Clair*; one of these gave its name to the de Clair family. The name *Sinclair* is, of course, also a corruption of Saint-Clair.

The form *Clare*, closer to the original Latin, was used by the Normans of the family who came to this country. 'Red' de Clare was head of the branch that settled in Ireland, giving his name to County Clare; the English branch gave its name to Clare in Suffolk.

When a daughter of this line married Lionel, son of Edward III, her husband was granted the title of Duke of Clarence, never given outside the Royal Family. 'False, fleeting, perjured Clarence,' who was popularly supposed to have been drowned in a wine-cask in the Tower of London, was a brother of Edward IV; his Christian name was George.

A Clarence Babington was christened at Hartlepool in 1593—an early example of the peculiarly English and American habit of giving a surname at the font; but it was only after the title had been revived for William IV, before he became king, that Clarence came to be taken generally as a personal name.

Clare and *Clarry* are used to-day as short forms.

CLAUDE represents the original Latin *Claudius*, as whittled down in French. It is a clan-name, probably meaning 'limping.' When, however, one of the clan became Emperor he was flatteringly assured that his name really meant 'glorious,' and was connected with the verb 'clueo,' 'to be spoken of, reputed' —which was most unlikely. It was under him that Britain was effectively conquered by Rome; his life-story is sympathetically told by Robert Graves in *I, Claudius* and *Claudius the God.*

Loyalty to the Imperial family made the name fashionable in the first and second centuries of our era. A chieftain of the Batavii, a Netherlands tribe, on accepting Roman sovereignty took the name Claudius Civilis. Contemporary with him, in the second century, was Claudius Galen, father of modern medicine.

In the sixth century the fame of St Claude of Besançon began the spread of the name in Western Europe; in France it was given to boys and girls alike. *Claudio* was, and still is, used in Italy: Shakespeare so named Hero's lover in *Much Ado about Nothing.* Claudio is also the modern Spanish version.

From France the name came to Scotland in the sixteenth century, and as *Claud* or *Claude* it has been used by Scots ever since; Field Marshal Sir Claude Auchinleck, Commander-in-Chief in India and in the Middle East during and after the Second World War, is a contemporary bearer. Claude Graham White, in 1913, was the first airman to risk flying by night, and the first air-fighter to mount a machine-gun on his plane during the First World War.

Shakespeare calls the usurper uncle of Hamlet Claudius. In the eighteenth century, Claudius Armgard, a German by origin, who was physician to George III, performed the first recorded successful operation for appendicitis.

But for world-famous bearers of the name we must look to France: Claude Debussy, the nineteenth-century composer, and Claude Monet, the Impressionist painter, are notable examples.

Claudie is the usual pet form to-day.

CLEMENT St Paul, in the fourth chapter of his Epistle to the Philippians, names a Clement ('merciful' in Latin) as one of his fellow-labourers. The fourth Bishop of Rome (first of fourteen popes of the name) is probably the same Clement. He is said to have been flung into the sea, weighted down with an anvil—a tradition that caused him to be regarded, particularly among Scandinavians, as a helper of sailors: hence the dedication of St Clement Danes in the Strand, originally built for Danish settlers in London. The present building, restored after bombing during the Second World War, is the R.A.F. Church, famous for its bells that ring *Oranges and Lemons*. St Clement's connexion with the anvil also led to his adoption as patron of blacksmiths. Joe Gargery's song at the forge in Dickens's *Great Expectations* shows how this tradition lingered almost until modern times. It runs:

> Hammer boys round—Old Clem!
> With a thump and a sound—Old Clem!
> Beat it out, beat it out—Old Clem!
> With a clink for the stout—Old Clem!

This short form goes back to the thirteenth century at least, with another, perhaps even earlier, Northern version, *Clim.* A ballad hero and outlaw who ranged the forests of Cumberland was celebrated as Clim o' the Clough (Clem of the Cliff). These abbreviations show the popularity of the name in England during the Middle Ages. It produced over fifteen surnames, all clearly recognizable.

Clement faded out at the Reformation, but was revived by the Victorians, many of whom had a particularly strong feeling for early Christian saints. Clement Shorter, the literary critic, Clement Davies, former leader of the Liberal Party, and Clement Attlee, second Labour Prime Minister and first Lord Attlee, were born in the reign of Queen Victoria.

CLIFFORD There are some four villages in England situated on slopes near ancient fords over rivers; one or more of these has given the surname Clifford.

As a Christian name, however, Clifford does not seem to have been used until the last century, though unaccountably it has become popular to-day.

Clifford Bax, the poet, and Clifford Curzon, the pianist, use the name in full; but it is most frequently heard in its short form. Examples are Cliff Richards, the jockey, and Cliff Michelmore, the television personality.

CLIVE is first recorded as a place-name in Shropshire in 1327. In meaning it is a variation of 'cliff' (compare the word 'de*cliv*ity'). General Robert Clive, whose family originated in this village, the hero of Arcot and Plassey in the mid eighteenth century, was virtually the founder of British India.

The General inspired the adoption of Clive as a personal

name, in the first place among British families living in India. It most probably gained a wider popularity through Thackeray's *The Newcomes*, in which the son of Colonel Newcome is given the name.

Clive Maskelyne, the conjuror, early in this century, and Clive Brook, the film star, more recently, are examples.

COLIN has two separate origins. In medieval France, whence it was introduced into England, it was a double diminutive of *Nicolas* (see p. 204); but in the predominantly Celtic areas of Britain it was a native name derived from 'cailean,' 'a young hound.' The collie dog may have got its name from the same word.

Colin is an hereditary name among the Campbell family; but the best known, Field Marshal Sir Colin Campbell, Lord Clyde, who has given his name and portrait to so many inn-signs, was really a Glasgow carpenter's son named Colin MacLiver, who took his uncle's surname. He fought in the Peninsular War, in China, India, and the Crimea, and was buried in Westminster Abbey in 1863.

Otherwise, both in France and in Britain, Colin early became a mainly peasant name, typified by Spenser's Colin Clout of the *Shepherds' Calendar* and other country poems.

To-day, however, the name has become general. Colin Gregory, British tennis champion in 1932, won this distinction at the unusually advanced age of forty-eight. Colin Cowdrey the cricketer is a well-known contemporary sportsman, and there is the novelist Colin McInnes.

Bearers of Welsh origin may perhaps derive their name from their native name *Collwyn*, 'hazel grove.' Collwyn, son of Tango, was founder of a tribe in North Wales in the eleventh century.

Colin has also been used to take the place of *Columba.* This is the Latin form of the Celtic *Colum*, meaning 'dove.' The sixth-century St Columba, a stormy monk of royal blood, was banished from Ireland after causing a tribal feud, and sentenced to convert as many souls as he had caused to die. He founded his missionary centre on the island of Iona, from which the whole of Northern England, as well as Western Scotland, was evangelized. His contemporaries called him *Colum* (or *Colm*) Cille, 'dove of the church.'

Colin Tampon is the Swiss national nickname, as John Bull is used for England.

CONAN Still a name honoured in Ireland, Conan means 'intelligent.' Its first recorded bearer seems to have been a legendary seventh-century chieftain, Conan (or *Conal*) Moal, 'Conan the Bald.' Having made a vow never to receive a blow without returning it, even when he found himself in the infernal regions and given a buffet by the Devil, he shouted 'Claw for claw,' and hit back, giving rise to the proverbial Irish expression: 'Claw for claw, as Conan said.'

Conan Meriadec in the fifth century A.D. led the British emigration to Brittany; it is said that the Breton badge of an ermine took its rise from the weasel that fled for refuge under his shield, and so became his mascot. Four dukes of Brittany bore the name after him.

An early British Bishop of London is said to have borne the name, but it inevitably died out in England after the Saxon invasions, and though, like many Celtic names, it was used after the Norman Conquest, it had no famous bearer before Sir Arthur Conan Doyle, the young Irish doctor in Birmingham who had so few patients that he took to story-telling to make ends meet, and so created Sherlock Holmes.

Conn—which is often used for Conan—is said to be derived from the old Celtic *Kunovals*, meaning 'high and mighty,' which is better known as Shakespeare's *Cymbeline*. Shakespeare's play is based on legend; nevertheless, *Cunobelinus* appears on ancient British coins, as the name of a real and powerful ruler in Southern England.

CONRAD means 'bold advice,' 'conja-rad' in Old German. It seems to have been taken as a personal name by the Southern German tribe of the Suevi, whose name survives in Swabia, where St Conrad was Bishop of Constance in the tenth century.

Conrad of Hohenstaufen, Duke of Swabia and King of Jerusalem, Naples, and Sicily in the thirteenth century, was so greatly beloved that his subjects gave him the affectionate diminutive *Conradin*. Defeated by the ruthless Charles of Anjou, he was publicly executed; this roused such a storm of pity and indignation that the name was spread in sympathy throughout German-speaking lands, where it has taken on such short forms as *Kunz*, *Kunzel*, *Kuno*, *Curt* and *Kurt*, all used to-day as separate names.

The English Mercian King *Cenred* shows the Anglo-Saxon version of the name, but it was never used here to any extent, though a Conrad Nye was rector of Foxley in Wiltshire in the fifteenth century. No other bearer is traceable in this country until modern times; the best known, Joseph Conrad, the master of sea stories, was of Polish origin, his real name being *Teodor Jozef Konrad* Korzeniowski. Wisely, having chosen to write in English, he used the English form of his two middle names for his nom-de-plume. In. W. S. Gilbert's *Ruddigore* Conrad Murgatroyd is given as the name of a baronet ancestor, suggesting that the name still had a somewhat aristocratic flavour in late Victorian times. To-day Conrad is common enough to have recognized short forms in *Con* and *Connie*.

CONSTANTINE *Constans*, meaning 'persevering,' was a favourite name among the Romans in later Imperial times, and had the secondary forms *Constantius* and *Constantinus*. It was the last which was destined to become most used, through the first Emperor who officially tolerated Christianity. Constantine was reputedly the son of the British princess Helena, daughter of 'Old King Cole' of Colchester, and named his sons by each of the three different forms.

This tradition, whatever truth there may be in it, early gave Constantine a vogue in Britain, with *Cystennin* and *Cystenian* as later Welsh variations. The name was particularly popular in Cornwall. It was taken by a Cornish missionary to Scotland in the sixth century, in whose honour the Pictish King Constantine Mac Fergus was christened; he bequeathed it to three of his successors before the tenth century.

Constantinus occurs in Domesday Book, and the name in various forms continued in use in England until the seventeenth century. In Ireland it was taken to replace *Conan* (see p. 83) and similar names; the modern writer Constantine Fitzgibbon shows its use there to-day.

Constantinople, of course, means 'Constantine's city,' from the Emperor who founded it as the 'New Rome.' The Russians, who regarded themselves as the heirs of the Roman Empire of the East, naturally favoured his name; it was also borne by the late King of Greece.

Constant is sometimes used in this country—probably rather with the literal meaning of the Latin 'constans' than from the name of Constantine's third son: Constant Lambert, best known for his *Rio Grande*, was a lively experimental composer earlier in the present century.

CRISPIN, connected with our word 'crisp,' means in Latin 'curly-headed.' Two brothers, *Crispinus* and *Crispinianus*, shoemakers of Soissons, in France, were put to death in the third century for preaching and practising Christianity; they were immersed in a tank of molten lead.

It was on their feast-day, October 25, that the battle of Agincourt was won by Henry V. Shakespeare, basing his words on historical fact, includes in the warrior-king's rousing speech before the fight the lines:

> And Crispin Crispian shall ne'er go by,
> From this day to the ending of the world,
> But we in it shall be remembered.

Both *Crispin* and *Crispinian*, the latter in various forms, were used in the Middle Ages in England. Crispin has survived, *Crispian* is less common.

St Crispin's Church in Bermondsey, South London, has been chosen in modern times as the religious headquarters of the shoemakers of England. A gigantic pair of shoes is hoisted on its flagstaff on the Saint's Day.

CUTHBERT There were formerly a number of English names beginning with the Anglo-Saxon word 'cuth,' meaning 'famous': *Cuthman*, 'famous man'; *Cuthred*, 'famous counsel'; *Cuthwin*, 'famous friend,' and so on. The word is still found in the adjective 'uncouth,' now applied to awkward and uncultured people; originally it meant merely 'unfamiliar' or 'not known.' The only name of this class in normal use to-day is *Cuthbert*, 'famous-bright,' in Anglo-Saxon *Cuthbeorht*. The Scottish county town Kircudbright, meaning 'church Cuthbert,' and pronounced 'Kirkoobry,' shows another development of the name, as does Cotherstone, meaning 'Cuthbert's stone,' in Northumbria. *Cuddie* Headrigg, showing the Scottish pet form, is a whimsical character in Scott's *Old Mortality*.

St Cuthbert was a Northumbrian shepherd-boy in the seventh century, when the kingdom of Northumbria included not only England north of the Humber, but Scotland nearly up to the Highlands. He became a monk of Melrose, and later prior, before he was forced, much against his will, to become bishop of the whole kingdom. His shrine at Durham was the Northern rival to that of St Thomas of Canterbury in the South.

Naturally, it was in the North that his namesakes were most numerous: Admiral Collingwood, Nelson's comrade-in-arms who took command after his death at Trafalgar, was a Northumbrian.

CYRIL (*Kurillos*) is a name of Greek derivation, connected with the word 'kyrios,' meaning 'lord': 'lordly' is, perhaps, the best rendering.

There were two celebrated Christian teachers of the name in the fourth and fifth centuries: St Cyril of Jerusalem and St Cyril of Alexandria. More generally remembered is a ninth-century St Cyril. With his brother Methodius he took Christianity to the Slavs, for whom he devised the alphabet known as 'Cyrillic,' enabling sounds peculiar to Russian and kindred languages to be written as they are to-day.

The name only came into regular use in England during the last century. Dr Cyril Garbett was Archbishop of York in the 1940's. The Cyril in E. Nesbit's *Five Children and It* is the eldest boy of a family in the early years of this century; the author's choice of his name is a sign of its popularity at the time.

To-day Sir Cyril Hinshelwood has the double distinction of having been elected President of both the scientific Royal Society and the Classical Association.

Cyriack, or *Syriack*, is a name of similar meaning. From the saint of this name—a child-martyr, *Cyriacus*, of the early Church—the French Military Academy of St-*Cyr* is named. Cyriack Skinner was a friend of the poet Milton.

The Welsh form is *Girioel*. The only short form of Cyril is *Cy*, shared with *Cyrus*.

CYRUS This name is one of the few, apart from those of Jewish origin, used to-day in the West but derived from Asia. It was the name of the Emperor of Persia who allowed the Jews to return to Palestine from their captivity in Babylon. Its original form seems to have been derived from the Persian 'khuru,' meaning 'throne.' The Greeks rendered it *Kuros* (probably from its similarity in sound to their 'kyrios' (see *Cyril*, p. 87).

The first recorded bearer was the founder of the Persian Empire, about 500 B.C. His namesake, Cyrus the Younger, who flourished about a century later, employed ten thousand Greek mercenaries to fight for him. Their march across Asia Minor to the coast is recorded by their leader Xenophon in his *Anabasis*, or "March up-country"; Xenophon also wrote a treatise which he called *The Education of Cyrus*, describing the ideal training for a ruler. The heir to the Persian throne to-day is Prince *Khooroo*.

Cyrus was first used in England in the seventeenth century, but only by Puritans. In America it has become popular: *Cy* and *Cyro* are used there as pet forms.

DANIEL *Dan*, Hebrew for 'judge,' and name of one of the Tribes of Israel, is sometimes used by itself as a personal name; but even when the bearer is commonly known as Dan this is generally the short form of Daniel, 'God is Judge.'

Daniel the prophet, according to the book of the Old Testament that goes under his name, was cast into a den of lions for refusing to deny his faith, but emerged unharmed, later to interpret the mysterious letters of fire in Belshazzar's banqueting-hall that announced the doom of Babylon. In the apocryphal books of the Old Testament Daniel appears as the first detective-hero. He cleared the reputation of the beautiful Susanna, and exposed the trickery of the priests of Bel, who pretended their idol ate its offerings, by strewing ashes to show their footprints when they came to steal them.

The name seems only to have come into general use in the twelfth century, giving the short form *Dannet*; it survived the Reformation, and its best-known bearers have lived since the seventeenth century. Daniel Defoe, author of *Robinson Crusoe*, has also been claimed as the founder of our Secret Service. When sentenced to the pillory for his attacks on Church and State, he was pelted by the London populace, who adored him for his democratic principles, not with garbage and stones, but with flowers.

Daniel Lambert of Stamford, who died in 1809, still holds the record for weight: nearly fifty-three stone. Kipling gives the short form of the name to the chief boy character in *Puck of Pook's Hill*. Dan Leno, the Victorian comedian, created the pantomime dame.

In America Daniel Webster, born in 1782, was a notable politician and orator: his collected works fill eighteen volumes; Dan Boone the frontiersman rivals Davy Crockett as a folk-hero. *Danny* Kaye, the film comedian—*Danill* Kaminsky—

is of Polish origin. His real name resembles the *Danilo* of the former Montenegrin princely family.

The Irish have taken Daniel as a substitute for their native *Domhnall*, 'world ruler' (see *Donald*, p. 97). Daniel O'Connell, known in Ireland as 'The Liberator,' was the leading representative of his country's interests in the British Parliament during the early nineteenth century. *Danny Boy*, with its haunting tune, *The Londonderry Air*, is perhaps the most popular of Irish songs.

In Wales the name has absorbed the native *Deiniol*, 'attractive' or 'charming,' and is still much used. St Deiniol, in the sixth century, founded two famous abbeys, both known as Bangor ('white choir'), one on the Menai Straits, the other on the Dee.

"A Daniel come to judgment," a proverbial saying implying a just verdict, is used by Shakespeare in the trial scene of *The Merchant of Venice*, when Portia gives her decision on Shylock's claim for his "pound of flesh."

DAVID Dodavehu is the Hebrew for 'beloved of Jehovah': the earliest known bearer is the slayer of the giant Goliath who became second King of Israel, traditionally also the author of the Psalms.

Absorbing the Celtic forms *Dahi* and *Dathi*, 'nimble,' David early became popular in both Scotland and Wales. The sixth-century St David was Bishop of Menevia, now known after him as St David's. A teetotaller and vegetarian, he was known to his contemporaries as 'the water man,' and the leek, which grows wild in profusion round his village cathedral, is a fitting symbol for him. When his bones were discovered in the last century he was found to have been six foot four in height. His countrymen call him *Dewi* Sant, 'David the saint,' but do not favour this form of the name, preferring *Dafydd*, with the short forms *Dai* and *Deio*. Dafydd ap Owain was a Welsh chieftain of the twelfth century, and three great bards, all known as Dafydd ap Gwilym, lived in the fourteenth and fifteenth centuries. David of the White Rock (y Garreg Wen), otherwise David Owen, recorded on his deathbed a tune he had heard in a vision. Scott wrote words to it under the title *The Dying Bard*.

David Lloyd George successfully directed British policy during the First World War, and was rewarded by an earldom. David Jones to-day is in the first rank of British artists, and Dai Rees is a notable golfer.

David I of Scotland, who ruled during the tenth century, was canonized for his lavish donations to the Church, causing his descendant, who became James I of England, to call him "a sair (sore) saint for the Crown." David II reigned from 1324 to 1371. Of later Scottish bearers the most famous are Sir David Brewster, who made important discoveries regarding the polarization of light and invented the kaleidoscope, and David Livingstone, who evangelized Central Africa.

In England David is not to be found before the Norman Conquest, but the surnames *Davy*, *Davit*, *Daw*, *Dakin*, and *Deakin* were all medieval short forms. David Garrick was our foremost actor of the eighteenth century, though in modern times the name was not popular until recently, when it leapt into favour: in 1958 and 1959 it had second place of all male names, beaten only by John. Princess Margaret's son, Viscount Linley, is named David Albert Charles. David was chosen partly because of the Welsh connexions of Lord Snowdon, and also because it was the Christian name of the late Sir David Bowes-Lyon, brother of Queen Elizabeth the Queen Mother.

The popularity of the name in fiction is shown in Scotland by David Balfour in Stevenson's *Kidnapped* and *Catriona*, in America by E. N. Westcott's *David Harum*, in England by *David Copperfield*, the hero and narrator of Dickens's greatest novel. Earlier in the present century David Lawrence (better known as D. H. Lawrence), a Nottinghamshire miner's son, became a novelist and poet of the first rank.

Taffy, like 'Thavies' for Davies, is an English attempt to pronounce the name in the Welsh manner; *Davy* is the Old English pet form: *Dave* is modern.

'Davy Jones' sounds like a Welshman, but is probably a corruption of the West Indian negroes' 'Duppy (=ghost) Jonah.' To sailors he is the Devil, who uses the sea-bed, his locker, as a mass-grave. Davy Crockett, the ballad hero, was an historical American frontiersman, whose exploits have become famous on both sides of the Atlantic.

The "Star of David" is the national emblem of Israel, a six-pointed figure composed of two triangles.

DENIS This name is often spelt *Dennis*, or *Denys*, as in Old French; it has been worn down in the course of ages from the Greek *Dionysios*, derived from *Dionysos*, 'the divine one of Nysa.' Better known as Bacchus, this god was protector of the vine, and was worshipped at the grape-harvest revels, where the dancing and singing of ballads developed into the Greek drama. Though there were stories of his birth in Greece, Dionysos was generally regarded as a foreign divinity. Arrian, a writer who accompanied Alexander the Great on his Asiatic campaigns, identifies Nysa with a mountain in Afghanistan, and describes the celebrations held there in the god's honour by the Greek army. It is a fact that the district was famous for its grapes and wine until the inhabitants became Mohammedans late in the nineteenth century.

The adjectival form, Dionysios, was used in Greece and Sicily in classical times: the best known, Dionysios, tyrant of Syracuse, is said to have ordered a tube to be bored connecting his bed-head with the quarry prison, whence his victims' groans could be heard as a lullaby.

The first Christian of the name was the Areopagite, or Senator, of Athens converted by St Paul, as can be read in the seventeenth chapter of the Acts. He was later identified with *Dionysius*, the first Bishop of Paris, who became patron saint of the Counts of Paris, and later of France. The Abbey of Saint Denis, outside Paris, was built to enshrine his relics, and became the royal burying place: there was kept the royal standard and the Oriflamme, and 'Montjoie St Denys!' became the French battle-cry. Denis of Burgundy is the cunning crossbowman companion of Gerard in Charles Reade's *The Cloister and the Hearth*, with his heartening catchword "Courage, mon ami, le Diable est mort!" ("Courage, my friend, the Devil is dead!")

The name came to England towards the end of the twelfth century, sometimes in the form *Dionis*: an odd example is a *Deenys* Scorchebefe in the fifteenth century. But for a notable bearer we have to wait until the present day, with Denis Compton, the cricketer.

Dennis seems to be the usual Irish spelling, the name replacing the old native *Donnchadh* (see *Duncan*, p. 99).

Diot, a medieval French diminutive of *Dion*, became a surname in England but in the course of time was changed into *Dwight*. A John Dwight left Essex for New England in the seventeenth century, and founded a numerous family. From him descended Timothy Dwight, parson and poet, best known in America for his song of the Revolution, *Columbia*. He became President of Yale University in 1795, and, like Dr *Chauncey* of Harvard, was honoured by his students' choice of his surname for their children. In the following century Dwight Moody was associated with Ira Sankey in the com-position of their famous Gospel Hymns, and in our time Dwight David Eisenhower was appointed Supreme Com-mander of the Allied Forces in Europe, becoming in 1952 President of the United States.

DENZIL is hardly a common name, but has been used, always with Cornish connexions, at least since the seventeenth century, when Denzil Holles held down the Speaker of the House of Commons in his chair, to prevent his adjourning the sitting as ordered by Charles I.

A variation is *Denzell*, but neither form can be satisfactorily interpreted. It seems generally agreed that the first part of the name comes from the Celtic 'dinas,' meaning 'stronghold'; the second syllable may come from the Old Cornish 'uhel,' 'high.' Another interpretation is 'fertile upland.'

The modern Cornish place-name Dinah's Hill is clearly a corruption of the name: Cornish is to-day a dead language.

DEREK Originally recorded as *Thiudoricus*, from the Old German 'theuda,' 'people,' and 'ric,' 'ruler,' this name has nothing to do with *Theodore* (see p. 253); it is a Germanic name used by the Goths. *Theodoric* the Great ruled in Northern Italy in the fifth and sixth centuries A.D. He came to be a magnet for legends among the southern Germans, who called him *Dietrich* of Bern (Verona) and made him a dragon-slayer who killed twelve champions for the reward of one rose and one kiss.

Though both a *Theodric* and a *Tedrick*, apparently both

Saxons, appear in Domesday Book, the name did not persist, at any rate in records, until it was reintroduced by Flemings engaged in the wool trade in the fifteenth century, and in the course of time it changed from *Dederick* to *Derric*. From the French form, *Thierry*, we get the surname Terry (the Christian name *Terry* is generally a short form of *Terence*). But in the seventeenth century it fell into disfavour, possibly on account of a notorious Tyburn hangman of the time. This bearer is said to be the origin of the use of 'derrick' for a pivoting crane.

Somewhere about the beginning of the present century the name came back into favour, and in various forms. The Chancellor of the Exchequer in 1960 was Mr *Derick* Heathcoat Amory; the Minister of Health was Mr *Derek* Walker-Smith. The fifteenth-century forms *Deryk* and *Deryck* have also been revived, and even *Derrick* and *Deric* are used. *Dirk* Bogarde, the film-actor, of Dutch origin, has the usual Netherlands form, a shortening of the official *Diederik*. Derek Ibbotson, the athlete, and Derek McCullough, 'Uncle Mac' of the B.B.C. children's programmes, show that this form is the commonest in present use.

Derry and *Rick* are present-day pet forms, also *Dekker*.

DERMOT This name is really *Diarmaid*, which like most Old Irish names has several alternative forms: *Diarmid*, *Diarmit*, *Diarmuid*, and *Diarmuit*. Its meaning is perhaps 'free from envy,' or possibly 'without orders,' which implies 'free man.'

The legendary Diarmaid eloped with Grainne, Queen of Tara; but having been tracked down, he was compelled by the lady's husband to hunt a savage boar, and met his death: a common theme in legends, as seen in the Greek story of Meleager.

Dermot McMurrough was King of Leinster in the twelfth

century, spreading his name particularly in Tipperary and Limerick, where it became shortened to *Derby*, whence '*Darby* and Joan,' describing a happy old married couple.

DESMOND, originally 'Deas Mumhain,' means 'man from South Munster,' and was at first a surname only; it seems not to have been taken as a personal name in Ireland before the nineteenth century, or in England before the 1880's. The name appears first among the McCarthy family: Desmond McCarthy was a well-known man of letters during the nineteenth century.

DOMINIC may either mean 'belonging to the Lord,' or 'born on Sunday,' from the Latin 'dies dominica,' meaning 'day of the Lord.'

The Dominicans, the order of preaching friars founded by the saint in the early thirteenth century, were known in this country as Black Friars, from their black cloaks. The London station and district of Blackfriars stand on the site of their principal monastery. St Dominic is often shown with black and white dogs at his feet: a punning allusion to 'Domini canes.' 'the Lord's hounds.'

St Dominic was a Spaniard; his name is consequently most popular in his own country, as *Domingo*. The Dominican Republic, formerly San Domingo, has its name from him. So, from their black-and-white plumage, has a species of penguins.

Dominic was never a common name in England, though occurring often enough in the Middle Ages to have such varying forms as *Dominick*, *Dominy* and *Domenyk*. At the Reformation it died out except among Catholics; but recently there have been signs of its general revival.

In Ireland it has been more frequently used, often as a substitute for *Domhnall* (see the following entry).

DONALD This name is in reality the Gaelic *Domhnall*, meaning 'world-ruler,' identical, it has been claimed, with Caesar's Gallic chieftain *Dumnorix*: the Romans were never able to record a 'barbarian' name without altering it. Appropriately, it was borne by six Scottish kings, Donald I being the first Christian ruler of the Scots; so many royal bearers naturally popularized it, and there was a ninth-century St Donald of Forfar.

Eventually the name became so widespread that Scott's caustic Lowlander Cuddie Headrigg, in *Old Mortality*, refers to it as a typical kilted Highlander's name, with his "a' the Donalds and Duncans and Dougalds that ever wore bottomless breeks." Shakespeare's *Donalbain*, in *Macbeth* was actually *Domhnall Ban*, 'Donald the White.' The Irish form is *Donal*.

Among present-day bearers, Donald Campbell, who achieved a water-speed record of 260 miles an hour in 1959, is a Scotsman. Walt Disney's endearingly cantankerous Donald Duck shows that the name is common in the United States. Dr Donald Soper, President of the Methodist Conference, is London-born; Sir Donald Wolfit, the Shakespearean actor-manager, comes from Nottingham.

There is an old Celtic name *Donn*, meaning 'brown' (we still use the word 'dun'); the popular *Don* of to-day is usually, however, the short form of Donald. In the case of the American Don Marquis, though the bearer's father was a Donald, Don is the poet's official name. Don Thompson was Olympic walking champion in 1960.

Sir Donald Bradman, the Australian cricketer, is also generally known as Don. In fact, his fellow-countrymen call him 'the Don.' This is a play on words: the Spanish 'don' (from the Latin 'dominus,' 'Lord') means 'sir,' and is not a name at all. It is in this sense that university lecturers are known as 'dons.'

DOUGLAS was originally a place-name, Dubh Glas. 'Dubh' means 'water,' 'glas' was used indifferently for dark blue, dark green, and grey: accurate colour-names are comparatively modern. 'Dark water' seems the best rendering.

One 'dark water' is mentioned as the site of a Northern victory of King Arthur, and it is found again in Devonshire as Dawlish. Douglas, in the Isle of Man, and Douglas in Lanarkshire are both named from their 'dark water.'

Giving its name to the Scottish clan that lived near one of these dark streams, by the early seventeenth century Douglas had also become a girl's name and, as Camden the antiquarian tells us in his name-list, published in 1605, already counted English bearers.

Famous among a famous clan was Sir James, known among the Northern English as "the Black Douglas," among the Scots as "Good Sir James"; he was one of Robert Bruce's chief supporters. Another branch of the family was known as "the Red Douglases," on account of the prevailing colour of their hair.

Dr Douglas Hyde became first President of Eire in 1938; he was among the first modern poets to write in the Irish language. Douglas Bader, a hero of the Battle of Britain, is perhaps the best-known bearer in England.

Duggie and *Doug* are pet forms.

DUDLEY in Worcestershire was 'Duda's meadow'; the Saxon Duda of Mercia founded Tewkesbury Abbey.

But the Dudley family, who rose to fame under the Tudor dynasty, gave the name currency; Robert Dudley, Earl of

Leicester, was Queen Elizabeth's favourite. *Dud* Dudley, in the seventeenth century, first smelted iron with coal. Sir Dudley Pound was Chief of the British Naval Staff from the beginning of the Second World War. The only fictional bearer of interest in English literature is found in Algernon Blackwood's humorous book, *Dudley and Gilderoy*, in which Dudley, a country-house cat, with his accomplice Gilderoy, a parrot, make their way unassisted to London.

Nowhere does the short form *Dud* seem popular to-day—perhaps because 'duds' is a slang word for old clothes and for explosives that fail to go off. But there is no connexion between the slang word and the name Dudley.

DUGALD, in Gaelic 'dubh gall,' meaning 'dark stranger,' was originally applied by the Celts to a Dane, in contrast with *Fingal*, 'fionn gall,' 'fair stranger,' used for the fair-haired Norwegians. Later it became so much acclimatized that in Scotland *Dougal* was used as the Lowland nickname for a Highlander. Dougal is also used as a personal name: the red-haired savage who led the "Gorbals Diehards" in John Buchan's *Huntingtower* was a Dougal.

Dugald Dalgetty, the pedantic old soldier in Scott's *Legend of Montrose*, is one of the raciest of all the great novelist's characters.

DUNCAN 'Donn chadh' in Gaelic and 'donn cean' in Irish both mean 'brown warrior.' Duncan, as we now pronounce it, was the name of two Scottish kings. The first reigned from 1034 to 1040, when Macbeth murdered him.

Shakespeare's picture of the venerable sovereign murdered by his ungrateful thane is unforgettable, but hardly historical: Macbeth's claim to the throne was at least as good as his victim's, and the latter was no older than his murderer.

Though the name is almost confined to Scots, a Somerset *Donecan* is recorded in Domesday Book. The Irish form has been ousted by *Dennis*.

To-day Duncan Grant is one of our most distinguished Scottish painters; the name seems still a Scottish preserve.

DUNSTAN, an Anglo-Saxon name, presumably means 'hill-stone.' St Dunstan, in the tenth century, was an energetic Archbishop of Canterbury, statesman, Church reformer and a skilful musician and artist.

Legend has it that being tempted by the Devil while at his furnace, Dunstan seized the fiend's nose with his pliers, causing him to take flight to Tunbridge Wells, where cooling off his proboscis gave the waters their sulphur-content.

DYLAN the Dark, 'son of the wave,' as the name is traditionally interpreted, was a legendary Welsh hero, born to the sea-god. He leaped into the sea "as soon as he had been baptized," and when he died the waves lamented him. It seems likely, however, that the name is also connected with 'dylanwad,' meaning 'influence'—so many names have double meanings. The correct pronunciation is 'dillan.'

Dylan is rare outside Wales; but the poet Dylan Thomas, best known for his *Under Milk Wood*, the radio story-poem of a day in a small Welsh harbour town, has spread the fame, if not the use, of the name.

EDGAR 'Rich' and 'spear' are the two components of the Anglo-Saxon *Eadgar*. The prefix 'ead' seems to have been almost peculiar to the royal family of Wessex and their descendants.

Edgar the Peaceful, Alfred's great-grandson, was the first publicly recognized King of England. He strengthened the English navy, and united eight lesser kings under him: they made the first recorded 'eight,' rowing him up the Dee to Chester, to ratify their alliance. Edgar Aetheling, the last legitimate Saxon claimant to the throne, died in the early twelfth century.

Edgar was never common after the Conquest; but Shakespeare, thinking of it as an 'ancient' name, incongruously gave it to an Ancient British character, the Edgar of *King Lear*.

The choice by Scott of Edgar as the name of the Master of Ravenswood in *The Bride of Lammermoor*, published in 1819, marks the period of its revival. Since then it has spread to the Continent, and across the Atlantic. Edgar Allan Poe, originator of detective tales in which the problem is solved by reasoning, and a master of the horror story, was born as early as 1809. The modern American author Edgar Rice Burroughs created *Tarzan*, and Edgar Wallace, an English back-street urchin, became a best-seller of the 1920's.

The first syllable, *Ed*, is the usual short form.

EDMUND The name is a compound of the Anglo-Saxon words for 'prosperity' and 'guardian': 'ead' and 'mund.' *Edmond* is the French version, but has been used in England since the Middle Ages.

The first noteworthy Edmund was King of the East Angles, shot to death by the Danes in 870 for refusing to renounce Christianity; from him the abbey and town of Bury St Edmunds were named. Edmund the Magnificent, King of England, died in 946; Edmund Ironside, son of Ethelred the Unready, ruled for less than a year after closing the Danish wars by his treaty with Canute.

After the Norman Conquest, though Saxon names in general were frowned on, the two royal saints, Edward the Confessor and Edmund, were regarded as more saintly than Saxon, and so the name was passed on in the Royal Family, and has never fallen out of use; it was the last name of the late Duke of Kent.

The first non-royal bearer of interest was St Edmund Rich, a native of Abingdon who became Archbishop of Canterbury. He died in 1240. Edmund Spenser wrote his *Faërie Queene* in the great days of Queen Elizabeth; the seventeenth-century astronomer Edmond Halley identified and named Halley's Comet; Edmund Kean was unrivalled in the early nineteenth century for his acting of Shakespearean parts; Edmund Cartright, who lived from 1743 to 1823, invented the power-loom for cotton spinning; Edmund Burke was among the great Parliamentarians of the eighteenth century.

In our own day the New Zealander Sir Edmund Hillary owes his knighthood to his conquest of Mount Everest in 1953; Edmund Rubbra, the composer, has revived the old English musical traditions of the sixteenth century.

The Irish also favour the name, in the form *Eamon*, or *Eamonn*. Eamonn de Valera is the virtual founder of the Irish Free State.

Edmund shares the short forms of Edward except *Ted* and *Teddy*.

EDWARD 'Weard' and 'mund' in Anglo-Saxon have identical meanings, so that Edward, like Edmund, means 'guardian of prosperity.'

The first King Edward, "the Elder," was son and successor of Alfred the Great; another King Edward, "the Martyr," was stabbed on his stepmother's orders as he drank a cup of wine after hunting, so that her own son Ethelred might become king in his place: a tragedy both for Edward and for England.

But to the Saxons it was Edward the Confessor, their last undisputed native ruler, who became the symbol of their national pride. Henry III built the present Abbey Church of Westminster and enshrined the royal saint's body there, and giving the name to his elder son, Edward I, set the seal on the fusion of Norman and Saxon.

Three Edwards occupied the throne of England continuously from 1272 till 1377. Since the death of Edward III five sovereigns have borne the name: the last, as Duke of Windsor, is alive to-day, though he abdicated in 1936.

Edward has spread to all ranks and professions. Edward Alleyne was the prosperous Elizabethan actor who founded Dulwich "College of God's Gift." In the seventeenth century Edward Cocker wrote a book on commercial arithmetic with such care that 'according to Cocker' is a synonym for accuracy. Edward Gibbon's *Decline and Fall of the Roman Empire* is the greatest English historical work of the eighteenth century: his friends addressed him as *Eddard*, the polite pronunciation of the period, which survived among old-fashioned speakers well into the 1800's. Edward Lear was not only the author of *The Book of Nonsense* but a painter of the first rank. Sir Edward Elgar, at the turn of the century, was the leading English composer.

The oldest pet form of Edward seems to be *Ned*: *Neddy* was the pet name for donkeys; *Neddie* is also found, with *Ed* and *Eddie*. *Ted* is of more recent use, as is *Teddy*. Teddy Boys took their name from the notion that their narrow trousers and other eccentricities of clothing were a revival of the fashions of the time of Edward VII. The Teddy-bear, however, is named after the American President *Theodore* Roosevelt.

In Ireland *Eamon(n)* is used for both Edward and Edmund. In Wales *Iorwerth* or *Yorath*, a combination of 'ior,' 'lord,' and 'gwerth,' 'worth,' is taken as the equivalent of Edward; it has an old diminutive, *Iolo*.

EDWIN, from the Anglo-Saxon 'ead,' 'prosperity,' and 'wine,' 'friend,' is alphabetically the last of the 'Ed-' names. St Edwin, first Christian king of Northumbria, was killed in battle against Penda of Mercia in 633. Edwin is reputed to have given his name to Edinburgh (Edwin's Burgh).

After his time the use of the name seems to have declined, and by the twelfth century it had almost vanished except as a surname.

The eighteenth century revived it; from this period dates Oliver Goldsmith's ballad *The Hermit*, whose hero and heroine, Edwin and Angelina, became type-names for sentimental lovers, as the captions of old *Punch* drawings show.

The name became popular in the time of Queen Victoria. Sir Edwin Landseer designed the Trafalgar Square lions, and painted innumerable dogs and stags. Dickens chose *Edwin Drood* for the title of his last, unfinished novel; and the poet Edwin Waugh, the "Lancashire Burns," died in 1890.

Arnold Bennett gave the name to the hero of his Staffordshire novel *Clayhanger*, published in 1901. Sir Edwin Lutyens was an architect, designer of the Cenotaph in Whitehall and of the familiar red telephone-booth. He and Sir Edwin Lankester, pioneer of comparative anatomy, were both born in the mid-Victorian age; since then Edwin has tended to become uncommon, though it is still found, appearing also as *Edwyn*. Its pet forms are shared by Edgar, Edmund and Edward.

Edwulf, or *Edulph* ('prosperity-wolf'), given in Camden's seventeenth-century list of names, is now unknown; it is probably a garbled *Adolphus*. *Edred* ('prosperity-counsel') was used by E. Nesbit for the boy hero of *The House of Arden*.

ELIAS The name *Elijah*, though it may linger among old-fashioned Protestants, is of more historical than present-day interest. It was a longer form of *Eli*, 'high,' made by adding 'Jah,' (Jehovah, 'the Lord'). The Greek version of Elijah was *Elias*.

A body of hermits who settled on Mount Carmel, in Palestine, claimed the Prophet Elias as their founder. The hermits became known in the thirteenth century as the Carmelite Friars, and Elias gained the status of a Calendar saint.

The first form of the name recorded in England is *Elis*, at the end of the twelfth century, indicating the origin of the surname Ellis. In the thirteenth century the French *Elie* appears. Chaucer uses *Elye*. It was the Puritans who took to using Elijah. But Elias persisted: Elias Ashmole, in the seventeenth century, founded the Ashmolean Museum at Oxford.

The bridge expert *Ely* Culbertson shows Chaucer's version of the name to be used in America.

Elisha ('the Lord is Salvation'), on whom fell the mantle, and authority, of his teacher, Elijah, was called by the Greeks *Eliseus*, a name so much resembling Elias that there was doubtless often confusion between the two.

Elihu ('God is the Lord') was one of Job's comforters; this name was not used before Puritan times. Senator Elihu Root, of the United States, was awarded the Nobel Prize for Peace in 1912.

Eleazar ('the Lord is my helper') was one of King David's captains. Adopted by the Puritans, his name is still found occasionally in America.

ELMER This may appear to be a typical American name; but its earliest known form was the Anglo-Saxon *Aethelmaer*, 'noble-famous,' common in England before 1066. There was a Saxon Abbot Elmer, or *Almer*, of Canterbury; and a Saxon Aethelmaer invented a primitive glider, which crashed owing to a defective tail fin. The name was Frenchified by the Normans into *Aylmer*—though this form may also have been derived from the Norse *Hjalmar*, 'helmed warrior,' and so have a double origin and interpretation.

But the old Elmer reappeared as a surname. Two brothers of the Elmer family settled in New Jersey, played an active part in the War of Independence, and so bequeathed it, as a personal name once more, to the United States.

Sinclair Lewis used the name as typically American for his novel *Elmer Gantry*, published in 1927. As a film, it gained wide popularity.

ENOCH, said to mean 'dedication,' was the name of Adam's descendant, the father of Methuselah. A book of heavenly revelations was attributed to him by the Jews after their return from Babylon.

A Welsh chieftain in Anglo-Saxon times named *Enog* was sentenced to have his right hand cut off for crossing Offa's Dyke into Saxon territory; but no other example is recorded in England until the Puritans began to favour it. Enoch became frequent among their descendants, particularly in the North and in the Midlands. Enoch Arden, in Tennyson's poem of the name, was a seaman who returned after years of adventure to find his wife remarried; he left his home once more without revealing himself, and died of a broken heart. Enoch was the first name of the great novelist of the Potteries, Arnold Bennett, who flourished at the beginning of the present century, and the name is still used.

St Enoch's Station in Glasgow gets its name from an old church, whose actual dedication was to St Thenew, mother of St Mungo.

ERASMUS is a Greek name meaning 'desired.' St Erasmus, who gave it popularity, is a shadowy figure, a bishop supposed to have been put to death by disembowelling, perhaps in the second century, which made him patron saint of stomach-sufferers. The windlass supposed to have been used in his execution made him a favourite among Neapolitan sailors, who call him St *Elmo*, and name the electrical discharges seen at mastheads before and after storms 'St Elmo's fire.'

The greatest purely historical bearer of the name was the Dutch Erasmus, the sixteenth-century scholar and translator of the New Testament from the original Greek. His real name was *Gerhard*, which he chose to translate as if it meant 'desire,' though its correct interpretation is 'spear-hard' (see p. 125).

The name was also known in England by the sixteenth century: an Erasmus Paston died in 1540. Sir Erasmus Earle lived from 1590 to 1667, and was the great-grandfather of Erasmus Darwin, scientist and poet of the eighteenth century (grandfather of Charles Darwin).

Like the similar *Erastus*, which has much the same meaning, Erasmus was a favourite for slaves in America, who were frequently called by high-sounding classical names; but it generally became shortened to *Rasmus*, just as Erastus was turned into *Rastus*. In Denmark, however, Rasmus is the normal form.

ERIC is usually said to mean 'ever-ruling,' from the Old Norse 'Eyrekr,' used as a personal name. In modern

Norwegian it is *Eirik*. But as 'ey' is an old word for 'island,' as in Anglesey ('Angles' Island'), *Eyrekr* may equally well be explained as 'island-ruler'—most suitable for Vikings.

There was a Gothic chieftain in Spain called *Euric*; the Danes have had six kings of the name; the Swedes boast fourteen, among them St Eric, treacherously killed by Magnus of Denmark in 1151. Eric the Red, a Norseman, founded a colony in Greenland in 986, and gave it its inappropriate name, probably to attract immigrants.

To link the name with England, we have Aesc Eric, son of Hengist, and in Domesday Book there is an *Iricus*: this suggests that, though unrecorded in Anglo-Saxon times, the name was in use among Scandinavian settlers.

After the eleventh century, not a single example of the name has been found in England until the nineteenth century. It was in 1858 that Dean Farrar published his school-story *Eric, or Little by Little*. Rider Haggard's heroic Norse romance *Eric Brighteyes* provides a stormy contrast to the good Dean's moral tale.

The name is used in America, with short forms *Air* and *Erie* (*Rickie* has been heard in England); though the best-known bearer there seems to have been Prince Eric—a bull, who recently fetched the record price of 100,000 dollars. In England Eric Kennington was official war artist in the Second World War; and Eric Partridge is a fertile writer on names and words.

ERNEST is one of the few names that explains its own meaning; though *Ernust*, the original Old German form of the word, may also mean 'vigour.'

The earliest bearer of importance seems to have been Duke Ernest of Swabia, born in the late tenth century. It was always a favourite aristocratic name in Germany, eventually taken into general use, and now shortened to *Ernst.*

In 1655 *Ernestus* is mentioned in an English treatise on names, but is there noted as German. Ernest only became naturalized in England after the Hanoverian kings had introduced it as a family name used from the time of their tenth-century ancestor, Ernest the Valiant, Margrave of Austria. Ernest Augustus, Duke of Cumberland, became King of Hanover on the accession of Queen Victoria. It was about the time of his death, in 1851, that the name became general in Britain.

Sir Ernest Shackleton, the Antarctic explorer, was born in 1874. Oscar Wilde suggested the name in the punning title of his comedy *The Importance of Being Earnest,* produced in 1899, in which the hero's chance of marriage depends on his having been christened as Ernest. Lord Rutherford the physicist, another Ernest, made his name in the present century.

The German-speaking Swiss have a partiality for the name. Ernest is the second son of the castaway Swiss Family, in the book known by that odd English title *The Swiss Family Robinson*: he was, we are told, "an intelligent and well-informed boy." Ernest Bloch, now the greatest musician of America, was Swiss by birth. Ernest Hemingway, the American author, who died in 1961, had an international reputation.

Ern and *Ernie* are the short forms. The use of 'Ernie' in connexion with British Government Premium Bonds comes from the initials of the words 'Electronic Random Number Indicator Equipment,' which suggests the name.

ESME This name is a Scottish borrowing from the French *Esmé*, which was derived from the Latin 'aestimatus,' meaning 'esteemed'; though it was so often spelt *Aymie* that it came to be mistaken for a form of the French 'aimé,' 'beloved.'

Its first use in Britain, as far as is known, was when the French mother of the Duke of Lennox gave it to her son Esme Stuart, baptized in 1542. The Duke handed his name on to his son and grandson, from whom it spread widely, north of the Tweed, only crossing the border late in the nineteenth century, and remaining a distinguished but uncommon name.

There is a name actually derived from the French 'aimé' (or rather from the Latin 'amatus,' the original form of the word), and that is *Amyas*, familiar to readers of Charles Kingsley as the name of Amyas Leigh, hero of *Westward Ho! Amias* is recorded as far back as the twelfth century, and there was a diminutive *Amiot*.

ESMOND, unlike *Desmond*, was not originally an Irish name; it may have two origins, and so two possible meanings. If it came from the Norse *Asmundr*, then it must mean 'divine protection,' and be a parallel to the Anglo-Saxon *Osmund* (see under *Osbert*, p. 210). But it is from the Old English *Estmund*, which is found in the Middle Ages, its meaning is 'grace-protection.'

The present-day use of the name, as Esmond, is probably due to Thackeray's historical novel *Henry Esmond*, dealing with eighteenth-century life and politics. Its political connexion cropped up again in 1919, when Esmond Harmsworth was elected for Thanet at the age of twenty-one: the youngest M.P. of this century. Esmond Knight, a brilliant actor, blinded at sea during the war, by sheer persistence made himself a first-class performer of 'character' parts.

EUGENE, *Eugenius* in Latin, was derived from the Greek adjective meaning either 'well-born' or 'born lucky.' Four

Popes have used the name, the first, who died in 657, being St Eugenius.

The spread of the name in Western Europe, however, is due to Prince Eugene of Savoy, who became so bored with Court life at Versailles that he forsook Louis XIV and fought against him with Marlborough in the War of the Spanish Succession. But in spite of his questionable behaviour towards the French, his name has been much used in France.

In early Scottish history, Eugene is claimed as a royal name; but, as with *Aeneas* for *Angus* (see p. 51), this was a scholar's substitute for some such name as *Eoghan.* The Welsh claim that Eugenius produced *Owain* (*Owen*) seems, however, correct. Three Owains occur in the ancient legends of the *Mabinogion*, and Owain Glyndyfrdwy, better known in England as Owen Glendower, in the fifteenth century made a bid for Welsh independence that all but succeeded. In Ireland Eugene replaced *Eoin*, the Old Irish form of *John.*

Eugene Aram, a Knaresborough schoolmaster and expert in the study of languages in the eighteenth century, murdered a fellow-townsman to whom he owed money; he was later taken as the subject of a novel by Lord Lytton, and of a grim poem, *The Dream of Eugene Aram*, by Thomas Hood. A pleasanter, but purely imaginary character is the Eugenius who is crony to Uncle Toby in Laurence Sterne's great novel *Tristram Shandy*. Earlier in the present century, Eugene Sandow was the most prominent physical culture expert: he could tear a pack of cards in two with his bare hands. To-day Eugene Goossens, of Belgian origin, is a notable composer and conductor.

Eugene Field, the American children's poet of the late nineteenth century, is best known for his *Wynkin, Blynken and Nod.* Eugene O'Neill is the most important American playwright of recent years. The usual abbreviation, *Gene*, is shown by

Gene Tunney, the most intellectual and, in his time, the most highly paid heavyweight boxer.

EUSTACE The Greek *Eustachios*—'plentiful harvest' is perhaps its best interpretation—was changed by the Romans into *Eustathius* or *Eustatius*, the name of a soldier-saint, probably of the second century. Little is known of him but romantic legends, in which he is converted by a vision of a cross-bearing stag, loses all his possessions, his wife and children; is happily reunited with them, only to be roasted alive in a brazen bull. As a soldier and huntsman he greatly appealed to the feudal age, and became a popular name-giver in France in the early Middle Ages, as St *Eustache*.

The Normans brought the name to England, one prominent example being Count Eustace of Boulogne (see *Algernon*, p. 46). It was never popular, though it never went entirely out of use. The Victorians revived it for its aristocratic flavour.

The Eustachian tubes that connect the ear with the throat are named after the Italian Renaissance physician *Eustachius*.

EVELYN This name, in slightly differing forms, has been used for both sexes. Connected with the French 'aveline,' 'hazel-nut,' the ancient Celtic fruit of wisdom, it occurs—as a woman's name only—in the twelfth and thirteenth centuries. It then became a surname.

As a man's name, Evelyn was given for the first time, as far as can be verified, to Evelyn Pierrepont, first Duke of Kingston, born in 1665: his mother was a member of the Evelyn family, from which also came the seventeenth-century diarist and traveller, John Evelyn.

Evelyn Waugh, the novelist, is the best-known English bearer of the present century.

EVERARD The Old German *Eburhard*, now *Eberhard* or *Ebert*, means 'boar-strength.' The Anglo-Saxons had a different form, *Eoforheard*. In Domesday Book, if we take away the artificial Latin -us ending we find the Norman form *Ebrard*. But later versions spelt with a v show that the Saxon pronunciation did not die out.

The North-country Digby family regularly used the name: an Everard Digby in 1581 published the first English book on swimming, and Sir Everard Digby was involved in the Gunpowder Plot.

In the Scottish Lowlands the name was changed into *Ewart*. In fact the name seems predominantly Northern: William Ewart Gladstone, the Liberal statesman, four times Prime Minister in Queen Victoria's reign, is the most notable example. Ewart Grogan in 1898 made the first direct journey from the Cape to Cairo.

FABIAN The Roman clan of the Fabii presumably derived their name from an ancestor who cultivated beans, in Latin 'fabae'; though they preferred to think of it as coming from 'foveae,' pits for trapping wolves.

Fabius "Cunctator," the 'delayer,' wore down the morale of the Carthaginian invaders of Italy by harassing them from the rear and refusing pitched battles. From this the Fabian Socialists in 1884 took their name, advocating a programme of quiet, persistent pressure to secure the nationalization of land and capital.

Pope Fabian in the third century, a martyr, as were all the first thirty-three Popes, spread the name in Western Europe. His fellow-martyr Sebastian, a soldier, has far more namesakes.

FELIX in Latin has rather the meaning of 'lucky' than of 'happy.' Sixty-six saints rejoice in the name. Its earliest bearer of note was Antonius Felix, the Procurator of Judea, who tried St Paul, as recorded in chapters 23 and 24 of the Acts.

A Burgundian St Felix first brought the name to England. He evangelized East Anglia in the seventh century, and gave his name to Felixstowe; but the name was never used in England before the Norman Conquest. Subsequently Felix was often used, generally as *Felis* or *Felice*, but more often as a feminine name; *Felyse* is also recorded. In Ireland it usurped the native *Phelim*, 'ever good.'

There have been no celebrated English bearers, though Felix Mendelssohn, who dominated British music during the Victorian age, spent much time in England. The best-known examples in the English-speaking world have been imaginary: George Eliot wrote a political novel, *Felix Holt*; Longfellow, in his *Golden Legend*, tells the story of Felix the monk, who listened entranced to the singing of a bird for a hundred years, that seemed to him "but a single hour." On the screen Felix the Cat was the first popular cartoon figure.

The only short form seems to be *Lix*.

FERDINAND is a compound of the Old German 'fardi' and 'nanthi,' 'journey' and 'venture.' Though originally a northern European name, it only came into prominence among the Gothic invaders of Spain, and later with the kings of Castile.

Ferdinand III, father of Edward I's queen, Eleanor, is the one saint of the name. Better known is Ferdinand V of Aragon, through whose marriage to Isabella of Castile Spain became a single nation in the fifteenth century. Cortes, conqueror of Mexico, another Spaniard, used the form *Hernando*; the Portuguese *Fernando* Magellan in 1519 began the circumnavigation of the globe, which he did not live to complete, giving his surname to the bleak sea-passage that divides South America near its southern tip.

Other internationally famous bearers were Ferdinand de Lesseps, the French engineer who artificially separated Africa from Asia by the Suez Canal, and Ferdinand Foch, leader of the Allied Armies against Germany in 1918.

In England Ferdinand was used during the Middle Ages only in French versions, from which come such surnames as Farren and Farrant. The Spanish and Italian *Ferdinando* became fashionable in the time of Shakespeare, who used it for the princely lover of Miranda in *The Tempest*, and for the King of Navarre in *Love's Labour's Lost*. Real bearers in Elizabethan England probably owed it to the brief Spanish influence of the reign of Mary Tudor. It was then, and remained, an aristocratic name, kept up in Northern and Midland families.

The best-known bearer of the present century must be Walt Disney's endearing Ferdinand the Bull, who preferred smelling flowers to fighting in the bull-ring.

Pet forms are *Ferd*, *Ferdie*, and *Nandy*.

FERGUS 'Ver gusti,' in ancient Celtic, signified either 'manly choice' or 'supreme choice.' The oldest known forms of the name are the Irish *Feargus* and the Gaelic *Fearghas*.

A Feargus, late in the fifth century, with his brother Angus, led the Scots from Ireland to the country since called Scotland; they took with them to Scone the Stone of Destiny, now in the Coronation Chair. Ten Celtic saints bore the name.

It is in Scotland that Fergus is popular to-day. That it has long been so is proved by the common surname Ferguson. *Fergie* is the short form.

But the name has not been forgotten in Ireland, where Feargus is still the normal spelling. The Irishman Feargus O' Connor was one of the leaders in England of the Chartist Movement of 1838, which demanded Parliamentary reforms, such as universal suffrage and voting by secret ballot.

FRANCIS The Franks, who gave their name to France, boasted that they were the only 'free men,' in contrast to the civil-service-ridden Gauls of the Roman Empire. As a personal name in England the word seems to have been first given to the three *Franco*s and one *Francus* in Domesday Book. This shows that the form *Frank*, generally looked upon as an abbreviation of Francis, is actually older. No form of Frank, however, seems to have been particularly popular in medieval England.

Le Franceys, a surname, must have been first given as a nickname, and so was Francis—or rather its original form, *Francesco* (Italian for 'little Frenchman'). Giovanni Bernardone, son of a merchant of Assisi, was so called by his friends on account of his 'frenchified' airs. These, and everything but his gaiety, he abandoned when he adopted poverty and the grey, cord-girt peasant's frock that became the uniform of his followers, the Franciscan friars. In England they became known as Greyfriars; and their preaching and poverty, contrasted with the cloistered and comfortable life of monks, made them the most beloved religious order before the Reformation.

In spite of the reputation of St Francis and his followers, his name was little used in England before the sixteenth century, when it became popular, as exemplified by Sir Francis Drake, the Devon seaman; Sir Francis Walsingham, the Elizabethan statesman, and Francis Bacon, Lord Verulam, inventor of a new system of logic and of cold storage, lawyer and man of letters. After this the name practically died out until the nineteenth century; though Francis Moore in 1700 started the popular *Old Moore's Almanac*, which continues to be sold to this day.

Meanwhile on the Continent the name had been given new fame by the Spaniard Francis Xavier (pronounced 'Zayveer'), an early Jesuit and saint, whose missionary journeys took him to Japan and India; he was born at his mother's castle of Xavier, in the Basque country. Many Catholic boys are baptized *Xavier*, one of the very few names beginning with an x. St Francis of Sales was a sixteenth-century Frenchman, whose lively correspondence caused him to be nominated patron saint of journalists.

English bearers since the revival of the name have been prominent in many professions. Sir Francis Galton, inventor of fingerprinting, was born in 1822; Francis Thompson, the poet, in 1859; Sir Francis Younghusband, the first Englishman to penetrate to Lhasa, forbidden capital of Tibet, in 1863.

But many celebrated characters have been either officially named, or at any rate always known as, Frank: Sir Frank Brangwyn, the painter, for instance, and Sir Frank Dyson, inventor of radio time-signals. Frank Lloyd Wright, one of the greatest architects of this century, and Frank Sinatra, the singer, are examples from the United States.

Franklin has been claimed as a diminutive of Frank, but is far more probably the medieval English word for a landowner of free but not noble birth. Becoming a surname, as with Benjamin Franklin, the American statesman, it was changed to a personal name in his honour, and borne, for instance, by Franklin Delano Roosevelt, thirty-second President of the United States.

The old Frank is, of course, used normally as the short form for Francis, but *Frankie* and *Fran* are other variants.

FREDERICK Two old German words, 'frithu' and 'ric,' were combined to make a name meaning 'peace-rule'; its Anglo-Saxon form was *Freodhoric*, latinized into *Fredericus*. This looks so like the present-day name Frederick that it is surprising to find that after the Norman Conquest it died out. But though not recorded, it is probable that the native version was still used; a *Fred* is mentioned in 1306.

However, the name was not common in any form in England; Germany was its chief home. *Friedrich* Barbarossa, 'red-beard,' the stormy Crusader, never died, the people said, but slept in a cave, where his beard grew through the stone table before him. Frederick the Great, in the eighteenth century, created the power of Prussia, an achievement much regretted since by other countries; and nine Danish kings have borne the name.

Friedrich Schiller was among the greatest German Romantic poets and playwrights. *Frédéric* Chopin, Poland's greatest composer for the piano, was of French origin.

It was from the Continent, with the Hanoverian kings, that Frederick came back to England. George II, for instance, called his eldest son by the name. Not over-popular, this Prince of Wales, who was killed by a blow from a tennis ball before he could succeed to the throne, was given the jesting epitaph:

Here lies Fred,
Who was alive and is dead:
Had it been his father
I had much rather;
Had it been his brother,
Still better than another;

Had it been his sister,
No one would have missed her;
Had it been the whole generation,
All the better for the nation:
But since 'tis only Fred
Who was alive and is dead,
Why, there's no more to be said.

It was in the nineteenth century that Frederick became most popular. Sir Frederick Leighton, President of the Royal Academy, was born in 1830. Field Marshal Lord Roberts was a Frederick affectionately known by his soldiers in the Boer War as "Bobs." He was born in 1834. In the middle of the century Frederick Winser invented gas-lighting for streets. Frederick, "the slave of duty," is hero of W. S. Gilbert's *Pirates of Penzance*, produced in 1879. Frederick Delius, the composer, died in 1934; Sir Frederick Banting early in this century discovered insulin.

Frederic, the French spelling without the accents, is a not infrequent English form: *Fred*, the commonest short form, is often used officially. Sir Fred Hoyle is the best-known English astronomer to-day; Fred Archer, the jockey, is another example of the short form. The American film-star *Fredric* March shows another, less-known form of the full name. *Freddie* and *Freddy* are as common as Fred. *Fredk.* is an old written abbreviation.

GABRIEL More common that *Raphael*, but far less common than *Michael*, Gabriel is one of the three angelic names in normal use. Its meaning is 'man of God.' According to the first chapter of St Luke's Gospel, the angel Gabriel was the divine messenger who announced to the priest Zacharias the birth of his son, John the Baptist, and to Mary the birth of Jesus.

Gabriel is recorded in England during the Middle Ages, and occasionally since the sixteenth century. The best-known English bearer is a character of fiction: Gabriel Vardon, the kind-hearted locksmith in Dickens's *Barnaby Rudge*. *Gabriel Conway* names a novel by Bret Harte about early settlers in California.

For historical bearers we must look to the Continent. Gabriel Metsu, one of many Dutch examples, was a seventeenth-century painter of middle-class families. Gabriel Fahrenheit, a German physicist, born in 1686, improved the thermometer by using mercury. Gabriel Lippmann, a Frenchman, was a pioneer of colour photography in the nineteenth century; *Gabriele* d'Annunzio, a colourful figure of our own century, was the Italian poet who led a private army in 1919 to capture Fiume from the Yugoslavs.

The angel Gabriel has seized on the imagination of the American Negro, as the trumpeter who will announce the Last Judgment, "tooting on his horn," as the 'spiritual' expresses it.

Gabe, *Gabby*, *Gabey* and *Gabay* are all short versions.

GAVIN *Gwalchmai*, 'hawk of the plain,' was King Arthur's nephew, according to the Old Welsh *Mabinogion* stories. *Gawain*, or *Gawen*, a later Welsh form of the name, seems to be a shortened version; it means 'little hawk.' As Sir Gawain, Gwalchmai became one of the best-known figures of romance. There is an English story of *Sir Gawain and the Green Knight* which is not found in either French or Celtic collections.

Sir Gawain is also sometimes referred to as *Walwain*. This suggests that his name was considered in England to be identical with the Old English *Walwyn*, 'friend in battle.'

But it is in Scotland that the name has chiefly survived, as

Gavin, perhaps through the Norman *Gauvin*. The Dunbar and Henderson families frequently used it. The first Librarian of the British Museum, in the eighteenth century, was *Gowin* Knight.

Galahad is another 'hawk' name—in this case 'hawk of battle.' Sir Galahad's name, owing to the legends of the Holy Grail, has become associated with such superhuman virtue that, in spite of its manly meaning, parents have fought shy of giving it.

GEOFFREY Like *Bertram* and *Bertrand* (see p. 68), *Geoffrey* and *Godfrey* have since the Middle Ages become confused, and it is difficult to be sure how many Geoffreys recorded in history were originally *Godafrid* ('guda' and 'frithu' in Old German meant 'god-peace'), and how many were *Gaufrid* ('gavja,' meaning 'district'). Besides, Gaufrid seems to have absorbed other names, such as *Walahfrid* ('traveller-peace') and *Gisfrid* ('pledge-peace'). At all events Geoffrey is the more popular to-day.

Geoffrey Plantagenet, father of Henry II, seems to have been known as Godafrid: *Godefrith* was hereditary among the Counts of Anjou. But the leader of the First Crusade is now known as Godfrey de Bouillon; Geoffrey of Monmouth, the twelfth-century historian, was a *Gaufridus*. There was a *Goffrid* of Croyland in the thirteenth century.

Of English Geoffreys, Chaucer is without doubt the most celebrated. It was he who in the late fourteenth century fixed the 'English of London' as our received form of speech when he decided to write his *Canterbury Tales* in the dialect used at Court. He also set rhymed metre as the pattern of normal English poetry.

Jeffery and *Jeffrey* are old written forms of the name, still used.

Sir Jeffery Hudson, three feet nine inches high, was served up in a pie-dish to Charles I and his Queen at dinner; Jeffrey, Lord Amherst, in the eighteenth century helped to end the threatened French supremacy in North America. Jeffery Farnol was an historical novelist popular in the 1920's.

Jeffery and Jeffrey have given several surnames. Thomas Jefferson was third President of the United States, elected in 1801, spreading *Jefferson* as a personal name.

Sir Godfrey Kneller, Court painter to Charles II, was of Dutch origin. As *Gottfried* the name has always been common in Germany, where Geoffrey is unknown in any form. Gottfried Leibnitz in the seventeenth century was a mathematician who invented a cheerful philosophy, claiming that "everything is for the best in the best of all possible worlds."

Godfrey seems to have no accepted short form. Geoffrey has both *Geoff* and *Jeff*. The second is more common in America; Geoff is preferred in England.

Godwin, 'god-friend,' was among the commonest of pre-Conquest names. Earl Godwin, who was the virtual ruler of England under Edward the Confessor, has left his name to the Goodwin Sands, once a tract of land, now a sandbank off the Kentish coast—and as a common surname.

Godric, 'god-ruler,' was so popular among the Saxons that it was given as a nickname to Henry I for his supposed English sympathies.

GEORGE was the Greek 'georgos,' 'tiller of the ground'—that is, 'farmer.' Virgil, the Roman poet, called his Latin poems dealing with farming the *Georgics*.

St George, a Roman army officer, was put to death for his Christianity at Lydda, in Palestine, probably in A.D. 303. His courage caused him to be known as "The Great Martyr," yet few facts are known about him. 'St George who swinged the dragon' refers to the legend that he killed a monster about to devour a princess. Many saints are shown trampling on a dragon symbolic of evil, and simple minds assumed that this was an historical fact. The Crusaders learned to venerate George in the East, particularly after his supposed appearance to rally the Christian forces at Antioch in 1107.

George thus became the ideal figure of chivalry: knights were dubbed "in the name of St Michael and St George." In 1348 Edward III put his new Order of the Garter under his patronage—St George's Chapel, Windsor, is still the headquarters of the Order. The badge of the members, representing the saint, is known as "the George." His red cross appears as the principal charge on all British ensigns.

Though St George was officially proclaimed "Protector of England," with a public holiday for his feast, by Archbishop Chichele in 1415, his name was seldom used, even in the Royal family; the first to receive it was Edward IV's brother, George, Duke of Clarence (see p. 78). It was only the succession of the four Hanoverian Georges that finally 'naturalized' the name. "*Georgy* Porgy, Pudding and Pie" is a mysterious character—certainly one of the Hanoverian family, but he has never been identified.

Well-known English Georges all date, therefore, from some time not earlier than 1714: George Romney, a painter once regarded as the equal of Reynolds, was born in 1734; George Stephenson, the railway pioneer, in 1781. Lord Byron, the poet, was born in 1788, and died while fighting for the independence of Greece in 1824: his names were George Gordon.

The name persisted in popularity: George du Maurier, author of *Trilby*, and *Punch* illustrator, was born in 1834; Thackeray calls the most sympathetic character in his novel

Vanity Fair George Osborne. The famous music-hall comedian G. H. Elliott, "the chocolate-coloured coon," owed his first name to having been born in the George and Dragon Inn at Rochdale, in Lancashire, the county which has also produced the two well-known comedians George Formby, father and son.

These examples stretch from the eighteenth century to the present day, when George continues in use, helped by the example of our two twentieth-century kings, George V and George VI. Among historic bearers of the name we must not leave out George Washington, founder of the United States.

In the North, and in Scotland, there is a special pet form, *Geordie. The Muckin' o' Geordie's Barn* is a traditional Scottish folk-song; Tynesiders are known by the general name of Geordies. But in parts of Scotland there is an unexpected pet form, *Dod*, or *Doddy*. The Irish use *Seiorse* as the full name, the Welsh, *Sior*. In writing, George has the common abbreviation *Geo. Yorick* is a Danish version. The Yorick whose skull Hamlet picks up in the graveyard in Shakespeare's tragedy had been the King's jester: "Alas, poor Yorick!" has become a proverbial expression, and Sterne uses Yorick as the narrator's name in *Tristram Shandy*. The first name of Major Gagarin, the pioneer space-man, is *Yuri*, a Russian version of George.

GERALD comes from the Old German 'gairu-vald,' meaning 'spear-force.' St *Gerhold's* name—an early example—seems hardly suitable for his career, for he was a Saxon monk who settled in Ireland, founding Temple Gerald Abbey. And, strangely enough for so Germanic a name, the best-known bearers of the name in English history were members of the Fitzgerald family that came from Italy before the twelfth century. Some of them migrated to France, then to England, and finally to Ireland, where, as Earls of Kildare, they wielded almost royal powers.

In Wales the name was used as early as the twelfth century, when Gerald de Barry (*Giraldus* Cambrensis), Archdeacon of St David's, half Welsh, half Norman, vividly described his country and its people in his travel-book. *Gerallt* is to-day the normal form of the name in Wales.

The modern use of Gerald in England, where it died out in the thirteenth century, is probably derived from Ireland, and is fairly widespread. Sir Gerald du Maurier, the actor, born in the nineteenth century, is an early example, and the choice of the name by E. Nesbit for the chief boy character in *The Enchanted Castle* shows its popularity in the earlier years of this century.

Gerry and *Jerry* are both used as short forms. *Gerold* is chiefly found in America.

GERARD in origin, differs only slightly from Gerald, being a combination of 'gairu,' 'spear,' and 'hardu,' 'hard.' Gerard seems to have been brought over by Norman immigrants to England even before the Conquest, as several examples are noted in Domesday Book as having lived in the time of King Edward the Confessor. It spread rapidly after 1066, such surnames as Garrard and Garrett showing to-day how the name was pronounced in the Middle Ages; *Garret* is an Irish Christian name to-day.

There is a Welsh name, *Gareth*, familiar from Tennyson's poem *Gareth and Lynette*, and meaning 'gentle,' from 'gwaredd,' according to some authorities. But its similarity to Garrett is too close to avoid suspecting that it is really a variant of Gerard. *Gary* and *Jarry* have probably also the same origin.

In England Gerald is far more common than Gerard, except

among Catholics, who are often given the name of the eighteenth-century Italian saint Gerard Majella. Otherwise bearers probably owe it to the prevalence of the name in France, where it has been popular ever since the medieval romance of *Girard* of Roussillon. Conan Doyle gives this name to his typical Gascon soldier of Napoleon's army, Brigadier Gerard.

Gerard Manley Hopkins, the poet who wrote *The Wreck of the Deutschland*, though quite unknown when he died in 1889, had a revolutionary influence on the forms of English verse. *Jerrard* Tickell, the present-day author, has a not uncommon alternative form of the name.

Gerard shares its short forms with Gerald (see p. 125). *Jerry* was used for a German during the last war. Jerry-building, for shoddy construction, seems to come from the name of a Liverpool contractor of the last century.

GERVASE, when used in Western Europe, may be derived from Old German 'ger,' 'spear,' and 'vas,' 'vassal,' probably applied to an armed retainer. Since, however, the remains of two supposed first-century martyrs, *Gervasius* and *Protasius*, were discovered at Milan in the fourth century by St Ambrose, it seems probable that, in Southern Europe at any rate, Gervase was connected in meaning with the Greek 'geras,' 'old age.'

The spread of the name was certainly due principally to the martyr, particularly among English Churchmen; we find Gervase of Chichester in 1170, Gervase of Canterbury in 1188, and Gervase of Tilbury in 1212—all three were priestly chroniclers. But there were enough married laymen of the name in England after the Conquest to leave behind them such surnames as Gervis and Jarvis, showing differences in pronunciation: Jervas was another form. *Jarvie*, the old pet form, was used especially in Ireland, and became a slang name for a cab and its driver.

Jarvis was used in the seventeenth century in England, and occasionally *Jerfast*.

GIDEON This Hebrew name, according to modern authorities, means 'having a stump for a hand' (the older interpretation was 'hewer'). There is no indication, however, in the Book of Judges that the Hebrew leader who first bore the name was maimed. He was the conqueror of the Midianites, and picked his followers from those who kept hold of their weapons even while drinking.

Gideon was not used before the Reformation in England, when it helped to fill the gap created by the disuse of saints' names. Besides Great Britain, France and America seem to be the only countries where the name has ever found much favour.

The Pilgrim Fathers took the name across the Atlantic, where it has been more popular than in this country. Gideon Wells was a co-founder of the American Republican Party. "The Gideons" are a philanthropic society, of American origin, which distribute Bibles gratis, for the use of travellers in hotels.

Rare in England after the seventeenth century, the name lingered on in country districts; Mary Webb in her novel *Precious Bane* suitably names the rustic lover Gideon Sarn.

GILBERT The Old German *Gisilbert*, from 'gisil-berhta,' 'bright pledge,' suggests the hope of parents that their son would continue the family line.

The name is recorded in Domesday Book almost in its original form, and soon became popular enough to occur in the Robin Hood legends: Gilbert of the White Hand was one of the outlaw's companions. The twelfth-century St Gilbert of Sempringham, in Lincolnshire, is the only Englishman to have founded a religious order, the Gilbertines; he died a centenarian. A Scottish St Gilbert, Bishop of Moray in the following century, was the last canonized Scotsman. But north of the Border the name was probably a corruption of 'gille Brighid,' 'servant of (St) Brigid.' The word gillie is still used in Scotland for a sportsman's attendant.

Gilbert à Becket was the father of the great saint of Canterbury. The country clergyman Gilbert White wrote the entertainingly gossiping *Natural History of Selborne*, his own Hampshire village, in the eighteenth century. Gilbert Jessop was a brilliant cricketer at the beginning of this century. The name has also been borne by a family of architects, beginning with Sir George Gilbert Scott, born in 1811, who restored most of the cathedrals in England, by his son, and by his grandson, Sir Giles Gilbert Scott, who died in 1959. Australian-born Gilbert Murray became not only a celebrated classical scholar but a leading advocate for international peace: he died in 1957.

The pet form *Gib* has not only given surnames such as Gibbs and Gibson, but also the old pet name for a cat: to gibber, in fact, means to caterwaul. Other pet forms are *Gil*, *Gillie*, *Gibbie*; even *Bert*.

GILES St Giles is said to have been an Athenian named *Aegidius*, 'wearer of the aegis (=goatskin),' emblem of the goddess Athene. He left Greece to become a hermit in France, and was only discovered when the hind on whose milk he lived was pursued to his hermitage by a royal hunting party. It is said that his Greek name was turned into *Gidie*, then into *Gide*, and finally became *Gilles*, the usual French form. But there is no proof of this, and it is tempting to think that the saint took the Celtic 'gille,' meaning 'servant,' from humility.

Giles is regarded as the patron of beggars and cripples: hence the London church of St Giles Cripplegate. The London parish of St Giles was formerly the poorest quarter of the town; like St Giles', Oxford, it lay on the outskirts, where the poorest people congregated. Edinburgh, however, claims St Giles, to whom its Cathedral is dedicated, as its patron saint.

An especially French name, Giles does not appear in England before the end of the twelfth century, when Giles of St Albans, our first-mentioned astronomer, was born. But, in spite of the dedication of 162 ancient parish churches, the name, possibly from its association with beggars, is rare in old records. Later it became associated with countrymen: hence "Farmer Giles." Giles, the present-day cartoonist, comes from rural Suffolk.

The most famous, or rather infamous, bearer was Gilles de Rais, the original Bluebeard. A companion of Joan of Arc, he later took to witchcraft and was burned at the stake. Our own Sir Giles Gilbert Scott, who died in 1959, won the competition for designing Liverpool Cathedral at the age of twenty-two.

GORDON is a place in Berwickshire, whose lords were heads of the clan of their name.

Before 1885 Gordon was not used as a personal name, except among the family connexions, as in the case of Lord Byron, the poet, who was christened George Gordon because his mother was a Gordon heiress. But after the tragic death of General Gordon at Khartoum, it spread so rapidly that notable examples must rather be chosen than sought. It is as frequent in England as in Scotland.

Gordon Selfridge, early in this century, brought transatlantic methods of salesmanship to England; Gordon Bottomley, at about the same time, wrote spectacular historical plays in verse; Gordon Russell, in the 20's, was famous for his furniture designs; Professor Gordon Childe to-day is our greatest expert in pre-history; Sir Gordon Richards, the trainer and former jockey, connects the name with sport.

GREGORY 'Watchman' is the meaning of the Greek 'gregorios,' first made famous as a personal name by two Eastern saints, Gregory of Nazianzen, a preacher and religious writer, and Gregory of Nyssa, "the Wonderworker," both of the fourth century. But it was St Gregory the Great, first Pope of the name, who spread the name in the West. Having seen slave-boys from England in the Roman market-places, he was seized with the longing to convert their country, but being unable to leave Rome after his election as Pope, he sent St Augustine.

Before the Conquest Latin names were little used outside monasteries, and we find no Gregory in England before the twelfth century, when it became popular enough to give a number of surnames, chiefly from the pet forms *Greg* and *Grig*.

Though Shakespeare gives the name to two servants, so 'Popish' a name naturally fell out of favour at the Reformation. It is in fact a particularly papal name, counting sixteen bearers, the most notable being Hildebrand, or Gregory VII. In 1077 he made the Emperor Henry IV wait three days and nights outside his gate, barefoot and in his shirt, before he would release him from excommunication.

Gregour was the normal English form of the name in the Middle Ages, just as *Gregor* is still in German-speaking countries. The Austrian Gregor Mendel, another clerical bearer, in the last century discovered the effect of genes on heredity, starting a revolution in the science of biology by experiments with the peas in his monastery garden. In our own times

Gregory Peck, the versatile film-star, shows the use of the name in America.

In common speech a 'Gregory tree' was a seventeenth-century term for the gallows, as Derrick had been a hundred years earlier, and again on account of a celebrated hangman. "Gregory Powders," named after the doctor who first prescribed them, were the terror of Victorian children with stomach troubles. Gregorian is used in more than one connexion: Gregorian music is the official Church music, reformed, if not originated, by Gregory the Great. The Gregorian calendar, which corrected a serious error in computing the exact length of the year, was inaugurated by Pope Gregory XIII in 1582; it ensured that the equinox should fall on the actual day when darkness and daylight are of equal length. It was not adopted in the British Isles till 1752.

GUY is said to be derived from the Old German 'wit,' 'wide,' or perhaps from the similar German 'witu,' 'wood.' It appears in England only after the Conquest, but as the forms it took, *Wido* or *Guido*, had no patron saint to make them acceptable to the clergy, they became identified with the Latin *Vitus*, 'lively,' which, it must be admitted, provided a more satisfactory meaning.

Guy and *Vitus* were thereafter regarded as the same name, Guy persisting in England and France, Vitus in German-speaking countries. Vitus Behring, a Dane, discovered the Behring Straits in 1728. An early English Guy, though he may have been no more than a legendary figure, was Sir Guy of Warwick. Having slain the monstrous Dun Cow, and the giant Colbrand, he went on pilgrimage, returning to live a hermit's life in a cave near Warwick, still to be seen there. The name persisted until disgraced by Guy Fawkes. In America such expressions as 'a regular guy' suggest that it has there no unfavourable connexions—rather the reverse.

Walter Scott's novel *Guy Mannering* is set in the eighteenth century. Charlotte Yonge chose Guy for the hero of her *Heir of Redclyffe*.

St Vitus was a Sicilian boy, martyred about the year 300. Pilgrims to his shrine expected cures for their nervous ail-ments: hence the name of the disease known as St Vitus' Dance, known in France as "la danse de Saint Guy."

Notable bearers seem lacking to-day, particularly in this country. Guy's Hospital in London takes its name from its founder, Thomas Guy: in this case a surname. *Guido* is the Italian version, occasionally used as a pet form. It brings to mind Guido of Arezzo, who originated the gamut, or musical scale, in the eleventh century, and Guido Reni, the painter. Guy de Maupassant, who died in 1893, was the French master of the short story.

HANNIBAL The tradition that the Phoenicians used to trade for tin in Cornwall seems to be supported by the Cornish use of Hannibal, a Phoenician name meaning 'grace of Baal,' as a personal name. Early Cornish parish registers include numerous *Hannyballs*. The surname Honeyball occurs in the Midlands, probably used by Cornish settlers.

The first historic Hannibal was the Carthaginian general who crossed the Alps with elephants, and all but put an end to the power of Rome. Starved of men and supplies by his ungrateful countrymen, however, he failed and later committed suicide.

HAROLD 'Here-weald' in Anglo-Saxon means 'army-power'; Harold is therefore 'weald-here,' or *Walter*, reversed.

Tacitus, the Roman historian, mentions a Dutch, or rather Batavian, *Chariovaldus*, the earliest record of the name.

St *Harald*, first Christian ruler of Denmark, met a violent end at the hands of his pagan adversaries in 986. There was also a "Little St Harold," a boy reputedly killed by Jews at Gloucester in 1168—but this story may well have been a piece of anti-Jewish propaganda.

Harold, or Harald, was a popular Scandinavian name; Harold Harefoot was our second Danish king, succeeding Canute in 1035. Harold II, the last Saxon king, killed at Hastings in 1066, was partly of Danish blood. Harold was also the name of several kings of Denmark, Sweden, and Norway.

Harold continued in use even after the Conquest, taking various forms, including *Eral* (suspiciously like *Errol*); but, like so many other Old England names, it soon died out, to be revived in the nineteenth century.

In modern England we have Harold Monro, who established the *Poetry Review* in 1911, and opened the Poetry Bookshop. Harold Golombek has three times been chess champion of the United Kingdom; Mr Harold Macmillan was Prime Minister from 1956 to 1963.

Harry, though properly a form of *Henry*, is so much used for Harold that it is often difficult to discover the bearer's official name.

HARVEY The real derivation of Harvey is from the Breton *Haerveu*, later *Hervé*, meaning 'battle-worthy.' In one form or another the name is common throughout France. But there was a Germanic name, *Harivig*, 'army-battle,' with which it may have been confused.

St *Hervé*, or *Huvarn*, was a fifth-century Breton. Born blind, he became a bard, like so many blind men in primitive society and his songs are still remembered.

There are eleven Hervés (*Herveus*) in Domesday Book; two had held land in the reign of Edward the Confessor, and may have been Saxon Harivigs. After the Conquest the name became common; by the end of the thirteenth century it had produced several surnames. *Hervey* was a popular form.

Harvey as a personal name came into use in the nineteenth century. One of the Harvey family was a friend of Dr Johnson, who paid him the sublime compliment: "Call a dog Harvey, and I will love him."

The name is well known in America. Harvey Cushing is the leading brain surgeon of the United States; but probably better known is Harvey the rabbit, invisible 'hero' of Mary Coyle Chase's fantastic play *Harvey*, made famous in London by Sid Field.

HECTOR, 'hold-fast,' prince of Troy, was killed by Achilles and his body dragged by his slayer round the walls of Troy. But in the Roman-inspired Middle Ages Achilles was forgotten, while Hector became a hero of romance, Sir *Ector*. The expression 'to hector,' meaning to browbeat, took its meaning from the domineering manner of the Trojan hero in early popular drama.

A fancied resemblance of Hector to the Old Gaelic *Eachan*, 'horseman,' and to the Old German *Hagtar*, 'horse of Thor,' caused it to replace both these names, particularly in Scotland, still the chief home of the name. Hector Boece, in the early sixteenth century, was the first Scottish historian of repute. In modern times, Hector Munro, better known as "Saki," was the author of short stories whose understanding of adults' weaknesses and small boys' ways of thinking are perpetually entertaining.

HENRY 'Haimi-ricja,' 'home-ruler' in Old German, does not seem to have produced an Anglo-Saxon form, though 'haimi' has given us both the 'ham' for place-names and 'home' as the house one lives in. By the time of its first appearance in England, in Domesday Book, it had changed into *Henricus*, which in normal use must have been pronounced either as *Henric* or as the French *Henri*. It came to be pronounced as *Harry*, in an attempt to give it the French sound. The seals of our first six kings of the name spell it *Herry*, and it is known that all our kings of the name were called Harry. "Bluff King *Hal*," as Henry VIII was called, shows the old short form. Henry, a renewed attempt to imitate the French pronunciation, came into fashion only in the sixteenth century.

For some time Harry was confined to the upper classes. In a list of Wat Tyler's companions in the fourteenth century the name does not appear. The reputation of Harry of Monmouth, Henry V, eventually popularized it.

In France and Germany, too, *Henri* and *Heinrich* remained aristocratic. In France, where four King Henris suffered a violent end, the name came to be regarded as unlucky. Of the several German Emperors of the name, the first, Henry the Fowler, died in 936; Henry II, who died in 1024, was canonized in 1152; but the medieval animal epic of *Reynard the Fox*, in which the cat is called *Heintz—Heinz* is the German short form most commonly used to-day—shows that the name had spread early among the common people. Heinrich was hereditary among the Princes of Reuss. The present holder of this title is Prince Heinrich LXXIV! In Portugal Henry was also a royal name; Prince Henry the Navigator was a pioneer, in the fifteenth century, of exploration along the western Atlantic coasts.

Important Englishmen of the name came later. In 1610 Henry Hudson discovered the great bay named after him in Canada; Henry Purcell was the last musician of the traditional English school before it was swamped by Handel and his followers in the eighteenth century. Sir Henry Bessemer, in the nineteenth century, revolutionized steel production with his "Bessemer Converter." In the later years of the century, and after, Sir Henry Rider Haggard and Sir Henry Newbolt, one with his romantic travel-tales, the other with his patriotic verses, became familiar to all boys, and their elders.

In our own century Sir Henry Wood inaugurated his popular Promenade Concerts. Henry Moore is the most prominent English sculptor, Henry Cotton the best-known golfer.

The United States also claim more than one famous Henry. Henry Wadsworth Longfellow, in the nineteenth century, was to his fellow-countrymen their native Tennyson; Henry James, the most important American-born novelist, died in 1916. To-day Harry Pilsbury is an international figure in chess. Harry Truman was the thirty-third American President. America also has its own special pet form of the name—*Hank*, from the Dutch *Henk*; *Hen* is also used.

HERBERT The Old German 'heri-berht,' 'army-famous,' was not a common Anglo-Saxon name, though a St *Here-beorht* lived as a hermit on an island in Derwentwater. The Normans first popularized it; *Herbertus* Camerarius, who came over with the Conqueror, founded the famous Herbert family. The spelling *Harbert*, also found, probably indicates the usual pronunciation (compare 'clerk'). Herbert of Bosham was a companion of Thomas à Becket, and wrote his life; but after the thirteenth century the name went out of favour.

The nineteenth-century revival of the name was probably, as usual, due to the fashion of giving aristocratic Christian names to little Smiths, Browns, and Robinsons. The memory of George Herbert, the country parson of the seventeenth century, whose hymns have never ceased to be favourites, must, however, also have encouraged the spread of the name.

Herbert Spencer, born in 1820, was a brilliant philosopher, and first urged the inclusion of science subjects in schools. Herbert was the second name of Lord Kitchener of Khartoum, War Minister in the First World War, and creator of a volunteer army. Herbert Morrison, once an errand boy, is now Lord Morrison of Lambeth. Herbert Howell, the musician, is known both as conductor and composer. Herbert Hoover was the thirty-first President of the United States.

To-day the Australian *Herb* Elliott, the world champion miler, uses the commonest short form of the name. Another short form is *Herbie*, while *Bert* and *Bertie* are shared with both *Bertram* (p. 68) and *Albert* (p. 42).

HEREWARD, the Old English 'here-weard,' meaning 'army-defence,' is the name made famous by Hereward the Wake, the Saxon who led the resistance movement in the Fens against William the Norman.

The Wake family revived the name; but bearers who can claim no descent from the original bearer probably owe it to Kingsley's *Hereward the Wake*, published in 1865, named after the champion of Saxon independence.

HILARY, a name used for both sexes, is from the Greek 'hilaros,' 'cheerful,' like our own word 'hilarious.'

St Hilary was Bishop of Poitiers in the fourth century; but it was probably chiefly on account of his championship of the Romanized Gauls against their barbarian invaders that his name was handed down, as *Hilaire*. The Greek *Hilarion* was widespread in the Christian East.

The earliest English record of the name, in 1199, refers to a woman, and there are numerous instances of it up to the end of the sixteenth century, as used by both women and men, and with various spellings: *Hillary*, for instance, survives as the surname of Sir Edmund Hillary, conqueror of Mount Everest. As a man's name Hilary seems to have survived longer than it did as a woman's, being referred to as *Hilarie* in 1655. It was only in the last century that it came back into favour, first as a male name—though to-day it is probably again more used for girls than boys.

The Jersey place-name St Helier, from the local hermit saint of that name, has been translated in Latin as Hilary, but it is probably not the same name at all.

Hilaire Belloc, versatile writer of prose and verse, yachtsman, author of the juvenile classic *Cautionary Tales* with its mock-moral "awful warnings," was the son of a Frenchman: hence the French form of his name.

Hilary Term at Oxford University, and the Hilary Sessions of the Law Courts, formerly both began on St Hilary's day, January 13.

HORACE With Terence, Horace has been our most popular Latin name, apart from those of saints. Its meaning is uncertain, but may be connected with 'hora,' the Latin for 'hour' or 'time.' As one of the earliest Roman names, its origin has been forgotten.

The Roman clan of the Horatii was celebrated for three

brothers who fought the three Curiatii from the rival city of Alba. *Horatius* "Cocles," the 'one-eyed,' held the bridge over the Tiber against the Etruscan army; Macaulay tells this story in his *Lays of Ancient Rome*. Quintus Horatius Flaccus, a freed slave's son, ranks with Virgil as one of the greatest Latin poets.

The use of Horace as a Christian name seems to have begun in Renaissance Italy, as *Orazio*. Shakespeare names Hamlet's friend *Horatio*. The lines:

> There are more things in heaven and earth, Horatio,
> Than are dreamt of in your philosophy

are the classic reply to a sceptic. Though the name had been given to children in England since the middle of the sixteenth century, Horace Walpole, the great letter-writer and collector of antiques in the eighteenth century, had the French form, which became normal in this country, in spite of Horatio, Lord Nelson, victor of Trafalgar, and Horatio Herbert, Lord Kitchener.

The name is not particularly popular to-day in either form, though in America it has a short form, *Hod*. Horace Greeley was a prominent American nineteenth-century agitator for the freedom of slaves and the right of every citizen to vote.

HOWARD, used as a personal name only since comparatively recent times, most probably comes from the 'hog-warden,' an official in the Middle Ages who superintended the pigs of the district; though there was also an old name in France, *Houard*, meaning 'worker with a hoe.' The Howard family are first heard of in the thirteenth century, in the Sussex Weald, a great agricultural district. The head of the Howards is the Duke of Norfolk, hereditary Earl Marshal of England.

As a Christian name Howard came into use during the nineteenth century, often no doubt, among connexions of the family; and its aristocratic connexions brought it into favour, the original meaning having been forgotten. To-day it has become so popular that it has lost any flavour of snobbery.

Sir Howard Florey was awarded the Nobel Prize for his medical researches, particularly into penicillin, in 1945. Howard Spring, the novelist, is best known for his book *Fame is the Spur*.

HUBERT is most probably purely Germanic in origin, from 'hugu,' 'mind,' and 'berhta,' 'bright.' There was an Anglo-Saxon *Hygebeorht*, but it was never popular. St Hubert, a huntsman, converted like St Eustace (see p. 112) by the vision of a cross-carrying stag, became Bishop of Liége in 708, and the combination of noble birth, hunting, and holiness naturally made him a fashionable patron saint and name-giver among the feudal aristocracy. November 3, his feast-day, was the opening day for stag-hunting, in times when venison was almost the only fresh meat during the winter months.

To Hubert, in Domesday Book, the name had added another form by the end of the fourteenth century: *Hubard*, whence "Old Mother Hubbard." Chaucer's Friar in the *Canterbury Tales* was a *Huberd*. *Hobart* was another variant, found in Yorkshire. Hubert de Burgh, the best-remembered bearer in England, appears in *King John*, sent to put out the eyes of Prince Arthur, in one of Shakespeare's most affecting scenes. He was a real Earl of Kent and Chief Justice of England. Hubert Walter, his near-contemporary, was Archbishop of Canterbury. These two indicate the high-water mark of the name in this country.

The name was most used in Flanders, where the eighth-century saint had lived. Two Flemish brothers, Hubert and Jan van Eyck, were the first artists successfully to use oil in painting, an innovation that made it possible to paint on canvas.

Charlotte Yonge, in her *History of Christian Names*, claims that Hubert was a forgotten name in England before the 1800's. But it was revived in her time. Sir Hubert Parry, the composer, was the greatest British music teacher in the mid Victorian period. And to-day, though not a popular choice, it is found often enough, both here and in America.

Hugh is often used as a pet form of Hubert, which also shares *Bert* and *Bertie* with Albert, Herbert, and Bertram. *Huber* has also been noted as a rarer choice.

HUGH It is generally claimed that Hugh comes from the Old German 'hugu,' 'mind' or 'thought'; but the Old Celtic *Hu* or *Huw*, meaning 'fire' or 'inspiration,' is similar enough in sound to be a strong claimant. Most probably the name when used in Celtic areas was from the Celtic form, but elsewhere was the Germanic *Hugo*.

In both cases the name goes back to the legendary past. *Hu* Gadarn, "the Mighty," was a Celtic hero who brought the Cymri to Britain, where he settled them and taught them agriculture.

The French dynasty of the Capets, founded by Hugh (Hugo) Capet in 987, ruled until 1328. Hugh was also a popular 'Crusader' name. Hugh de Payens, about 1120, founded the Order of Knights Templars to protect pilgrims to the Holy Land.

The Normans introduced the name into England, where it again appears, in Domesday Book, as *Hugo*, a form still sometimes used. Common by the twelfth century, it was given still greater popularity through St Hugh of Lincoln, who even dared to make fun of Henry II, and got away with it. The magnificent Angel Choir of Lincoln Cathedral was paid for out of the offerings at his shrine. In the same building was a humbler memorial to "Little St Hugh," whose pathetic legend is told as *The Nun's Priest's Tale* by Chaucer, though its truth is more than doubtful. Kipling, in his tales of the Middle Ages in *Puck of Pook's Hill*, introduces a Hugh the Novice, to tell the story of an unwilling young monk. *Hugh the Drover* is an opera by Vaughan Williams.

The greatest, perhaps, of all historical bearers of the name was Hugo Grotius, the seventeenth-century Dutchman, actually called *Huig* van Groot, who worked out the "Law of Nations" by which international relations have ever since—at least, in theory—been regulated.

In our day Sir Hugh Casson, the architect, designed the Festival of Britain in 1951; Hugh Carleton Greene, brother of the author Graham Greene, was appointed Director-General of the B.B.C. in 1960.

An alternative spelling of the name is *Hew*. *Hughie* is the pet form.

HUMPHREY The history of Humphrey is like that of Gervase (see p. 126); both are Germanic names that became identified with Greek saints' names with which they had no real connexion, in order to 'Christianize' them. Humphrey is a compound, of which the meaning of the second part is clear; it is 'frith,' 'peace.' The first part is generally taken to be 'huni,' 'giant.' If however, it refers to the dwarfish Huns who terrorized Europe in the fifth century, the word must have gained this meaning on account of their monstrous cruelty, not their size. But such a contradictory combination as 'hun-

peace, is improbable; perhaps the 'hun' element is rather in the Anglo-Saxon 'hun,' a 'cub,' or 'hunig,' 'honey': 'honey-peace' is certainly an attractive combination.

But to connect the name with a saint it was taken as identical with *Onuphrios*, the name of a fourth-century Egyptian hermit, with an unknown meaning. This might explain the change of the f to 'ph.' *Humfrey* was the older spelling. The spelling *Umphrey*, sometimes found, also suggests Onuphrios.

The first record in England of the name is in Domesday Book, both with an n and with an m. It was at first confined to the nobility. Humphrey, Duke of Gloucester, son of Henry IV, "learned, wise, and void of ambition," was starved to death by his political opponents. At his reputed tomb in St Paul's Cathedral briefless barristers would linger in the hope of clients. Hence 'to dine with Duke Humphrey' came to mean having no dinner at all.

Sir Humphrey Gilbert, half-brother of Sir Walter Raleigh, was drowned off the Azores in 1583, after founding a settlement in Newfoundland, the earliest British colony; his dying words are proverbial: "We are as near to Heaven by sea as by land." He was the last famous bearer for over two centuries. The short forms were *Hump* and *Dump* (possibly the origin of "Humpty Dumpty"). Tobias Smollett's last novel, *Humphrey Clinker*, the story of a workhouse lad who makes good, was published in 1771, and shows the social decline of the name.

Sir *Humphry* Davy, inventor of the safety-lamp for miners, in 1815, restored the name to fame. According to one of E. C. Bentley's clerihews,

Sir Humphry Davy,
Abominated gravy.
He lived in the odium
Of having discovered sodium.

Dickens made use of the name in *Master Humphrey's Clock*, designed as a framework for several independent novels, such as *The Old Curiosity Shop* and *Barnaby Rudge*, supposed to be told as stories by the clock's aged owner. Marryat gave the name to one of the Beverley boys in *The Children of the New Forest*.

Humphrey Lyttleton, the present-day band-leader, is known as *Humph*.

IDRIS is a popular old Welsh name compounded of 'iud,' meaning 'lord,' and 'ris,' 'fiery.'

Idris Gawr, 'Idris the Giant,' was an astronomer and magician, son of King Gwyddno Caranhir, whose lands were flooded by the sea in the seventh century. Cader Idris, the mountain, is supposed to have been his observatory.

The syllable 'id' occurs in several Welsh names, such as *Idnerth*, 'strong lord,' *Idwal*, 'rampart lord,' *Idwallon*, 'scattering lord.' In the Welsh language the adjective always follows the noun.

INGRAM means 'Ing's raven.' *Ing* was an ancient deity of the Scandinavians, and has been identified with *Frey*, god of peace and fertility. He had a horse called "Bloody-hoof," a boar named "Gold-bristles," and a ship which could be folded up and carried in the hand; his wife was the beautiful Gerda.

Ing was also regarded by the Angles as their ancestor. It is extraordinary that, in spite of spelling the name of our country England, we still call it *Ing*land.

In Old German the name became *Ingilrammus*, which the Normans changed to *Ingelram*; Ingelram of Ponthieu was William the Conqueror's brother-in-law. This form came to be mistakenly interpreted as 'angel-raven,' and was therefore sometimes written *Engelram*, which eventually gave the French version *Enguerran*.

Whether through the French form, or directly from the older Ingelram, the name in England became Ingram, used right through the Middle Ages, and up to the seventeenth century. To-day, however, when found it is more likely to have been borrowed from Ingram used as a surname.

ISAAC In Hebrew *Yitschak* means 'laughter,' the name given by Sara, wife of Abraham, to her first-born, in her joy at bearing a son in her old age; though she had laughed in disbelief when the angels told her she would become a mother. The Greek translators of the Old Testament rendered Yitschak as *Isaak*; it was then Latinized into *Isaac*.

Isaak was popular among Eastern Christians; two Emperors of Constantinople and one Russian saint were so named. But in the West it was not much favoured before the Reformation.

In England it appears twice in Domesday Book. But it was generally looked upon as a Jewish name: Isaac of York, it is said, was condemned by King John to have all his teeth torn out, one by one, until he revealed the hiding-place of his treasure. Scott, in his *Ivanhoe*, borrowed this name for the father of the beautiful Rebecca, Jewish victim of Reginald Front-de-Bœuf. But Isaac was not exclusively Jewish, even during the Middle Ages, when *Isake* became a recognized form.

In the seventeenth century Isaac came into general favour. A Breton missionary in Canada, killed by the Iroquois with a tomahawk in 1646, was canonized as St Isaac Jogues. In England the reputed writer of the 'fisherman's bible,' *The*

Compleat Angler, was *Izaak* Walton, whose spelling of his name seems to have become fashionable from the Elizabethan age until some time in the following century. Sir Isaac Newton, greatest bearer of all, who discovered the law of gravity, lived from 1642 till 1727. The eighteenth-century Isaac Watts was the author of the hymn *O God, our Help in Ages Past.* Sir Isaac Pitman was the pioneer of modern shorthand writing.

The usual English short form of the name is *Ikey.* "Ikey Mo" (Isaac Moses) was a common nickname for a Jew: a sort of parody of Eskimo. *Ike* was the more common American short form, before it was taken over as an affectionate term for President Eisenhower.

IVOR *Ifor* is a Welsh name meaning 'lord' which has become anglicized as *Ivor.* Originally it was *Ior*, but was probably influenced by the Breton *Yves* and *Ivo*, brought over by the Normans. The learned novelist Virginia Woolf, however, suggests that it is a corruption of *Ibhor*, meaning a Spanish (Iberian) settler in Wales, which is not impossible. An Irish St Ivor, who was a companion of St Patrick, is now known as St *Ivory.*

But the Breton name had also been originally Ifor; Ifor ab Alan was a King of Brittany in the seventh century. In Wales Ifor has remained unchanged; Ifor Hael ('the generous'), in the fourteenth century, was a chieftain noted for his hospitality and love of music.

One of Charlemagne's knights is said to have been named *Yves*, and the historical *Ivo* Tailbois married the sister of Edwin and Morcar in the eleventh century.

In England Ivo became a favourite among Anglo-Normans; but though an *Yfore* occurs in the thirteenth century, the name did not remain in common use, in spite of the two Sts *Ives.*

The Cornish bearer who gave his name to the town was undoubtedly an Ifor; but the Huntingdon saint is said to have come from Mesopotamia!

Ivor Novello was the stage name of a popular actor and songwriter of not so long ago, who composed and wrote many popular romantic songs; Ivor Brown, the journalist and critic, is a present-day English bearer. Ivo is still occasionally used to-day, but Sir *Ivone* Kirkpatrick, Chairman of I.T.A., has an unusual variant of the name.

JACK, though properly the common short form of *John* (see p. 159), is so often used independently that it needs separate treatment.

Its likeness to the French *Jacques*, which is *Jacob* (see p. 149) or *James* (see p. 151), makes it natural to assume that this was its origin. But this is not so.

The history of Jack seems to have been as follows. In the Low Countries *Jan* became the popular version of *John*; *Jankin* became a pet form of Jan. In the French pronunciation of Jankin the n was scarcely sounded, and in England it disappeared entirely, leaving *Jackin*, which was in turn shortened to *Jakke*, *Jak*, and *Jack*. It should be remembered that in the Middle Ages wool was the most important English commercial product; but the Flemings were the principal weavers, so that there was a constant immigration of Flemings into this country, who introduced their names: the ending 'kin' shows the Flemish origin of any English name in which it occurs.

That the change from John to Jack actually happened is proved by an extract from the history of St Augustine's Monastery at Canterbury, written early in the fifteenth century, in which it is stated that the "Saxons" transformed *Thomas* into *Tomme* (*Tommy*) and *Johannes* into *Jankin* or *Jacke*. Jack had, at least a century earlier, become so common that it was used for any man or boy, as it is to-day in that horrible saying, "I'm all right, Jack!"

The Oxford Dictionary lists about eighty different uses of Jack as a common noun. Most of these show that it stands for a man, or boy, of the people: 'Jack is as good as his master' is a good example of this; the Jack is the lowest of the court cards in a pack; 'every man-jack' means every ordinary man, and so on.

In nursery rhymes and fairy tales Jack is the commonest of names for the 'hero.' This may be accounted for by the child's habit of insisting that every character in a tale must have a name. John, with its pet form, being the commonest name of all, it was natural for a hard-pressed story-teller to satisfy the demand for a name by using Jack. Hence Jack the Giant-killer, Jack and the Beanstalk, Jack Sprat, Jack and Jill. Little Jack Horner may have been a real person; he is said to have founded the family fortunes by stealing the deeds of the manor of Mells, in Somerset—a very substantial sort of 'plum.'

But Jack has spread to the animal kingdom as well. There for instance we meet the jackass, the jackdaw, jack used for a young pike, and the jackanapes, which is a monkey.

When used for a machine or tool jack was probably in the first place a piece of apparatus used to take the place of a man-servant. A jack for turning the spit in roasting was a substitute for the human turnspit, and the jack used for lifting took the place of the man who had previously done this job.

Another variant of Jack is *Jock*. Now regarded as purely Scottish, and used as a common term for a Scotsman, it was once used in England as well, with its own diminutive, *Jockey*, now only given to the rider of a racehorse. But the earliest recorded example was the Duke of Norfolk who was warned before the battle of Bosworth:

Jockey of Norfolk, be not too bold,
For *Dickon*, thy master, is bought and sold.

Only in Scotland, however, do we hear that expressive name for a turkey—a 'bubbly-jock.'

JACOB is the Hebrew 'aqob,' meaning 'supplanter,' or 'following-after.' Though the second meaning is the more probable, the first is more appropriate; the first bearer, younger son of the patriarch Isaac, supplanted his elder brother *Esau*, 'hairy,' tricking him out of his inheritance and his father's blessing, with the encouragement of his mother Rebecca, as the Book of Genesis tells us in Chapters 25–27. Jacob's behaviour was hardly honourable, but his initiative was more suited to the head of a growing tribe than the weakness of his senior. And it was to him that the new name of *Israel*, 'ruling with God,' was given, which passed to the whole of the Chosen People.

A favourite with the Jews after their return from captivity in Babylon, when so many of their ancient names were first revived, *Aqob* became *Jakobos* (with a long 'o') in Greek, naming two of the twelve Apostles, both of whom we know as *James*. How this change of form came about will be found in the next section; for though originally the same name, Jacob and James have come to be regarded as entirely separate, except that James is always translated into Latin as *Jacobus*.

Jacob occurs before 1066 in England, but, like most scriptural names, only in clerical circles. After the Conquest it seems to have been used almost exclusively by Jews, though the two Apostles commemorated on May 1 are referred to in one fifteenth-century document as St Philip and St Jacob.

It was only after the Reformation that Jacob came into use as a normal English name. This was because the translators of the Bible used Jacob for the Old Testament patriarch, keeping James for the two Apostles. The fashion for Old Testament names spread the one; loyalty to the Stuart kings popularized the other.

On the Continent a similar splitting of the name took place, even earlier than in this country. *Jacobus* de Voragine was a thirteenth-century Archbishop of Genoa; his collection of lives of the saints, known as *The Golden Legend*, is a medieval classic, later published by Caxton. In it each saint's life is prefaced by an 'interpretation' of his name. This is one of the earliest attempts to explain the meanings of names—ingenious rather than convincing in its odd derivations. But in Italian he was known as *Jacopo*. *Giacomo* was the alternative form (the villain of Shakespeare's *Cymbeline* is *Iachimo*). Spain has both *Iago* and *Jaime*. The French, however, were satisfied with *Jacques*, which Shakespeare used for four of his characters, notably the "melancholy *Jaques*" in *As You like It,* a name occasionally used for real people and recorded as early as 1306, as *Jake*.

In Wales and Cornwall *Iago* and *Jago* were regularly used, the Welsh having a peculiar pet form, *Ianto*. One Welsh Iago was among the seven kinglets who rowed Edgar of England on the Dee as a sign of their allegiance, in 973. Iago, the similar Spanish form, is given by Shakespeare in *Othello* to his most villainous villain; Captain Marryat named his novel *Jacob Faithful* after its leading character, and Virginia Woolf wrote a novel in the 1920's with the title *Jacob's Room*.

Jacob's Ladder is a reference to the vision seen by the patriarch of a stairway reaching from earth to heaven. The same name is given to a garden plant whose thin flowers and leaves hang down parallel, suggesting rungs. Jacobites were the followers of the exiled Stuart Jameses. Jacobins were the extremists in the French Revolution, who originally met in the old friary of St Jacques in Paris; the same name is given to a species of pigeon whose neck-feathers suggest a friar's hood. A jacobus was an English coin struck in the time of James I; Jacobean is the name given to the heavy style of furniture which was in fashion at the beginning of the seventeenth century.

The common short form of Jacob is *Jake*, never Jack. A Jake in America is a complimentary term for an Australian. The pet form *Jaikie* is used in Scotland.

Jacob Epstein, the sculptor, is one of the few famous British-born bearers of the Old Testament name: he was, however, of Jewish origin.

JAMES The early history and meaning of James are included in the previous section, under *Jacob*.

Of the two Apostles whom we call James, the first was brother of John and son of Zebedee. One of the most favoured of the Twelve, he witnessed both the Transfiguration and the Betrayal of Jesus; and though beheaded at Jerusalem by King Herod, as recorded in Acts xii, his body is supposed to have been taken to Spain, where he had preached, and buried at Compostela, known also as Santiago (St James). The numerous pilgrims to his shrine in the Middle Ages led to the saint himself being represented in pilgrim dress. The second Apostle, James "the Less," was head of the Church in Jerusalem, where he was put to death by being hurled from a lofty building, and then dispatched with a club.

Our English version of the name appears to have come from the late Latin *Jacomus*, which became *Giacomo* in Italy (see

Jacob, p. 150), and was further shortened to *Jaime* in Spain. Brought back by pilgrims, it occurs at least as early as the thirteenth century as *Iame*, with a pet form *Jamettus*. Chaucer, in the following century, speaks of "saint *Jame*." Shortly after the final s of the modern version appears in *Iamys* and *Jamys*, already with an alternative *Iames*.

But it was in Scotland that James first became a popular name, spread by five kings, before the sixth became James I of England in 1603. He was addressed as *Jeames*, which persisted as the usual English pronunciation until the nineteenth century, when it came to be regarded as vulgar, and was only retained as a type-name for a man-servant. This pronunciation explains the rise of the pet form *Jem*, or *Jemmy*, also used for a burglar's tool. *Jim*, *Jimmie* and *Jimmy* are more recent. *Jamie* is Scottish, but the Highlands have a special variant, *Hamish*, corresponding with the Irish *Seumas*, which is pronounced, and sometimes even spelt, as *Shamus*. *Jas.* is the traditional written abbreviation in England. 'Dago,' the American term for a South American, is a corruption of another Spanish form of James: *Diego*.

The name was naturally much used in Spain: two kings of Aragon in the thirteenth century were known as James the Conqueror and James the Just. Of the Scottish kings, James I was a distinguished poet, author of *The King's Quhair* ('quire,' meaning 'book'), verses composed while he was a prisoner in the Tower of London. The untimely deaths of his five previous royal namesakes caused James VI (James I of England) to call his successor *Charles*; but it was the family character rather than the Stuart choice of names that made the family unlucky. James II of England lost the throne through his obstinacy; his son James, the Old Pretender, failed utterly to inspire the Jacobite rising of 1715.

The first notable Englishman of the name was Lord James Audley, in the reign of Edward III; his exploits are chronicled by the historian Froissart. But the best-known bearers were later; Captain James Cook, for instance, in the eighteenth century, was the first British explorer with a scientific bent.

In more recent times Sir James Barrie created *Peter Pan*, at the beginning of the present century; the Welshman Jimmy Wilde was the greatest flyweight known in the history of boxing; Sir James Jeans was a great astronomer; James Joyce, an Irishman, wrote those remarkable novels *Ulysses* and *Finnegan's Wake*; Jim Laker, the England off-spinner, during the 1956 season took 9 wickets for 37 and 10 for 53 in a single Test match. Jimmy Edwards is one of our most individual comedians to-day.

Jim is better represented in literature than James, with Conrad's *Lord Jim*, whose name-hero spends his life atoning for an act of cowardice; Stevenson has Jim Hawkins in *Treasure Island*; and Jim is the old Negro friend of Huckleberry Finn.

JASPER Traditionally, the three Wise Men who were led from the east by a star to Bethlehem, with their symbolic offerings of gold, incense, and myrrh, were called *Melchior*, 'king of light,' *Balthasar* (a variant of *Belshazzar*), 'God defend the king,' and *Gaspar* (or *Caspar*), 'keeper of the treasure.' Melchior has seldom been used; Balthasar we find occasionally, particularly in Italy, as *Baldassare*: Shakespeare gives the name *Baltasar* to more than one Italian servant. Portia in *The Merchant of Venice* assumes the name when she appears in court disguised as a lawyer. But Gaspar has been used in many forms.

In the twelfth century the supposed relics of the Wise Men were brought to Cologne. But though all three names have been used in Germany, *Kaspar*, as he is called there, proved the favourite: "Old Kaspar" will be remembered from his irritating repetition of "It was a famous victory" in Southey's poem *The Battle of Blenheim*.

This name came to England from France, where it was changed to *Gaspard*, and here became *Jasper* (without any reference to the gem-stone of the same name). It must have been in fairly frequent use, as we have the surnames Jasper and Jesperson; but it is not recorded before the fifteenth century, when Jasper Tudor, "redoubted Pembroke," was the principal supporter of his nephew, Henry VII.

The people of the Middle Ages liked to think that each of the Magi represented one of the three races of mankind: Melchior, the white race; Balthasar, the brown; Jasper, the black. This may well be the reason why, in Victorian melodrama, Jasper was a type-name for the villain—generally a baronet, and always swarthy and black-moustached.

Though Jasper is the normally used English version of the name, the only notable bearer of the present century is Admiral Sir Caspar John, the First Sea Lord.

JEREMY Rendered as *Jeremiah* in the Authorized Version of the Bible, the traditional English form of this name is *Jeremy*, which at present is enjoying considerable popularity. The exact meaning of the name is not clear: it is a combination of 'Jehovah' and 'exalt' (Jiremejahu). Jeremiah the Prophet was so pessimistic in his *Book of Lamentations* over the ill-advised foreign policy of the Chosen People that a 'jeremiad' has come to mean any long tale of grief.

Jeremias, the Greek and Latin rendering, is found in English records as early as the beginning of the thirteenth century. Jeremy, formed by dropping the last syllable, became so common that it was recorded officially before 1240.

Among the Puritans Jeremias was revived, together with Jeremiah; it was in the seventeenth century that Jeremiah Horrocks discovered the Transit of Venus. But Jeremy was not forgotten; Jeremy Taylor was the greatest English preacher of Stuart times, Jeremy Bentham, who lived from 1748 to 1832, was a writer who claimed that the guiding principle in human life should be the greatest happiness of the greatest number. Jeremiah Meyer, a celebrated painter of miniatures in the eighteenth century, and Jeremiah Clark, who composed the *Trumpet Voluntary* so often wrongly attributed to Purcell, show that the Biblical version of the name continued in use side by side with the traditional form.

Nowadays Jeremy has spread—principally, it is supposed, owing to Hugh Walpole's series of 'Jeremy' books about a boy's childhood, his schooldays, and his dog. Another, very different Jeremy of fiction is the hospitable frog, Jeremy Fisher, in Beatrix Potter's nursery story of that name.

The short form *Jerry* is shared among Jeremys, Geralds, and Gerards, but there is no doubt that Dickens's Jerry Cruncher, the body-snatcher in *A Tale of Two Cities*, was a Jeremiah.

JEROME The Greek *Hieronymos*, from 'hieron onoma,' 'holy name,' is of pre-Christian origin: both a king of Syracuse and a celebrated philosopher bore it in the third century B.C.

What was meant exactly by 'holy name' among pagans is not known; it must have referred to some deity whose actual name was too sacred for mention. But after the foundation of the Christian Church it was especially favoured, as dedicating its bearer to the Holy Name of God ("hallowed be Thy Name"), and through Eusebius *Hieronymus* Sophronius, known to us as St Jerome, it became a 'holy' name in itself. St Jerome translated the Scriptures from Hebrew into the common, or 'vulgar,' Latin of the fourth century; hence his version is known as the 'Vulgate.' Jerome was a favourite subject for painters: scholar, hermit, cardinal, and owner of a pet lion, he gave scope for a wide variety of treatment.

The name occurs in twelfth-century England as *Geronimus*, but it was some time before its spelling settled down: in one thirteenth-century document the same man is recorded as *Gereminus*, *Germinus*, *Jereminum*, and *Jeremimum*, suggesting that it was uncertain whether he was a Jerome or a Jeremy. But it was most probably the Italian *Geronimo*, becoming *Jérôme* in French, that gave us our finally fixed version. In the classically-minded seventeenth century there was a tendency to revive Hieronymus, but it did not prosper. Slightly earlier, in a popular Elizabethan horror-play, *The Spanish Tragedy*, a *Hieronimo*, or *Jeronimo*, appears as chief character. A phrase from this play, "Go by, Jeronimo," became a catchword quoted by Shakespeare, Ben Jonson, and Dekker as a certain laugh-raiser.

Jerome K. Jerome, the English humorous writer, who died in 1927, is best known from his story of a Thames river holiday, *Three Men in a Boat*. The American Jerome Kern composed the music for *Show Boat*, including the famous *Ol' Man River*.

JESSE This name is first found as that of the father of King David of Israel: it seems to mean 'the Lord is.'

Barely if ever used before the Reformation in Europe, it became popular among Puritans, who carried it to America. In England it survived chiefly in Nonconformist circles.

Jesse Boot, who developed his small chemist's shop in Nottingham into the largest pharmaceutical concern in Britain, may be regarded as practically the founder of Nottingham University. Jesse Collings was a prominent Member of Parliament earlier in this century. But, true to its Puritan tradition, America has produced a larger number of well-known bearers: Jesse James was an outlaw, notorious for his railroad and bank robberies in the years following the Civil War. Jesse L. Laski, the film magnate, virtually founded Hollywood, the least puritanical town in the world.

Pet forms are *Jake* (shared with Jacob), *Jess*, and *Jessie*.

JOCELYN may have two origins. Possibly it comes from the Old German 'Gauzelen,' meaning 'a descendant of the Goths' ('Gothling'), or possibly from the Celtic *Josse*, meaning 'champion.' In all likelihood it is the result of a confusion between the two. It was used by Germans as early as the seventh century in several forms, including *Joscelin*, a spelling sometimes found in England to-day. Brought to England by the Normans, who included in their army a large Breton contingent, it was among them most probably the name of the Breton saint Josse, with the double diminutive ending -el-in.

However, the earliest and most numerous records of the name in the Middle Ages in England are spelt with a g, giving such surnames as Goslin and Gosling, though *Jocelyn* of Brakelond, in the twelfth century, wrote a famous chronicle of the Abbey of Bury St Edmunds, a mine of information about the way of life of his contemporaries. The name continued to be used, often confused with *Jocosus*, meaning 'merry.'

One form of the name—perhaps *Joceus*—was eventually changed into *Joyce*, now usually regarded as a girl's name. But it was always a male name until late in the last century. Joyce Cary, author of *The Horse's Mouth*, died in 1958.

The only notable use of Jocelyn in fiction seems to be in

Jeffery Farnol's historical romance, *The Gestes of Duke Jocelyn.* The most unexpected example in real life is the former President of Brazil, who built Brasilia as a new capital for his country, the only city expressly designed for air communications—Senhor *Juscelino* Kubitschek de Oliveira.

JOHN The Hebrew *Jochanaan*, meaning 'the Lord is gracious,' was the original form of John; it contains the same root-word as the feminine Hannah.

Popular among Jews after their captivity in Babylon, it owed its spread among Christians to two important New Testament characters. John the Baptist was Christ's cousin and forerunner, and St John the Evangelist was the "Beloved Disciple." His common title St John "the Divine" means, not 'godlike,' but 'learned in theology.'

The use of John as an ordinary name in Western Europe began only with the Crusaders, who found it was a favourite among Eastern Christians: the Greek form of the name was *Ioannes*, latinized as *Johannes*, the original in Europe of all later forms. Its popularity in the West is shown by eighty-two canonized saints, including two Englishmen, and a number of kings.

The first notable English bearer was St John of Beverley, an engaging Anglo-Saxon bishop of York; he encouraged sport among his students, and is claimed as patron of the deaf and dumb, having taught a deaf-mute boy to speak—not by miracle, but by careful training.

In the twelfth century John began to spread throughout Great Britain. But as a patron saint, and so as a name-giver, St John the Baptist was favoured far more than the Evangelist. He has five hundred ancient churches dedicated in his honour; the Evangelist can claim a mere hundred and eighty-one. And as it spread it began to take shorter forms, becoming *Johan* and *Jon*, both used by Chaucer towards the end of the fourteenth century. Our final form, John, is a compromise in spelling between the two. At the trial of John Wyckliffe, out of sixty-six persons listed as present, twenty-five were Johns. Probably the best-remembered bearer in the Middle Ages in this country is Robin Hood's companion, the gigantic "Little John," certainly a more popular figure than our one king of the name.

Early short forms have already been mentioned under *Jack* (p. 147), but the surnames Hancock and Hankin show that *Hans* (from *Johannes*), which is the usual German form, was also once used in this country, imported from the Continent. The French *Jean* must also have been known; the surname Jennings shows this. *Jan* survived in the West Country.

Any list of English Johns risks being tediously long; a full list would be endless. But a few may be of special interest. John Thweng, Prior of Bridlington, was the last Englishman to be canonized before the Reformation. A John Fisher, Bishop of Rochester in the time of Henry VIII, had his head cut off for refusing to admit royal supremacy over the Church; he was declared a saint in 1929. On the other side, John Hooper, Bishop of Gloucester, was burnt by Henry's daughter, Mary Tudor, for denying the Pope's supremacy. John Hawkins, the Elizabethan sea-captain, helped to defeat the Spanish Armada in 1588. John Milton was the greatest English poet of the following century; John Churchill, Duke of Marlborough, was the greatest English general in the time of Queen Anne. Sir John Moore has been immortalized by that sombre poem commemorating his burial at Corunna during the Peninsular War. John Keats, together with Shelley, stands at the pinnacle of English verse of the early nineteenth century.

Coming nearer to our own day, John Ruskin directed the

artistic taste and opinions of the mid-Victorians. He died in 1900, when John Galsworthy was beginning to write his novels picturing the changing life of England between the Victorian age and the 'twenties. John Ireland, the composer, was born in 1879. Twentieth-century achievements include the pioneer flight of John Alcock across the Atlantic from west to east, the establishment of the British Broadcasting Corporation under Sir (afterwards Lord) John Reith as first Director-General, followed by television, pioneered in this country by John Logie Baird. And to-day, as in the time of Wyckliffe, John still heads the list of Christian names in England, possibly in all Europe.

So it is not surprising that our national nickname is John Bull. This was taken from a satire by Dr John Arbuthnot, in which each nation is represented by an animal—the Frenchman being *Lewis* Baboon, the Dutchman *Nicholas* Frog. The original John o' Groats seems also to have been a Dutchman, Jan de Groot, who built a house on the north-eastern tip of Scotland in the reign of James IV. As his sons were always quarrelling about their rightful positions in the family, he had an eight-sided room constructed, containing an octagonal table, so that none could claim to sit above the rest.

Scotland, however, has its own version of John, which is *Ian* or *Iain*, sounding much like the Dutch pronunciation of *Jan*, which is 'yan.' General Sir Ian Hamilton commanded the Gallipoli expedition in the First World War. The author Ian Hay (actually Major John Hay Beith) made his name with his war book *The First Hundred Thousand*, published in 1915, but was particularly successful in his stories of youth, such as *Pip*, and plays such as *The Sport of Kings*.

In Irish, which has no j, John becomes *Sean*, pronounced, and sometimes spelt, *Shaun*. Sean O'Casey is best known for his play of Dublin life, *Juno and the Paycock.* Sir *Shane* Leslie, the historical writer, has another Irish spelling.

The Welsh sometimes spell John as *Sion*, often pronouncing it 'Shon,' with a long o. Sometimes they use *Evan*; but this may be a native name in origin, meaning 'young warrior.' The Welsh traditional song of *Jevan Dovy* seems to show a name halfway between John and Evan, and remarkably like the Italian *Giovanni.*

But in mentioning songs we must not leave out the greatest English hunting song, *John Peel*, commemorating an historical North Country huntsman, nor in any account of the name can one of Cowper's masterpieces of comic verse, *John Gilpin*, be forgotten.

Johnny and *Johnnie* are pet forms, as well as *Jack.*

JONATHAN is an elaboration of *Nathan*, meaning 'gift.' The first syllable, as in John, is a contraction of Jehovah, and so Jonathan may be interpreted as 'gift of the Lord.'

In Hebrew Jehovah (Yaweh), was, so to speak, the 'personal' name of God. God, as a general conception, was rendered by El. In this book forms of Jehovah have been translated as "the Lord," according to the practice of the Authorized Version of the Bible. *Nathaniel* (see p. 201) is therefore almost identical with Jonathan; *Theodore* has the same meaning in Greek.

The first known Jonathan was the son of King Saul. His friendship with David has given us the expression for two close friends, 'a David and Jonathan.' David's lament for Saul and Jonathan, recorded in the first chapter of the Second Book of Kings, is among the most moving poems in the Old Testament.

Before the Reformation Jonathan was little used; though

there is mention of an English *Jonathus* in 1213. But with the change of fashions in names at the Reformation it became relatively popular. Its best-known bearer was Jonathan Swift, the brilliant eighteenth-century writer of satires, and author of *Gulliver's Travels*, who became Dean of St Patrick's, Dublin.

Jonathan Trumbull, an eighteenth-century American, took a prominent part in the War of Independence. His opinions were so greatly respected that Washington's phrase, "Let us hear what Brother Jonathan says," is supposed to have been the origin of "Brother Jonathan" as a personification of the United States.

The Jonathan apple is also of American origin. A travelling preacher who toured the countryside used to carry with him a bag of apple-pips, which he planted wherever he went. Though a Jonathan, he was generally known as *Johnny* Appleseed, which shows the common pet form of the name, shared with John. *Jon*, a more correct abbreviation, is also an old spelling of John; *Jonty* is also occasionally used.

JOSEPH The dramatic story of Joseph, son of Jacob and Rachel, occupies the last fifteen chapters of the Book of Genesis. Joseph means 'increase' or 'addition'; he was Jacob's twelfth son.

In the New Testament Joseph is the carpenter husband of Mary, about whom we read in the early chapters of St Matthew and St Luke. There was also Joseph of Arimathea, who buried the body of Jesus; legend further connects him with Glastonbury and the Holy Grail.

There were other forms: *Joses*, a Greek adaptation, was the original name of St Barnabas; the Jewish historian of the siege of Jerusalem and the dispersal of the Jews in A.D. 70 called himself by the latinized form *Josephus*.

Once or twice Joseph occurs in England before 1066. Afterwards it was used fairly frequently, though in most cases by Jews. The surname Jessop looks like the Italian form *Giuseppe*: many Jews from Italy did settle in this country, until all were expelled by Edward I.

But the widespread choice of Joseph dates only from the seventeenth century; in spite of its saintly associations, it was previously not much favoured. In England the use of Old Testament names gave Joseph a new vogue during the Reformation period; on the Continent the previously neglected Joseph of Nazareth suddenly became regarded as a major saint, apparently through Spanish influence, the Spanish form being *Jose*, with the pet form *Pepe* (pronounced 'Paypay'). In Italy *Giuseppe* took the diminutive *Beppo*. Two German Emperors in the eighteenth century, and Napoleon's brother, King of Naples and of Spain, bore the name.

Of English bearers, one of the earliest was Joseph Taylor, a manager of Shakespeare's Company of Players. In the eighteenth century Joseph Addison edited *The Spectator*, the first successful English literary periodical. Fielding's novel *Joseph Andrews* was published in 1742. Joseph Mallord Turner, born in 1775, is one of the greatest landscape painters. Sir Joseph Paxton, in his design for the Crystal Palace that housed the Great Exhibition of 1851, discovered the possibilities of steel and glass architecture. Joseph Blanco White's sonnet *To Night* (1828) may be found in nearly every anthology of English verse. At the turn of the century Joseph Chamberlain reformed the Conservative Party, and, nearer our own day, Sir Joseph Thomson was a pioneer of nuclear physics.

Joe and *Jo* are short names. Joe Miller, the eighteenth-century comedian, gave his name to an expression for an often-repeated joke. Joe Davis is acknowledged as the century's greatest snooker player. Joe Gargery, the blacksmith in *Great Expectations*, is one of Dickens's most lovable creations. *Joey*, a less common pet version, became the common term for a circus clown through the great Joseph Grimaldi, who died in 1837.

JOSHUA was originally *Jehoshea*, meaning in Hebrew 'the Lord saves'; another form was *Hosea*, borne by one of the Minor Prophets. The first Joshua, one of Moses' early followers, succeeded him as leader of the Israelites, and under him they reached the Promised Land.

Joshua seems not to have been used in England before the sixteenth century. Joshua Sylvester, a poet born in 1563, is one of the earliest known bearers. Most famous is the painter Sir Joshua Reynolds, appointed first President of the Royal Academy by George III.

Common in America, the name has there had more than one out-of-the-way bearer. Joshua Slocum, in the last century, without radio, mechanical aids, or crew, made the epic venture recounted in his book *Sailing Alone Round the World*.

A later version of the name was *Jesus*. There is an ancient Jewish book of moral teaching, written some time after the return from Babylon, whose author was Jesus, son of Shirach. Jesus Christ was, therefore, not unique in bearing His name. Christians, as a rule, have tended to avoid using it in baptism, out of reverence. Nevertheless, in Spain and South America Jesus is a popular boys' name.

The common short form of Joshua is *Josh*: Josh White, the American negro folk-singer, is an instance. But *Jos*, shared with Joseph, is also not unusual.

JUDE Yehudi Menuhin, perhaps the greatest violinist of our century, shows a Hebrew form of the name, rendered as *Judah* in the Authorized Version of the Old Testament; it means 'praise.'

Judah was the fourth son of Jacob and Leah, bequeathing his name to the tribe (and later kingdom) which gave us the word 'Jew.' But there seem to have been no further bearers until the Jews of Judah, the only Tribe of Israel to return from captivity, encouraged the revival of ancient names, to remind themselves of their glorious past.

The greatest bearer of this period was *Judas* Maccabaeus, more correctly *Yehudah* the Maccabee. He championed the independence of the restored kingdom of Israel against the Syrians, and rebuilt the Temple in the second century B.C.

Any popularity the name may have won was forfeited among Christians by *Judas* Iscariot. Yet there was another Apostle of the name, the author of an Epistle. Some alternative form seemed desirable to distinguish him. So, on the Continent, his second name *Thaddeus* ('praise'), was taken, often used in Ireland as *Thady*. In England the difficulty was overcome by using *Jude*.

Notices are often to be read in the daily papers in which "thanks are given to St Jude." The reason for this custom is said to be that because St Jude was so long neglected he should now have plenty of time to spare for looking after modern clients!

Thomas Hardy chose the name for the chief character of his gloomiest novel, *Jude the Obscure*: Judas Maccabaeus turns up in the Masque in Shakespeare's *Love's Labour's Lost*, as one of the "Nine Worthies," or heroes of the ancient world.

JULIAN The Roman clan-name *Julius* is rare in England, except in the family who called themselves Caesar. The first English bearer of this Roman name was a judge knighted as

Sir Julius Caesar in 1603. A descendant and namesake of his was a notable Victorian cricketer.

The original Caius Julius Caesar, though his second and third names meant 'downy' and 'hairy,' was both clean-shaven and bald. He was a great general, whose account of the conquest of Gaul has been constantly used as a practical text-book by military commanders. He was also responsible for a revision of the calendar, known as the Julian Calendar. The month of July was named after him.

Both *Julius* and *Caesar* became common names in Italy as *Giulio* and *Cesare*, and in France as *Jules* and *César*. Jules Verne was the Frenchman whose science-fiction, in such works as *Twenty Thousand Leagues under the Sea* and *From the Earth to the Moon*, anticipated so many of the scientific facts of to-day. *César Birotteau* is one of Balzac's greatest novels.

In England, however, only the derived form *Julian* has become a normal name. The bad reputation of the pagan Emperor Julian, "the Apostate," who tried too late to stem the advance of Christianity, was counterbalanced by the reputation of his contemporary, St Julian the Hospitaller. Having accidentally killed his father, this Julian expiated his deed by devoting himself to helping poor travellers.

The name Julian came to this country in the thirteenth century. First recorded in the Latin form *Julianus*, it took such odd shapes in popular use as *Julyan*, *Jolanus*, *Jollan*, and *Jolin*. *Jolyon*, which was used by Galsworthy for one of the characters in his *Forsyte Saga*, is a North of England version. Julian, rather than Juliana, was used in the Middle Ages also as the feminine.

The name has come to the fore in our own century, with Julian Grenfell, the poet of *Into Battle*, Sir Julian Huxley, the zoologist, and Julian Bream, the guitarist. It is little known that the film comedian Groucho Marx is also in fact a Julian.

The pet form is *Jule*.

KAY *Caius*, or more correctly *Gaius*, was the first name, or praenomen, of Julius Caesar, derived from the Latin verb 'gaudere,' 'to rejoice,' and related to our word 'gay.'

The Welsh turned it into *Kai*, hence Sir *Kay*, who was King Arthur's foster-brother. John Masefield took Kay as the name of the young hero of his classic *The Midnight Folk*. It is also the name of the brother of Gerda in Hans Andersen's *The Snow Queen*.

The original form Gaius, found in the New Testament, was occasionally used in England after the Reformation. Caius College in Cambridge was named after John Caius, its founder in the sixteenth century, but is pronounced 'keys,' probably the founder's real English name.

As a pet form, *Kay* may stand for any name beginning with the letter K.

KEITH This now popular Scottish name is sometimes claimed to mean 'wind.' But it seems more probable that it is derived from an old Gaelic word for 'wood,' similar to the Welsh 'coed.'

Earlier *Keth*, it survives in more than one Scottish place-name. The Earls of Kintore, whose family seat was at Keith Hall, either called their home by their surname or took their surname from it. And so Keith came to be used, firstly by family connexions, then as a general Scottish personal name.

The Ballad of Keith of Ravelstone, by the Victorian poet Sydney Dobell, is an early use of the name; but for some time it was apparently not given in real life. Ian Keith Falconer was a missionary and expert in Oriental languages, who became Professor of Arabic at Cambridge. He also cycled from John o' Groats to Land's End. Keith was G. K. Chesterton's second name. Keith Smith in 1919 was the first to fly from England to Australia. To-day Keith Vaughan, the painter, and Keith Miller, the Australian cricketer, show that it has become a normal personal name, without any necessary Scottish connexion.

Kiki has been used as a pet form.

KENNETH is the anglicized descendant of the old Gaelic *Caioneach*, meaning 'handsome.' In Wales St *Cennydd* (pronounced exactly as we pronounce the name to-day) was a son of the sixth-century Gildas: *Cenydd* is now the usual Welsh spelling. In Ireland the name is known as *Canice*, from a fifth-century saint Caioneach, who gave his name to Kilkenny.

But the chief propagator of the name was Kenneth MacAlpine, the first king to rule over both Picts and Scots, who died about A.D. 860, through whom Kenneth spread all over Scotland. Scott took the name for his Crusading hero in *The Talisman*, Sir Kenneth.

Most modern bearers are of Scottish origin or extraction. Kenneth Grahame, author of *The Wind in the Willows* and *The Reluctant Dragon*, though he lived in England all his life, clearly showed his national origin in his surname. Sir Kenneth Clark, who has written many books on painting, has *MacKenzie* as his second name—MacKenzie meaning 'son of Kenneth.' Kenneth MacKellar is a popular Scottish ballad-singer of to-day.

Sportsmen of the name seem generally to prefer the short form *Ken*: Ken Wood, for instance, the athlete, and Ken Viljoen, South African cricket captain earlier in this century. Another and equally popular short form is *Kenny*.

KEVIN is an Irish name, widespread in its own country. Originally *Caomhghin*, an elaboration of *Caioneach* (see *Kenneth*), it means 'handsome by birth.'

St Kevin, or *Coemgen*, to whom its popularity is due, in the sixth century was abbot of Glendalough, 'the valley of the two lakes,' where the ruins of his settlement are to-day a favourite day's trip from Dublin. He spent many years as a hermit, and a popular ballad by Tom Moore asserts that he threw a young woman who came to visit him into the lake below his cave. According to a recent authority, however, he did nothing of the kind, but merely beat her with nettles for her curiosity, which, as this biographer adds, "was naughty of him." A pleasanter story tells of his bringing back to life the pet goose of King O'Toole.

The famous Irish song *Kevin Barry* refers to the boy who saved the Irish leaders in 1916, sacrificing his life by attracting the attention of the British soldiers besieging their hideout.

LAMBERT 'Landa' and 'berhta,' meaning 'land' and 'famous,' were combined to form the Old German name *Landebert*. An Archbishop of Canterbury named *Lanbriht*, who died in 791, shows an Anglo-Saxon version, but it was never common.

There was a German Emperor of the name in the late ninth century, but it was the seventh-century St Lambert, Bishop of Maastricht, who made the name popular in the Low Countries, whence it seems to have spread to England with the Flemish immigrants connected with the wool trade, at any rate by the thirteenth century, when *Lambard* became a common form. The pet forms *Lambin*, and even *Lambkin*, suggest that there was an imagined connexion between the name and the lamb in whose wool the Flemings dealt.

In the sixteenth century Lambert went out of favour in this country, possibly on account of the unsuccessful attempt to oust Henry VII by the pretender Lambert Simnel. It is as a surname that Lambert claims most of its historic owners.

Nevertheless, Lambert is common enough to have such modern short forms as *Bert*, *Lam*, and *Lamy*, both here and in the United States.

LANCELOT, both from its sound and from its associations, so strongly suggests the word 'lance' that it is difficult to believe it has any other origin. It has been claimed that it is connected with an old German measure of land; but this might well be the length of a lance (compare our 'rod, pole, or perch'), or with an old French word for a weaver's shuttle, which is shaped like a spear-head.

There is another possible origin: the old French word 'l'ancelle' (from the Latin 'ancillus,' feminine 'ancilla'), meaning 'servant.' But as a personal name Lancelot was first given to Sir Lancelot of the Round Table, by Chrétien de Troyes, the twelfth-century romance writer. In the Middle Ages any word that resembled another was supposed to be connected with it. So it is reasonable to suppose that Chrétien, in naming Sir Lancelot—the lance-bearer, and 'servant' of Queen Guinevere—had in mind the ideas both of servant and spear.

In England Lancelot was used mostly in the North, but gradually became a peasant name. Shakespeare in *The Merchant of Venice*, for instance, makes *Launcelot* Gobbo the servant of Shylock, who deserts his Jewish master to serve the Christian Bassanio. But there were also prominent bearers. Lancelot Andrewes, Bishop of Winchester in the reign of James I, was the foremost Churchman of his day; Lancelot Brown, in the eighteenth century, was the most celebrated English garden designer, and known as "Capability Brown." The contemporary Lancelot Hogben, popularizer of scientific subjects, is the author of *Mathematics for the Million*.

Launcelot is an alternative spelling: there are yet other variants, such as *Lancelyn* or *Lancelin*. But more common is the short form *Launce*, or *Lance*. Shakespeare used Launce for Proteus' servant in the *Two Gentlemen of Verona*, whose private talks to his dog Crab show Elizabethan humour at its broadest.

LAURENCE is a more correct spelling of this name than *Lawrence*, though at present both are equally common. The name was originally the Latin *Laurentius*, from Laurentium, the 'city of laurels,' in Italy. But the idea of the laurel as a symbol of victory was probably the principal reason for its spread.

Among Christians it became a favourite name through St Laurence, Archdeacon of Rome in the mid third century. When summoned to surrender the treasures of the Church to the civil authorities he asked for time to 'realize his assets,' as a businessman to-day would say. He then distributed all the funds and valuables among the poor, and when the appointed day arrived the Imperial officials were faced with a crowd of pensioners, as the 'treasure of the Church.' This naturally failed to satisfy them, and Laurence was sentenced to roasting alive on a gridiron. Yet even as he was dying his sense of humour did not desert him. "Turn me over," he called out to his executioners. "I am done on this side." The St Lawrence river is so named because it was discovered on his feast-day, August 10.

Like most Latin names, Laurence was rare in England before 1066, though it had been the name of the second Archbishop of Canterbury, who succeeded Augustine in 604.

There is only one example in Domesday Book; a century

later, however, the name was becoming common, giving, besides clearly recognizable modern surnames, such variants as *Laurie*, *Lowrie*, and *Larking*. Some 237 old English churches show the popularity of the deacon-saint and his name. Shakespeare uses Laurence for the kindly old friar who marries Romeo and Juliet. In *The Merchant of Venice* he gives the lover of Shylock's daughter, Jessica, the Italian form, *Lorenzo*. This was a favourite in Italy: Lorenzo de Medici, for instance, fifteenth-century ruler of Florence, and patron of art and scholarship in the heyday of his city, was known as Lorenzo the Magnificent. Lorenzo has occasonally been used in this country.

The best-known English example before modern times is probably Laurence Sterne, the eccentric eighteenth-century Yorkshire parson who wrote that racy novel, *Tristram Shandy*. Captain Scott's companion, Laurence Oates, walked out to certain death in an Antarctic blizzard to save his friends from starving. The present-day popularity of the name has probably been helped by the romantic figure of "Lawrence of Arabia," though in this case it was a surname. Lawrence Durrell is an outstanding present-day novelist who wrote the *Alexandrian Quartet*. Sir Laurence Olivier is generally admitted to be our foremost Shakespearean actor. He is familiarly known as *Larry*, the commonest short form, which he shares with Larry Adler, the virtuoso of the mouth-organ. *Laurie* and *Lawrie* are also used, and in Scotland also *Lowrie*. 'Tod-lowrie' in Scotland is used for a fox.

In Ireland the name has spread independently, through St Laurence O'Toole, Archbishop of Dublin, who died in 1180: during a famine he fed three hundred children daily. His baptismal name was *Lurcan*, or *Lorcan*, meaning 'fierce.' *Lanty* is a special Irish short form. *Lars*, found occasionally, is a Scandinavian version, like *Loren*, *Lorin*, and *Lauren*.

LEO is the Latin for 'lion.' This word is probably best known to-day as the fifth sign of the Zodiac: according to the astrologers, it gives its lion-like character to those born between July 22 and August 21. But as a personal name the Romans seem to have taken it from the Greeks, whose name for the king of beasts was 'leon.'

Six Emperors of Constantinople have borne the name, and thirteen Popes have taken it, from Leo the Great, who by sheer personal courage induced the Hun invaders to spare the city of Rome, to Leo XIII, the first world authority to codify the duties and rights of workers and their employers, in 1890. This has made the name popular among Catholics.

English bearers of the form *Leon* will generally be found to be of Jewish origin, using this Greek and Spanish version to replace the Hebrew *Levi* ('pledged'); it is a common practice among them to bear a Hebrew name privately, while officially known by a like-sounding Gentile name—*Isaac* becoming *Isidore*, *Benjamin* becoming *Bernard*, and so on. Leon Goossens, however, the leading oboeist of the present day, is of Belgian-Flemish extraction.

The name has never been common in this country. Dickens in *Pickwick Papers* caricatures the type of lady who chases celebrated characters, in the person of Mrs Leo Hunter (the 'lion-hunter')—her husband is of no consequence. Rider Haggard names the hero of *She* Leo Vincey: he is a romantic young Englishman who finds himself to be the reincarnated lover of Ayesha, the 'immortal' woman, ruler of an African tribe who 'crown' strangers with red-hot jars.

Leo is common in America, where *Lee* is used as a short form; but the extraordinary pet version *Metro* can only come from the roaring lion trade-sign of the Metro-Goldwyn-Mayer film combine.

LEONARD The Old German *Leonhard* is supposedly a compound of 'levon' and 'hardu,' two words meaning 'lion' and 'brave' (it is strange to find an animal not native to Northern Europe in a Germanic name).

Presumably, however, Leonard was not really an ancient name; its first recorded bearer was a sixth-century saint, converted from heathenism together with his royal master, the Frank Clovis. He devoted the rest of his life to looking after prisoners.

The popularity of the name in France is understandable, but its spread in England is not so clearly explained. However, after the twelfth century the saint became so popular over here that he can claim over 150 ancient church dedications, and the name has never died out. The surname Lennard shows that the pronunciation has remained unchanged since the Middle Ages, when surnames began.

The greatest Leonard was the Italian, *Leonardo* da Vinci, whose *Last Supper* and *Mona Lisa* are two of the most admired paintings in the world; he was actually more interested in scientific investigations than in the arts, producing models of man-powered aeroplanes, plans for fortifications, irrigation schemes, and innumerable practical designs for engines and instruments, preserved in his notebooks.

The first well-known English example in the present century is fictional: Arnold Bennett's irrepressible young man from the Potteries, Leonard Henry, known to his friends as *Denry*, hero of that entertaining novel *The Card*, which was published in 1911. In real life, and in our own time, we have Sir Leonard Lord, head of the British Motors' Corporation, and Sir Leonard Hutton, ex-Yorkshire and England cricketer. Like *Len* Harvey, the boxer, he is known by the short form of his name. An alternative pet form is *Lennie* or *Lenny*.

LEOPOLD is a compound of the Old German 'leudi' and 'balda,' meaning 'people-bold'; but there is no doubt that it owes its present spelling to the influence of other names in which Leo means 'lion.'

Its chief home was Austria, where seven rulers bore it before the end of the fourteenth century. The first is regarded as a saint, the fifth was the captor of Richard the Lionheart. From Austria the name spread throughout the German-speaking countries, and so to many ruling houses of Europe; there were two Emperors of the name, one in the seventeenth, the other in the eighteenth century.

The name reached England through Queen Victoria's uncle and adviser, King Leopold of Belgium, himself of German origin; she called her third son, the Duke of Albany, after him, and during her reign Leopold became common enough in England to produce the pet form *Poldie*.

The best-known example of the last century was probably Leopold von Ranke, the great German historian. At present the Polish-born Leopold Stokowski is a leading orchestral conductor in the United States.

James Joyce, the Irish writer, chose Leopold Bloom as the chief character in his extraordinary novel *Ulysses*, which draws a parallel between the events of one day in this Dublin Jew's life and the adventures of the ancient Greek seafarer.

LESLIE is by origin an Aberdeenshire place-name, Lesslyn or Leslie, whose owners took their surname from it. The head of the family was ennobled in 1457 as Lord Leslie. John Leslie, Bishop of Aberdeen, was a champion of Mary, Queen of Scots. Various old spellings are found, such as *Lesley*, *Lesly*, and *Leslie*.

Leslie became a popular name for English boys in the

nineteenth century: Lesley was taken as the girls' form. To-day both are still widespread, and by no means prove a Scottish connexion. Sir Leslie Stephen, alpine climber, philosopher, and author, was born in 1832. Leslie Howard, the famous English actor, was killed in 1943 when the plane he was travelling in was shot down by the Germans; the use of the name for non-Scots had its rise between the birth of the first example and the death of the second. To-day, Leslie Durbin is one of our finest craftsmen in gold and silver: Leslie Charteris is the popular author of the thrillers whose hero is the engaging but unscrupulous 'Saint.'

The short form *Les* has been preferred by many bearers: Les Ames, for instance, the pre-war England wicket-keeper.

LIONEL, like *Lancelot* (p. 170), seems to be a medieval name, given to one of King Arthur's knights, a cousin and companion of Sir Lancelot, and means 'young lion.'

Edward III, a romantically-minded king, gave the name to his second son, afterwards Duke of Clarence, and this form has persisted to the present day. Its survival seems to be due to its lasting popularity in Northern England, though to-day it has no special local flavour. *Linnell* was a medieval form suggesting a careless pronunciation of the name.

Lionel Johnson, best known for his poem *By the Statue of King Charles at Charing Cross*, died in 1902; he is an example of the revival of the name in the nineteenth century. Lionel Twiss, a British pilot, broke the air-speed record with 1132 m.p.h. in 1956.

Lyonel is a somewhat uncommon variant.

LLEWELLYN This name is more correctly spelt *Llywelyn*, generally taken to be a combination of the Welsh 'llew,' 'lion,' and 'eilun,' 'likeness'; but if it is an ancient name the first part is more probably from 'llyw,' meaning 'leader,' or from the Celtic god Lugh, later Luel, from whom we get the last syllable of Carlisle (Caer Luel).

Llywelyn, son of Iorwerth, Prince of All Wales, married a daughter of King John of England; he is known as Llywelyn the Great. His grandson, Llywelyn, son of Griffith, took the title of his grandfather, but failed to justify his claim; he was defeated and killed in a battle against the army of Edward I, in 1282.

The name was used in England, but changed to *Leoline*, even by Welshmen; in the seventeenth century, Sir Leoline Jenks was Principal of Jesus College, Oxford. Another form of the name found at that time is *Lewlin*. Shakespeare's *Fluellen* in *Henry V* shows an English attempt to pronounce the Welsh correctly. But it may have been a recognized form, as *Floyd* is for *Lloyd* (see below). Coleridge calls the father of the heroine of his eerie poem *Christabel* Sir Leoline, without any suggestion that it is a Welsh name; Leoline is still used occasionally in England.

Short forms of Llewellyn are *Llew*, *Llelo*, and *Lyn*, the third of these being sometimes taken as an official name. Sir Lyn Ungoed-Thomas was Solicitor-General in a recent Socialist Government. *Lewis* is sometimes used as a substitute.

The author of the novel *How Green was My Valley*, who wrote as Richard Llewellyn, was in fact Richard David Vivian Llewellyn Lloyd.

LLOYD The popular Welsh name *Lloyd*, or *Lluyd*, equally common as a surname, is a form of the adjective 'llwyd,' meaning indifferently 'brown' or 'grey.' It was used as a title of the sea-god Llyr, probably the original of the legendary King Lear.

'Dark-complexioned' probably gives the best interpretation: the name is particularly favoured by Welsh gipsies. As a surname in England, owing to the difficulty of the English in pronouncing 'Ll,' it has often become *Floyd.*

Notable examples seem to have been given Lloyd rather as a second than as a first name. David Lloyd George was the Prime Minister largely responsible for the winning of the First World War; the foremost American architect of this century was Frank Lloyd Wright. It was, however, the first name of Robert Louis Stevenson's stepson, who collaborated with him in several novels, the American Lloyd Osbourne.

Floyd is more common as a personal name in America than Lloyd. Floyd Patterson is the present world heavyweight boxing champion.

LOUIS Although *Lewis* was formerly the normal English spelling and pronunciation of this name, as it still is in Wales (see *Llewellyn*, p. 177), the French *Louis* seems now to prevail in England; even the French pronunciation, "Louee," is now normal. Neither, however, was the original form; this was *Chlodovech*, from 'hlod' and 'vig,' Old German words for 'glory' and 'fight.'

The real founder of the Frankish monarchy, *Chlodowig*, had his name latinized either as *Lodovicus* or as *Clovis*, later simplified into the present Louis, the most popular French royal name from Charlemagne's son Louis the Pious, who was born in 778, to Louis-Philippe, who died, an exile in England, in 1850. Most admired was Louis IX (St Louis), the ideal medieval king, lawgiver, just judge, and Crusader; most magnificent was Louis XIV, the "Sun King," who built the palace of Versailles; most pathetic was little Louis XVII, who died in the Temple prison in 1795, after his father, Louis XVI, and his mother, Marie-Antoinette, had been guillotined.

As a pre-eminently French name, Louis claims many famous French bearers. Louis Daguerre, for instance, early in the nineteenth century, gave his name to that primitive form of photography the daguerrotype; Louis Blériot was the first man to cross the Channel by aeroplane: this was in 1909, and he took thirty-seven minutes to do it; Louis Braille, blind himself, invented the Braille alphabet for blind readers.

In England *Lewis* is the first discoverable form of the name, though *Lowis* was sometimes used in the Middle Ages. The Latin *Ludovicus* has survived here and there, in such forms as *Ludovic* or *Ludovick*, probably from German connexions (the German form is *Ludwig*, first name of the great musician Beethoven). But Lewis was normal until comparatively recently—Shakespeare even calls his French bearers by this form; though he has an Italian *Lodovico* in *Othello*, and uses *Lodowick* in *Measure for Measure*.

No great English historical characters have had the name; but Chaucer compiled his *Treatise on the Astrolabe* in English for his son Lewis, "for Latin ne canst thou yet but small, my little son." For another famous English Lewis we must come to the nineteenth century, when Lewis Carroll wrote *Alice's Adventures in Wonderland* and *Through the Looking-glass*. His real names, however, were Charles *Lutwidge* Dodgson, showing an uncommon variant.

Robert Louis Stevenson, though Louis was only his second name, is an interesting example as an early use of the now prevailing French version.

Louis is the normal form used in America, where Louisiana is a reminder that in Louis XIV's time a great part of the present United States was in French possession. This territory was bought from France in 1803 for 15,000,000 dollars.

Strange to say, its first American Governor was Meriwether Lewis. Louis Armstrong, the "grand old man" of jazz, is the most widely known American example of to-day.

An unexpected variant of the name is *Aloysius*, originally a French name 'à Loys,' meaning 'son of *Loys*' (yet another old version). It is used in Southern Germany to-day as *Aloys*; but the Latin version is best known, from the Italian Jesuit saint Aloysius Gonzaga, who lived in the early days of the Order, and died at the age of twenty-three; he is, so far as is known, the only canonized billiard-player. *Trader Horn*, a best-seller of the 1920's, is the story of a real character, Aloysius Horn.

Lou, less often *Louie*, and occasionally *Lewie*, are used as pet forms; *Lew* is yet another, which, at least since the time of Lew Wallace, the American author of *Ben Hur*, has become an independent name.

LUCIUS Lucia, or Lucy, is to-day far commoner than the masculine *Lucius*; the syllable Luc- in both is connected with the Latin word 'lux,' meaning 'light,' as in *Lucifer*, 'light-bearer.' Both Lucius and Lucia are said to have been given originally to children born at daybreak.

Lucius Apuleius was a Latin author of the second century A.D., who wrote *The Golden Ass*, in which the narrator is turned into a donkey for his curiosity. Three early Popes were named Lucius, one of them a martyr; and there were several related names, such as *Lucianus* and *Lucentius*. *Lucian*, a Syrian Greek, wrote *The True History*, a satire on travellers' tales, in the second century A.D.

There was an old English tradition that an ancient British King Lucius in the second century became a Christian with all his people; but there is no contemporary evidence for his existence. Yet even though the British tradition was firmly believed until modern times, Lucius was never used as a name in this country before the Renaissance. Shakespeare has several forms for minor characters in his plays; but Lucius Cary, Lord Falkland, is the only notable English example in history. Hating any form of violence, he nevertheless took part in the Civil War on the Parliamentary side, and rode willingly to certain death at the battle of Newbury.

Though only occasionally given in England, Lucius was a popular Irish name, substituted for several native ones. Sheridan, in his play *The Rivals*, appropriately introduces Sir Lucius O'Trigger.

America has the special short form *Lush*.

LUKE, in the Greek of the New Testament, is given as *Loukas*, said to mean 'man of Lucania.' In Latin *Lucanus* certainly had this meaning; there was a Roman poet, generally known as *Lucan*, who wrote a long historical poem called *Pharasalia*. But it is Loukas, latinized as *Lucas*, which was the name of the writer of the third Gospel.

It is an odd coincidence that the Romans called the elephant a "Lucanian ox," for St Luke's symbol is an ox. He was given this emblem because he emphasizes in his Gospel the patience of Christ (patience was regarded as the special characteristic of oxen). Besides being a writer, St Luke was a doctor: St Paul describes him as "the beloved physician"; he is therefore one of the patron saints of doctors. St Luke is also said to have been a painter, and numerous ancient pictures of the Madonna were supposed to be his work; he is therefore claimed as the patron of painters.

Luca della Robbia, the fifteenth-century Italian sculptor and modeller, is best known for his relief plaques of children; Lucas

Cranach was a late-medieval German engraver. In these cases, and many others, the name was no accidental choice; until the seventeenth century at least, artists were regarded as craftsmen, and the calling was passed down from father to son; any painter would be likely to give the name of his guild's patron to his child. No famous doctor, however, seems to have borne the name.

In England there seem to be no examples of the name before the twelfth century, *Lucas* being the earliest recorded form. *Luke* and *Luk* are mentioned a century later, *Luck* becoming a common version.

Luke Hansard (1752–1828), who was printer to the House of Commons, produced the official reports of Parliamentary debates that still bear his surname. In America, where it was introduced by the Pilgrim Fathers, Luke has often been used.

It has never been popular in England, possibly on account of its resemblance to the old word 'lukewarm,' meaning 'tepid,' though this adjective has no connexion with the name. There are, however, signs that recently Luke has been gaining favour, along with *Matthew* and *Mark*, which are now in fashion.

LUTHER Though generally given nowadays in honour of the great German reformer Martin Luther, this name was not a surname in origin, but a combination of the Old German 'hlu,' 'hear,' and 'herja,' 'people,' once a common personal name. *Clotaire* (Old German *Hlotar* or *Chlotar*) was the eldest son of Clovis, the first Christian King of the Franks. The last survivor of his family was *Lothair*, ruler of Lotharingia (which contained the province now called Lorraine), who succeeded to his territory in A.D. 855. Three early German Emperors were called after him.

There was a Saxon king named *Lothar*, and the surname *Lowther*, meaning 'a man from Lorraine,' may have occasionally been used as a given name. But Luther in this country is confined to Nonconformists. In the United States, where Lutherans are the most numerous Protestant body, the name is frequent; the French reformer John Calvin (his surname means 'bald') also has his namesakes there, notably President *Calvin* Coolidge, who succeeded President Harding in 1924. The best-known Luther of this century is the American plant-breeder Luther Burbank, who died in 1926. The American pet form is *Loot*.

The Italian form, *Lothario*, is found in three seventeenth-century English plays. In the earliest, *The Cruel Brother*, by William d'Avenant, the bearer is characterized as haughty, gallant, and gay, and two later plays give the name to a similar character. 'A gay Lothario' has consequently become a general expression for any young man of this type.

Benjamin Disraeli wrote a novel with *Lothair* as its title; the hero is a high-minded young gentleman of the name. The chief interest of the book to-day, however, is that the leading characters are portraits of well-known people of the 1860's.

MADOC, or *Madog*, is a Welsh name meaning 'fortunate'; it has an Irish form, *Maidoc*.

There was a St Madoc, a disciple of St David; but the most notable bearer was Prince Madog ab Owain of Gwynedd, in the twelfth century. He is said, but without any great probability, to have discovered America; Southey wrote a long narrative poem describing his expedition.

The name seems to have spread from Wales into the West of England; a *Madoch* is recorded in Domesday Book, and other bearers are found in the thirteenth and fourteenth centuries, giving such surnames as Madox and Maddocks. *Madox* was given as a family name to the nineteenth-century historical painter Madox Brown; his grandson Ford Madox Ford wrote novels of the First World War, and one of the liveliest historical stories of this century, *Ladies Whose Bright Eyes*.

MAGNUS 'Magnus' is the Latin adjective meaning 'great.' Though there were seven early Christian saints of the name, the spread of Magnus is due to *Charlemagne* (Carolus Magnus); his title 'Magnus,' 'the Great,' was thought by his contemporaries to be a personal name, and so suitable for noble bearers.

St Olaf of Norway had his son and successor baptized Magnus, and this king, "Magnus the Good," codified the laws of his country. Six of his successors inherited the name, the last becoming ruler of a united Norway and Sweden in the fourteenth century.

The name has not been uncommon in Germany. Magnus Hirschfeldt, for instance, was a famous investigator of the glandular system early in the present century.

In Ireland Magnus, introduced by the Norsemen, has taken the form *Manus*, whence the surname McManus. In England the name is practically unknown. In Scotland, however, particularly in the Shetlands and Orkneys, it is a favourite on account of St Magnus, Earl of Orkney, who was killed in 1141 and is buried in Kirkwall Cathedral.

Scott's *Pirate* is a story concerned with the daughters of the appropriately named Shetlander Magnus Troill. *Magnus Merriman* is the title-hero of a modern novel by Eric Linklater set in the Scottish Isles.

MALCOLM, a favourite Scottish name, is the Gaelic 'mael Colum,' 'servant of St Columba.' Though it appears in Domesday Book, as *Malcolum*, and was used occasionally in England during the Middle Ages, it was rare outside Scotland until comparatively recent years.

Four Scottish kings have borne the name. Malcolm I came to the throne in 936. Malcolm III is more generally remembered (from Shakespeare's tragedy) as the son of Duncan who with Macduff defeated Macbeth. Known as Malcolm Canmore ('big-head'), he married the Saxon princess canonized as St Margaret of Scotland. Malcolm IV, who died unmarried in 1165, was known as Malcolm the Maiden.

In our own century Sir Malcolm Campbell was the first motorist to exceed 300 miles an hour; Sir Malcolm Sargent is one of our leading orchestral conductors.

MARK *Marcus* was used by the Romans both as a personal and as a family name. Probably derived, like *Martin* (see p. 188) from Mars, the Roman war-god, it may be rendered as 'warlike.'

Shakespeare's *Mark Antony*, Caesar's friend and Cleopatra's lover, was actually *Marcus Antonius* (see *Antony*, p. 52). Marcus Aurelius was the philosopher-emperor whose *Meditations* are still read by serious-minded people. Marcus Tullius Cicero was the greatest Roman orator. Marcus Tiro was the earliest known shorthand writer: he took down dictations from both Cicero and Caesar. Its notable bearers seem to have popularized the name, not only among the Romans, but also among the Greek-speaking peoples; even to-day *Markos* is one of the most popular names in Greece.

As a Christian name, in the literal sense of the phrase, we owe the use of Mark to the second Evangelist. St Mark eventually became Bishop of Alexandria, capital of Roman Egypt. But after the Mohammedans had conquered all the Near East his body was stolen by Venetian merchants under the noses of the Moslems; they carried it off, shouting that the coffin was a crate of pork, meat unclean to Jews and Mohammedans alike. His great church in Venice is one of the wonders of the Christian world, and even to-day every fifth Venetian is said to bear his name. It is therefore not surprising that *Marco* Polo was the name of the Venetian traveller who visited the Far East in the thirteenth century; he brought back the first factual description of China and the adjoining countries.

St Mark's symbol is a winged lion, typifying Christ as King. This was the design stamped on Venetian coins; and as the Venetians became during the Middle Ages the bankers of Europe, the coin then most in circulation became known as a mark. The English mark was worth 13*s*. 4*d*.

The first known British bearer of the name was a certain Marcus, proclaimed Roman Emperor by local troops in A.D. 406. His reign lasted less than a year, and he never left the country. It does not appear again till the thirteenth century, and then both as Marcus and Mark, but it was never a favourite, possibly on account of the treacherous King Mark of the Arthurian Legends, the villain in the tale of *Tristram and Iseult*. But the nineteenth century, in its search for unusual names, revived it, both as Mark and as Marcus. Marcus is particularly favoured among Jews, though by no means confined to them. Marcus Stone, the Victorian painter, and Marcus Morris, the only clergyman to have edited a 'comic,' show it as the name of a Christian.

In the nineteenth century Sir *Marc* Isembard Brunel, whose form of the name indicates his French origin, constructed the Thames Tunnel and produced the first set of machine-tools. Dickens shows that the name was normal in his time by calling the irrepressible optimist of *Martin Chuzzlewit*, who shares the hero's dismal adventures in America, Mark Tapley.

Mark was also not uncommon in the United States. The best-known American example is Samuel Clemens, who used as his pen-name Mark Twain, from the Mississippi boatmen's cry of "Mark Twain," meaning the minimum safe depth of two fathoms.

A name derived from Marcus is *Marcellus*, 'little Mark,' especially frequent among the Claudian clan, and providing two saints to the Calendar, one an early Pope, both martyrs. *Marcello*, in Italy, and *Marcel*, in France, are common, the latter being used occasionally as an English boy's name. Marcel Dupré was one of the greatest organists of this century, and a French hairdresser of the name invented the Marcel wave for ladies' hair, in the days of bobs and shingles, by using his curling-tongs reversed.

MARMADUKE is predominantly a Yorkshire name. It is first recorded in Domesday Book, in the case of a pre-Conquest *Melmidoc*, which may be the Celtic *Maolmadoc*, 'servant of Madoc' (see p. 183), or possibly another Celtic name, *Meriadoc*, 'sea leader.' Like *Chad* (see p. 73), it suggests that there was a strong survival of Celtic stock in Northern England.

By the thirteenth century the name had become *Marmaduc*, the usual medieval spelling, which with a Northern pronunciation easily became *Marmaduke*. As a lengthy and, from its last syllable, an aristocratic-sounding name, it might be supposed that Marmaduke has been chiefly used by noble families; yet this is not so. It is practically confined to Yorkshire, but not to any particular class, and is common enough to have been given the short form *Duke*; *Marmy* has also been noted.

The American name *Duke*, as instanced by the band-leader Duke Ellington, has no connexion with the Yorkshire name, but is taken purely for its noble sound, like *Count* (Count Basie is another jazz musician) and *King*, in a country where there are no titles of nobility. More common in the United States is *Earl*; but this may be due to a confusion with *Errol*, easily explained by the American rolling of the letter r. *Prince* Littler, however, is the foremost English organizer of pantomimes. *King* C. Gillette invented safety razors.

MARTIN Martinus is presumably, like *Marcus*, derived from Mars, so meaning 'warlike'; though as St Martin, the first known bearer, was a native of what is now Hungary, the name may be of unknown non-Latin origin.

The saint was a fourth-century soldier, best remembered by the story that he cut his military cloak in two, giving half of it to warm a beggar he once met on a winter night: he is generally represented holding this garment. Later he became Bishop of Tours, in France. Five Popes, the first in 649, took his name.

In England his popularity in the Middle Ages is shown by over 170 old churches dedicated to his name, notably St Martins-in-the-Fields, in London. Martinmas, or Martlemas, is his feast-day. It falls on November 11, known since 1918 as Armistice Day: a happy coincidence, if we remember that Martin was a soldier before he became a man of peace. The mild weather prevailing about this time gave it the old name of 'St Martin's little summer.'

The Scottish St Martin of Bullions is a counterpart of the English St Swithun. If it rains on his day, July 4, wet weather is predicted for the next forty days.

Martin is found in England by the beginning of the thirteenth century, and has never fallen altogether out of favour. Diminutives were *Martel*, *Martlet*, and *Martinet*. The type of weasel known as a marten has no connexion with the saint, although *Marten* is an occasional spelling of the name; but the bird known as the martin has its name from him.

The best-known bearer of the name is the German reformer Martin Luther, so that, unlike most saints' names, it has equal popularity among Protestants and Catholics. The most famous English bearer was Sir Martin Frobisher, one of the many explorers who tried to find a north-west passage through America to the East. He was Drake's Vice-Admiral in his West Indian expedition, and fought against the Armada.

There were no prominent bearers in England between the seventeenth century and the Victorian age; but the general use of the name in the nineteenth century is shown by Dickens's choice of *Martin Chuzzlewit* as the title for the novel containing such immortal characters as Mr Pecksniff and Sairey Gamp; and Ballantyne's selection of *Martin Rattler* to name one of his best-known boys' stories. Sir Martin Harvey was one of our leading actors at the beginning of the present century.

Martyn is the Welsh version, but found more as a surname than as a Christian name. *Martinet* is a French pet form. Colonel Martinet, who reorganized the French army under Louis XIV, was so ruthless in his methods that his name has come into general use for a strict disciplinarian; in France it is also given to the cat-o'-nine-tails. English pet forms are *Mart*, *Marty*, and *Martie*.

MATTHEW The Hebrew *Mattathiah*, 'gift of the Lord,' has given us two names: *Matthew*, from the Latin *Matthaeus*, and *Matthias*, which has never become common enough to change its original Greek form.

St Matthew the Apostle, writer of the first Gospel, was a tax-collector; before Christ called him from his unpopular profession he had been known as *Levi.* His symbol as an Evangelist is an angel in the form of a young man, typifying Christ's humanity. Traditionally he preached in Ethiopia and was beheaded there.

St Matthias was chosen to take the place among the Twelve forfeited by Judas Iscariot. His history is obscure, though his supposed body was found by the Empress Helena and enshrined at Trier in Germany.

Matthew, as a name in England, first appears in Domesday Book, in the Latin form *Matthaeus* and in the French form *Mathieu*; it is the French form which produced our present version. Its general popularity between the thirteenth and fifteenth centuries can be seen from the number of surnames beginning with Mat-, Mack-, Mass-, and May-; Macey, of French origin, is another. Matthias seems to have been used very little, if at all, before the Reformation.

The earliest notable Matthew in this country was Matthew Paris, a monk of St Albans in the thirteenth century. His three chronicles, covering contemporary events from 1200 to 1235, are a mine of information for historians, enlivened in the original manuscripts by delicate drawings, including a self-portrait. Matthew Parker was Queen Elizabeth's choice for the Archbishopric of Canterbury—the first English Primate appointed without the Pope's authority. Matthew Prior was a witty poet and diplomat in the reigns of William and Mary and Queen Anne. Matthew Boulton, in the reign of George III, financed James Watt; he also standardized the diameter of the halfpenny at one inch. The American sailor Matthew Perry opened Japan to commerce with the United States in 1854; Captain Matthew Webb was the first man to swim the Channel, in 1875, taking 21 hours 45 minutes. Matthew Arnold, who was born in 1822, is the poet of *The Forsaken*

Merman and *Sohrab and Rustum*; he died in 1888. Matthew Smith was one of our leading twentieth-century painters.

To-day Matthew is more common in America than in England. It has the pet forms *Matt* and *Mat. Matty* is a more English diminutive. But Matthew in Ireland is also often a substitute for *Mahon*, 'bear,' whence the surname McMahon.

MAURICE was the Latin *Mauritius*, meaning 'an inhabitant of Mauretania,' the Roman name for what we now call Morocco.

St Maurice, to whom we owe the spread of the name, was a soldier of the Theban Legion, martyred with 600 companions in Switzerland in the year 286. The Swiss resort of St *Moritz* shows the German version.

The name appears in England from the eleventh century, sometimes in the Old French version *Meurisse*, later, and more often, as *Morris* (a Morris dance is actually a 'Moorish dance'). William I's Chancellor was a Maurice: as Bishop of London he built Old St Paul's Cathedral, destroyed in the Great Fire. Another Norman bearer was Maurice Fitzgerald, who was one of Strongbow's chief companions in the conquest of Ireland, and who died in 1156. But the later form, Morris, was more normal until recent times.

After the Norman period distinguished examples of the name are rare in this country. Its use since the seventeenth century has probably been largely due to Prince Maurice, younger brother of Rupert of the Rhine, a Royalist hero of the Civil War; but its most celebrated bearers have been for the most part Frenchmen, such as the composer Maurice Ravel, who died in 1937, and the actor and music-hall star Maurice Chevalier in our own day.

The Welsh have a special form, *Meurig*, used far earlier than any form in England; Meurig ap Tewdrig was a Prince of South Wales in the fifth century. The last notable Welsh bearer was a Bishop of Bangor who died in 1139.

There is another old Welsh name, *Morus*. This appears to come from the parallel Latin word 'Maurus,' meaning 'a Moor.' As the name of one of the chief disciples of St Benedict, founder of the Western monks, it was popularized by them, particularly in France. The place-name Saint-Maur, derived from a famous French abbey, has given us the English surname *Seymour*, which in turn has become a personal name, as with Seymour Hicks, a leading light-comedy actor early in the present century.

MAXIMILIAN *Maximus*, as our word 'maximum' shows, means 'greatest.' It was a Latin title of honour given to successful military commanders, such as Quintus Fabius Maximus, who foiled the Carthaginian bid for supremacy in the Mediterranean. It came to be a personal name, perpetuated by several early saints, though none of them is well known. A Spaniard named Maximus, who had a British wife, allowed himself to be proclaimed Roman Emperor in A.D. 383. He settled veterans in Brittany and invaded the Continent, but never reached Rome. The Welsh still remember him as *Macsen* Wledig (Maximus the ruler), and Kipling tells some of his story in *Rewards and Fairies*. *Maxentius* and *Maximinus* were also used in late Roman times. *Maxim* is a modern variant.

Max, the English short form generally used for any of these names, will, however, often be found to be none of them, if the bearer's full name is known, but *Maximilian*.

There were two saints Maximilian. The first, a legendary character, was one of the "Seven Sleepers of Ephesus," who escaped martyrdom by hiding in a cave, only to wake a century later, when Christianity had become established. The second was a third-century bishop and martyr in what is now Austria, whose name was given to the son of the German Emperor Frederick III, born in 1459. A fanciful reason given for this choice is that it combined the names of the two great Romans, Fabius *Maximus* and Scipio *Aemilianus*, who followed up the successes of Fabius by destroying Carthage itself, in 146 B.C. The Emperor Maximilian, a reckless huntsman and daredevil fighter, was so greatly admired by the Austrians that they called him "our Max," and spread his name throughout the German-speaking area of Europe. The name was made familiar through one of the most popular of German juvenile classics, Wilhelm Busch's rhymed and illustrated stories of Max and Moritz, the original "terrible twins," translated since the mid nineteenth century into all European languages.

In 1954 Max Born was awarded the Nobel Prize for science, in recognition of his researches into the structure of crystals.

The only English bearer of note was the witty Sir Max Beerbohm, author and broadcaster, but even he showed his German origin in his surname. The Canadian newspaper magnate Lord Beaverbrook, who was previously known as Max Aitken, is not a Maximilian, his Christian names being William *Maxwell*.

Another pet form is *Maxy*.

MEREDITH In its Welsh spelling Meredith is *Meredydd* or *Maredudd*, with the accent on the second syllable. It is a combination of the Old Welsh 'mawredd,' 'greatness,' and 'iudd,' 'chief.' Its earliest recorded form seems to be *Margetud*, the name of a king of Dyfed in the early seventh, or late sixth, century.

Even in Wales to-day the name is more often a surname than a given name; but it is frequent enough as a Christian name to have the diminutive *Merry*. *Bedo* is another odd old diminutive, which is sometimes given as an independent name.

Though in his case it was a surname, no account of the name would be complete without mentioning the writer George Meredith, whose poems and novels covered the half-century between 1851 and 1901.

MERVYN, or *Mervin*, is probably a name with a double derivation. There was an Anglo-Saxon name *Maerwine*, meaning 'famous friend,' from which, it is said, we get the surnames Marvin and Marvyn; but far more famous is the Old Welsh *Myrddin*, which is the true Welsh form of *Merlin*.

Legend claims that there were two enchanters of this name, Myrddin Emrys (Merlin Ambrosius), who was King Arthur's magician, and Myrddin Wyllt (Merlin Silvestris), the 'Wild' Merlin, of whom little is known but his name. The town and county now called Carmarthen is said to be named after one of them, but it is probable that the wizard took his name from the town, for 'caer' means 'fort' and 'myrddin' 'sea-hill.' Merlin Ambrosius, however, is connected with the city by ancient tradition; the stump of his oak-tree, whose life is said to be bound up with the town's prosperity, still stands there.

The ninth-century Roderick the Great, King of South Wales, was the son of Myrddin Frych ('the freckled') and father of the second king of the name. And, until the close of the last century, Mervyn seems to have been regarded as having an aristocratic flavour; W. S. Gilbert, in *Ruddigore*, names one of the hero's ghostly ancestors Sir Mervyn Murgatroyd.

To-day the name is in general use. Mervyn Peake is a master of horrific illustrations for books, and a horrific writer as well, as the title of his romance *Gormenghast* suggests. Mervyn is also the name of two contemporary bishops, Dr Mervyn Stockwood of Southwark and Dr Mervyn Charles-Edwards of Worcester. Mervyn Cowie inspired the creation of big-game reserves in Africa.

If *Marvin* is used as a personal name it takes the pet form *Mar*; *Mervin* and *Mervyn* take *Mer* or *Merv*.

MICHAEL is the name given to the Archangel who led the heavenly hosts in the great battle described in the twelfth chapter of Revelations. His name is his war-cry: "Who is like God?" In the Book of Daniel he also appears as the guardian angel of Israel.

The feast of St Michael and All Angels, on September 29, shows its former importance by its old name, Michaelmas, still used for the third quarter of the legal year, and for the autumn term at the older universities. Geese being at their plumpest at this time, the Michaelmas goose was traditionally eaten on the saint's day.

In Christian times Michael came to be regarded not only as the conqueror of Satan, but also as the weigher of souls at the Last Judgment; hence he is often seen in stained-glass windows with the dragon of evil under his feet, and holding scales containing man's evil deeds in one pan and his good actions in the other. As a warrior angel he is the principal patron of soldiers, taking precedence even over St George. Nine Emperors of Constantinople bore his name, and five kings of Rumania, including the last.

The name came to England only in the twelfth century, and though usually written in its correct form, it seems to have been pronounced in the French manner, as *Michel* or *Mihiel*, giving rise to numerous surnames, such as Mitchell, Mighill (probably from the Spanish form *Miguel*), and Miall. *Miall*, in fact, seems to have been the pronunciation used in the seventeenth century; Samuel Butler's satire *Hudibras* contains, as two rhyming lines:

> At Michael's term had many a trial,
> Worse than the dragon and St Michael.

Miles Coverdale, the sixteenth-century translator of the Bible into English, signed himself in Latin as Michael.

The first Earl of Suffolk, in the reign of Richard II, was Michael de la Pole. He began his career as apprentice to a Hull merchant named Rottenherring. Michael Drayton, the author of the sonnet beginning "Since there's no help, come let us kiss and part," was one of the leading Elizabethan poets; he was a contemporary of Miguel de Cervantes, greatest of Spanish writers and creator of the immortal Don Quixote; a contemporary also of the French essayist Michel de Montaigne. The English Michael Faraday, in the early nineteenth century, was a pioneer of electromagnetism. Michael Tippett to-day is among our leading composers. But the greatest of all bearers of the name literally takes us back to the original: he is Michelangelo—"Michael the Angel"—the Italian painter, sculptor and poet.

The Welsh use a similar name for Michael—*Mihangel*, which is 'Michael Angel' contracted.

In Ireland, though rare before the seventeenth century—at any rate, in written records—Michael has become one of the commonest names, with the same pet forms as in England: *Mick*, *Micky*, and *Mickey*. These have been adopted in America, not so much as personal names, but as slang terms for an Irishman. To take the micky out of anyone is to make fun of him; the term for a pocket flask is a micky—presumably filled with

Irish whiskey. But the best known of all American Mickeys is the smallest; Walt Disney's Mickey Mouse. In Australia Mickey is used for a young bull, probably in allusion to the quick Irish temper. *Mogga* and *Spike* are recent pet forms.

An alternative form of Michael in Hebrew was *Micah* ('who is like the Lord?' instead of 'who is like God?'). Micah was one of the Minor Prophets. His name was much used by Puritans, which accounts for its choice by Conan Doyle in his historical novel *Micah Clarke*.

MILES, or *Myles*, was a shortened form of *Michael* in England; but it is also a separate name, derived from the Old German 'mil,' meaning 'beloved.' The Franks had such compound names as *Milhard*, 'beloved-bold,' and *Milberht*, 'beloved bright,' but the Normans used the simple forms *Milo* and *Milon*.

This name was also probably popularized because it happened to be identical with a Greek name, said to mean 'crusher,' whose most celebrated bearer was the Greek wrestling champion *Milo* of Croton who, having carried a live ox through the stadium at Olympia, ate it all in a single day. As an old man he tried to split an oak with his bare hands, but was caught fast in the crack and devoured by wolves.

The Normans brought the name to England. Though not a saint's name, it died out in the sixteenth century, to be revived by the Victorians, partly, perhaps, from the surname, partly from its popularity in Ireland.

After the Normans had introduced it into Ireland, Miles came to be substituted for the native *Maolmuire*, 'servant of Mary,' and *Maelmor*, 'majestic chief.'

An early example of the revived use of Miles is Longfellow's poem *The Courtship of Miles Standish*, which appeared in 1858.

Longfellow's fellow-countryman, the American-born Henry James, in his novel *The Turn of the Screw* makes a boy Miles and his sister victims of the ghosts of a pair of wicked servants.

Sir Miles Thomas is former Chairman of the British Overseas Airways Corporation, and Miles Malleson is a writer and translator of plays.

MONTAGUE 'Mont aigu,' in French, means 'pointed hill.' There are several places in France with this name, in some cases spelt *Montagu*. Drogo "de Monte Acuto" (the Latin translation of the words), probably took his surname from the 'pointed hill' near Caen, in Normandy, before William the Conqueror granted him estates in Somerset, where Montacute to-day is famous for its great mansion.

As a personal name *Montagu*—or now more commonly *Montague*—came in with the fashion for giving aristocratic names to the little Smiths, Browns, and Robinsons of the nineteenth century.

The pronunciation of the name is shown by the story of the army recruit who dared to correct the sergeant who called him "Montaig." "All right, Montague," answered the sergeant, "I'll put you down for fattigew!"

Montagu Rhodes James is an example of the less common spelling of the name. He was Provost of Eton, and created a new type of ghost story in his *Ghost Stories of an Antiquary*.

Monty, the pet version, is now more usually thought of as the nickname of Field Marshal Lord Montgomery of Alamein. Though no doubt many recent Montgomerys have been named in his honour, *Montgomery* was used as a personal name long before he became famous, usually from the Welsh county. Another occasional pet form is *Monte*, pronounced like Monty.

MORGAN, in its earliest known form *Morcant*, is a combination of the Welsh 'mawr,' 'great,' and 'can,' 'bright'; but it has absorbed another old name, *Morien*, meaning 'sea-born.'

Its first important bearer is better known from his name as rendered in Greek: *Pelagius*. The first recorded British heretic, he claimed that a man can lead a good life without any help from God.

Morgan has always been popular in Wales. Both the county of Glamorgan, and Morgannwg, the district between the Towy and the Wye, are claimed to have taken their names from rulers of the name.

MORTIMER The Mortimer family liked to derive their surname from the Dead Sea, 'morte mer,' in Palestine, where their ancestors had fought in the Crusades. Marlowe expressed this somewhat fanciful but picturesque derivation in his play *Edward II*:

> This tattered ensign of my ancestors,
> Which swept the desert shore of that Dead Sea
> Whereof we got the name of Mortimer,
> Will I advance you these castle walls.

But it is far more likely to come from a Mortemer in Normandy.

The Irish *Morty*, though it looks like a pet form of Mortimer, is in fact derived from *Murtagh* (see *Murdoch*, p. 201); yet even the Irish, before they revived their ancient names early in this century, used Mortimer as a 'long' form of their own old native name. *Mort* is a present-day pet version.

As a personal name in England, Mortimer is of recent use. The best-known example to-day is Sir Mortimer Wheeler, who by his books and television appearances has done more than any other expert to popularize archaeology.

MOSES is generally claimed to be a Hebrew name meaning 'drawn out,' in allusion to the infant Moses, who was drawn out from the Nile by Pharaoh's daughter, to become the law-giver of Israel; but the name is more likely to be of Egyptian origin, meaning 'born,' or perhaps 'my son.' Almost the whole of the Book of Exodus is devoted to Moses' history.

The name of their great leader was not used by the Israelites, but became widespread after the Jews had returned from captivity in Babylon. Their pronunciation of it was something like 'Mosha.' *Moshe* is the modern Hebrew version.

In England the name first appears in Domesday Book, in the form *Moyses*, as in the old Latin 'Vulgate' Bible. In ordinary use this became *Moyse*, which came to be pronounced as one syllable, *Moyes*, or *Moss*, and was by no means confined to families of Jewish extraction. The Welsh version is *Moesen*, pronounced 'Mo-aysen.'

It was only after the Reformation that Moses came into use in its present form, taken from the Authorized Version of the Scriptures. The name seems to have been used only by the humbler classes. In Goldsmith's *Vicar of Wakefield* Moses Primrose is the simple-minded son of the poor village clergyman, who exchanges the family horse for a gross of spectacles.

Mo is the common short form, though *Mose* is also occasionally used.

MUNGO was the nickname, meaning 'darling,' given originally by his affectionate followers to St *Kentigern*, the sixth-century bishop of Glasgow. He lived for a time in Wales, where he founded a monastery at Llanelwy (now St Asaph), and sent out missionaries as far afield as Iceland.

Mungo has not been used outside Scotland, except by bearers of Scottish origin. Scott, in *The Fortunes of Nigel*, introduces a sixteenth-century Sir Mungo Malagrowther. The most notable example in real life was the late-eighteenth-century Scottish explorer of the Niger, Mungo Park: his account of his adventures, *Travels in the Interior of Africa*, is a classic of travel.

Kentigern, in spite of its meaning, 'chief lord,' is rarely, if ever, used to-day, though it was formerly found in Wales, as *Cyndeyrn*, as well as in Scotland.

MURDOCH, a popular Scottish name, is another form of the Irish *Murtagh*; both were originally *Muireadhach*, meaning something like 'sea-man.' In Ireland it also became *Morty* (see *Mortimer*, p. 199). *Meriadoc* and *Meriadek* were other old forms; one sixth-century Welsh saint is recorded under both.

In Domesday Book a *Murdac* is found living in Sussex. It would be interesting to know how he found his way there: perhaps he was a seaman from Ireland or Scotland; perhaps the name had persisted since Celts lived in Sussex. Far more Britons remained in Saxon England than we are apt to imagine.

Murray is yet another 'sea' name. It may be geographical, from the Moray Firth, between Lossiemouth and Cromarty, also derived from the old Celtic word 'mor.' From this district the Scottish clan, known both as *Murray* and *Moray*, took its name.

The Bonnie Earl of Moray is a famous old Scottish ballad.

NATHANIEL *Nathan* is the Hebrew word for 'gift.' This was the name of the prophet who rebuked David for bringing about the death of Uriah, by putting him in the most dangerous post in battle, so that the king could marry Bathsheba, his widow. The full story may be found in the twelfth chapter of the Second Book of Samuel, with the dramatic accusation,

"Thou art the man!" Nathan has been used in English-speaking countries since the seventeenth century.

More common is the compound form *Nathaniel*, or *Nathanael*, whose meaning, 'gift of God,' is the same as that of *Jonathan*. Nathanael, the "Israelite without guile," is generally supposed to have been the Apostle *Bartholomew* (see p. 62).

A very early example of the use of Nathaniel in England is in Shakespeare's *Love's Labour's Lost*, where Sir Nathaniel is a grotesque but sharp-witted curate. In Dickens's *Pickwick Papers* Nathaniel Winkle is the sporting type whose incompetence leads him into one disaster after another.

Of bearers in real life the best known are Americans. "I only regret that I have but one life to lose for my country," Nathan Hale, a hero of the American Revolution, hanged by the British, exclaimed before he died. Nathaniel Hawthorne, the nineteenth-century novelist, wrote *The Tanglewood Tales*, a collection of Greek legends simplified for children—perhaps the best introduction to classical mythology.

An English writer, who took the usual short form of the name, was *Nat* Gould (a pen-name), who died in 1919; he produced some 130 novels, every one dealing with horse-racing. Nat seems particularly popular to-day among sportsmen and jazz musicians.

Nat is used for both Nathan and Nathaniel; *Nath* for Nathaniel; *Nate* and *Nathe* for Nathan.

NEVILLE is derived from Neuville, 'new town,' near Dieppe, in France. Gilbert de Nevil was one of the companions of William the Conqueror, and the family he founded produced numerous public figures—soldiers, landowners, judges, even two bishops, during the Middle Ages. Shakespeare, in *Henry VI, Part II*, alludes to:

The Nevilles all
Whose swords were never drawn in vain.

Besides *Neville* and *Nevil*, the form *Nevile* is also found.

Warwick "the Kingmaker" was Richard Neville, Earl ot Warwick, virtual ruler of England during the Wars of the Roses: his changing support of Yorkists and Lancastrians swayed the fortunes of each party.

But as a Christian name Neville has reached distinction only recently. Nevil Maskelyne invented the prismatic micrometer in the late eighteenth century; Neville Chamberlain was Prime Minister at the outbreak of the Second World War. Had he listened to the warnings of Sir Nevile Henderson, the diplomatic expert on German affairs, war might have been prevented. An earlier namesake of the Prime Minister was Colonel Neville Chamberlain, who invented the game of snooker.

Contemporary bearers are Neville Cardus, our greatest writer on cricket, and Neville Duke, a great test pilot.

Nevil Shute, after a successful career in engineering, became a novelist of the first rank: he died in 1960.

NICHOLAS The Greek *Nikolaos*, compounded of 'nike,' 'victory,' and 'laos,' 'people,' became *Nicolaus* in Latin. The form *Nicolas*, sometimes used to-day, is therefore less incorrect than the usual *Nicholas*.

St Nicholas, as we call him, was Bishop of Myra, in Asia Minor, during the fourth century. After his body had been removed to Bari, in Italy, he became one of the most popular saints. Having, among other reputed miracles, restored three dead boys to life, calmed a storm at sea, and saved three girls from slavery by secretly bestowing three bags of gold on their father, he is regarded as patron saint of schoolboys, sailors, and pawnbrokers, whose sign is three golden balls. He is also known as the patron saint of thieves, mockingly referred to as "St Nicholas' clerks." This is due to a confusion between his name and that of a German demon, the *Nix*, or *Nickel* (whence also the expression 'Old *Nick*' for the Devil).

It is from the German short form of his name, *Klaus*, that we get our Santa *Claus*. The Americans adopted it from the German and Dutch settlers in their country, who gave presents on St Nicholas' Eve, December 5, not on Christmas Day.

For so famous a saint surprisingly little is known about the life of Nicholas; but he is known to have shown one very human trait—when he became so exasperated with the heretic Arius that he knocked him out.

The first recorded bearer of the name seems to be one of the seven deacons mentioned in the sixth chapter of the Acts, of whom we know nothing further; though another New Testament character, *Nicodemus*, has a name of exactly the same meaning ('demos,' like 'laos,' is a Greek word for 'people').

Five Popes have taken the name, and there was a King Nicholas of Denmark, who died in 1134. Nicholas Breakspeare, of St Albans, who became Pope in the mid twelfth century, changed his name to *Adrian* (see p. 37). Two Emperors of Russia were named *Nikolai*; the second was murdered by order of the Soviet Government in 1918. Mr Krushchev has the diminutive form *Nikita*.

The name is found in pre-Conquest England. One appears in Domesday Book as holding land before 1066. It was not until the twelfth century that it became a favourite, usually in the French form *Nicol*, which is occasionally used to-day. It is at this time that the spelling with an h seems first to have been used. The short form *Colin* was also taken from France, but, as often as not, was really an old Celtic name (see p. 82).

The most celebrated bearers have not been Englishmen. *Niccolo* Machiavelli, the Italian Renaissance expert on state-craft, recommended such unscrupulous conduct among rulers that 'Machiavellian' has come to mean unprincipled and cunning. *Nicolaus* Copernicus was the Polish astronomer who at the beginning of the sixteenth century insisted that the sun, and not the earth, was the centre of the universe. In the early nineteenth century *Nicolo* Paganini, another Italian bearer, made a reputation throughout Europe as the most brilliant violinist of all time; there were no recordings, however, in his day to prove this claim to us.

Nicholas Wanastrocht, schoolmaster-cricketer in the mid nineteenth century, invented tubular batting gloves; he was an Englishman.

Apart from Nicholas Hillier, the Elizabethan miniaturist, and Nicholas Culpeper, the seventeenth-century expert on herbal remedies, the best-known English examples occur in literature. *Nick* Bottom, the weaver in *A Midsummer Night's Dream*, is, with Falstaff, Shakespeare's most celebrated comic creation. *Nicholas Nickleby*, with its harrowing descriptions of the Yorkshire boarding-school Dotheboys Hall, is one of Dickens's best-known novels. Nicholas Nye is a sad little donkey described in the poem of that name by Walter de la Mare. Nicholas Blake is the pen-name under which poet C. Day Lewis writes 'whodunits.'

Pet forms of Nicholas, besides *Nick*, are *Nickie* or *Nicky*, and occasionally *Nicco*.

NIGEL, like *Colin* (see p. 82), seems to be a name of mixed origin. There was an old Irish word 'niadh,' meaning 'champion,' which became *Niul*, and later *Niall*. Niall "of the nine hostages" was an Irish king of the fifth century. His descendants, the O'Neills, gave the Red Hand on their shield to the arms of Ulster.

There was also an Icelandic name *Njal*, possibly introduced from Ireland, and well known from a famous saga, *Burnt Njal*, whose Christian hero allowed himself to be burnt to death in his blazing homestead rather than resist his enemies. When the Normans came to France they may well have brought the name with them; though *Niel* was already used by the French as a short form of *Daniel* (p. 89).

At any rate, the name *Nel*, *Neel*, or *Nele* came to England at least as early as 1086, but was wrongly written in Latin documents as *Nigellus* (a Latin adjective meaning 'black') because of the resemblance in sound. Then, by dropping the Latin ending, this form became *Nigell* and *Nygelle*, and so our familiar *Nigel*. The form *Neal* became a surname, but is now used again as a Christian name.

The name was popular in England during the Middle Ages, so Conan Doyle appropriately named one of his historical novels *Sir Nigel*; but there were no outstanding examples.

In Scotland Robert Bruce's younger brother was called both *Nigel* and *Nial*, and Nigel continued to be used there. Scott's *Fortunes of Nigel* tells the story of a young Scottish laird who seeks redress from James I, but meets with a number of unpleasant experiences in the underworld of seventeenth-century London before his claim is granted. *Neill* and *Neil* seem to be the more favoured versions of the name to-day.

In modern fiction we have Nigel Strangeways, the hero of Nicholas Blake's detective stories, and Nigel Molesworth of those 'hideous revelations' of school life in *Down with Skool!* and its sequels, illustrated by Ronald Searle. Nigel Balchin is the author of powerful war-time novels.

It is generally supposed that the surname Nelson was originally 'Niel's son.' The memory of the hero of Trafalgar popularized *Nelson* as a personal name.

NOEL is a corruption of 'natalis.' 'Dies natalis' is the Latin expression for 'birthday' ('natal day'): it usually refers to Christmas, though the South African Natal was officially claimed as Portuguese territory by its discoverers on the birthday of the Blessed Virgin, September 8.

The French shortened 'natalis' to *Noel*, and the word eventually became a cry of joy such as 'alleluia' and 'hosanna,' with no connexion with a special feast-day; in one old Cornish carol it is even rendered as 'now well,' from the later English version *Nowell*.

Noël and Nowell have been given to children, both boys and girls, who were born about Christmas-time, from the Middle Ages till the present day. Captain Noel Chavasse, in the First World War, won the rare distinction of a Victoria Cross with bar. Noel Coward, the actor, playwright and composer, is a contemporary example.

Several feast-days besides Christmas have provided names for both sexes. Easter, or rather the Latin-Hebrew form, *Paschal* ('dies paschalis'), has produced the Cornish name *Pascoe*. *Pentecost*, another word for Whitsuntide, is rare. The straightforward *Christmas* is not unknown; Christmas Humphreys, Q.C., is the leader of the English Buddhists.

NORMAN A reader who has studied such names as *Montague* (p. 198) and *Algernon* (p. 46) might well imagine that *Norman* was another old aristocratic name, revived in the last century. But this is not the case. Norman, like *Franko* and *German*, was an old English name, meaning 'northern man,' even before the Conquest; all three must have been given originally as nicknames to foreign settlers. Domesday Book lists several men named Norman who had held land in the time of Edward the Confessor.

By the fourteenth century Norman seems to have died out as an English Christian name, though it continued to be used north of the Tweed. In the nineteenth century it had come to be looked upon as a sure sign of Scottish ancestry; but to-day it is firmly established on both sides of the Border.

Norman MacFadyen, a Scotsman, was a pioneer of town planning early in the present century. Norman Allen, a bass singer, reached the lowest note, an A, ever attained by the human voice; Norman Hartnell is the Queen's dress designer; Norman Wisdom is one of our funniest comedians. Norman von Nida, the ace professional golfer, is an Australian.

Nor and *Norm* are both used as short forms.

OLIVER, like the feminine Olivia, seems to be directly connected with the olive-tree; or so it has often been claimed. But this connexion was made far later than the appearance of the original name. This was *Anleifr*, an ancient Scandinavian combination of 'ancestor' and 'remains,' presumably given to a male child in the hope that he would carry on the family traditions. When we find that a Prime Minister of Iceland was a Mr *Olafur* Thor the connexion of *Oliver* and *Anleifr* is not so hard to understand.

In Scandinavia the name was shortened, and became *Olaf* or *Olave*. Olaf Trygvesson was King of Norway in the tenth century; St Olaf, who finally established Christianity in his country, was murdered by his pagan opponents in 1030. Two Danish kings of the name ruled Denmark, Northumbria, and Dublin, and it has continued to be used by Danish royalty.

Olaf was also used by Danes settled in England, where two

London churches were dedicated to the saint. They are now known as St Olave, Hart Street, and St Olave, Tooley Street (Tooley itself being a corruption of St Olave); but the name, at least in its northern form, did not survive the Norman Conquest.

When the Normans came south the old name came to be connected with the olive. The champion of Charlemagne who gave it its vogue in the Middle Ages was known in romance as *Olivier*, but among Germans of the eighth century, when he flourished, he was more probably called something like *Olafur*; he is always associated with his friend and rival, *Roland* (see p. 237). Shakespeare in Part I of *Henry VI* uses the phrase "England all Olivers and Rowlands bred."

It was as *Oliver* that the name reached England, this being the name of a landholder mentioned in Domesday Book, and the name continued to be used. In fourteenth-century Yorkshire we have a *Holiver* paying the poll tax, and the popularity of the name, at any rate in country districts, during the sixteenth century is shown by Shakespeare's choice of it for two characters in *As You like It*, Orlando's ruthless elder brother, and the hedge-priest Sir Oliver Martext. A popular ballad was licensed for publication in 1548 with the title O, *Sweet Oliver*. But after the Restoration, in the second half of the seventeenth century, in the reaction against Oliver Cromwell, England's only dictator, the name lost favour. Oliver Goldsmith, the author of *The Deserted Village* and *She Stoops to Conquer*, and other poems and plays, is a rare example from the eighteenth century.

This indicates, however, that the name never died out; and Dickens's early novel *Oliver Twist*, published in 1838, shows it was still used by humble people: Oliver was a workhouse orphan. The American writer Oliver Wendell Holmes is an example from across the Atlantic; his life almost spanned the nineteenth century. In the late-nineteenth-century boys' book *The Fifth Form at St Dominic's*, Oliver Greenfield is a principal character. By this time Thomas Carlyle's praise of Cromwell in his *Essay on Heroes and Hero Worship* had made the name generally acceptable.

A Bath Oliver is so called from the surname of Dr Oliver of Bath, who invented this biscuit in the eighteenth century.

Pet forms of Oliver are *Ol* and *Ollie*.

Olaf and Olave are still occasionally used in this country; Olaf Stapledon, earlier in the present century, wrote that extraordinary book *Last and First Men*, tracing the story of the human race step by step into the furthest imaginable future.

Another name, said to be a Welsh form of Oliver, is *Havelock* or *Abloyc*. The romance of Havelock the Dane was a medieval English favourite. Havelock Ellis was a pioneer of commonsense psychology.

OSBERT There are a number of Old English names beginning with the syllable Os-, a word used in Saxon times only in compounds, where it means 'god.' It is connected with the Scandinavian collective name for the gods of Asgard, the Aesir.

Most of the Os- names, such as *Osmund* ('god-protection'), *Osric* ('god-rule'), and *Osborn* ('god-warrior') are seldom used to-day. Three only—*Osbert*, *Oscar*, and *Oswald*—are at all common.

Osbert, which is 'os,' 'god,' and 'beorht,' 'famous,' was used chiefly in Northumbria, Os- being in that kingdom a favourite first syllable for royal names, as Ed- was among the Wessex royal family. As the Normans also used the name, Osbert did not lose favour until about 1400. The name is to-day hardly popular; but it has two notable bearers: Sir Osbert Sitwell, the poet and author, and Osbert Lancaster, cartoonist and satirist.

Pet forms of Osbert will be found under *Oswald* (p. 212).

OSCAR is 'os' and 'gar,' 'god-spear.' An Old Norse equivalent, *Asgeirr*, also existed, and both were used in England before the Conquest, when they began to die out.

The revival of the name came about through James Macpherson, a Scottish antiquary of the eighteenth century, who produced what he claimed to be translations of ancient Gaelic poems composed by *Ossian*, a bard and warrior of the third century, who had a son named Oscar (an unlikely name for an ancient Celt). The 'Ossianic' poems became everywhere so popular that Napoleon insisted on his godson, later King of Sweden, being called Oscar. A second King Oscar of Sweden reigned from 1872 to 1907. Oscar Strauss, the composer of light operas, is an example from Austria.

In the nineteenth century Oscar was revived in Ireland, where it had first been introduced by the Danes as *Osgar*, and was given by his poetically-minded mother to Oscar Wilde, the witty playwright and author of the 1890's. His behaviour, however, so shocked the late Victorians that Oscar has hardly been used since in England.

In America the name is popular. Oscar Hammerstein was the librettist of the musicals *Show Boat* and *Oklahoma!* Oscar Niemeyer is the architect of the most modern of all cities, Brasilia, capital of Brazil.

The 'Oscar' cinema trophy, awarded for outstanding achievements in the film world, was given this name through the chance remark by one of its first viewers that its appearance reminded him of his own Uncle Oscar.

Oscar shares its pet forms with the other Os- names, except *Ossy*, which is not used for the others: *Ocky* has been heard.

OSWALD, from 'os' and 'weald,' means 'god-power.' It was a Northumbrian royal name.

Oswald, King of Northumbria in the seventh century, was so generous that his friend St Cuthbert declared that his right hand should never decay. He defeated the Welsh at Heaven-field, near Hexham; but the enemy rallied, and with the help of Penda of Mercia defeated and killed Oswald at Oswestry, which owes its name to him. Oswald was revered as a saint; as a Christian hero he has been taken as the patron saint of the Church of England Men's Society.

A second St Oswald was Archbishop of York and Bishop of Worcester; he helped St Dunstan with his church reforms in the tenth century.

Oswald has never gone out of use. Chaucer's Reeve is an *Osewold*; this is one of several medieval forms—most of which tended to leave out the final letter, producing such surnames as Oswell. Shakespeare gives the name to Goneril's steward in *King Lear*. Out of place in ancient Britain, when the action of this tragedy is supposed to take place, it shows that the name was familiar in the time of James I, though probably looked upon as old-fashioned. In certain families it has been regularly used down to the present day. In E. Nesbit's *The Treasure Seekers* and its sequels Oswald Bastable is the boy narrator, creditably trying to be modest, but seldom succeeding.

Pet forms are *Ozzie*, *Ozzy*, and *Os*.

OWEN, or more correctly *Owain*, is one of the most popular Welsh names, originally the Latin *Eugenius* (see *Eugene*, p. 111), meaning 'well-born'; but it looks and sounds so like the Welsh word 'oen,' 'lamb,' that it has often been claimed to have that meaning.

Thirty-nine Owains are mentioned in ancient Welsh legends. Owen of Gwynedd was a twelfth-century chieftain; the real popularizer of the name, however, was Owain Glyndyfrdwy—Owen Glendower—who nearly became an independent king of Wales, but was defeated by Henry IV and subsequently disappeared from history in 1415.

There was a St Owen, or *Ovin*, disciple of St Chad, probably, like his master, of Celtic origin; he seems to be the earliest example in Anglo-Saxon England; but a *Uwen* is recorded in the *Anglo-Saxon Chronicle*. Several bearers also occur in Domesday Book, and in English records at least up to the sixteenth century, though it is impossible to decide whether they were all Englishmen.

In modern times the name is often used without any Welsh connexion. Owen Wister, the American novelist, shows its spread in the United States; his novel *The Virginian* gives a vivid picture of life in the West and has been successfully filmed. In England Owen Nares was regarded in the 1920's as the best-looking man on the British stage.

A name that looks very like Owen is *Ewen*, or *Ewan*. Probably derived from the Celtic *Eoghain*, 'youth,' it was once used in England. But as names are not usually chosen by scholars, those which look alike have often been regarded as identical. If *Eugenius* could become *Owain*, *Owain* could easily become *Ewen*. *Evan* (see *John*, p. 161) may also have been confused with both Owen and Ewen.

PATRICK St Patrick, Apostle of Ireland, was baptized *Sucat*, probably meaning 'warrior'; he adopted the Latin name *Patricius*, 'nobleman,' at his ordination.

He was a Celt. As his earliest biography calls his birth-place Banaven Taberniae, which cannot be identified, but looks like something or other 'of the Tavern,' Patrick's real place of origin is unknown—though he is generally thought to have been born at or near Dumbarton. It was certainly near the sea, for he was captured as a boy by pirates and sold as a slave in Ireland. He managed to escape, but his conscience would not let him stay at home while the pagans in the land of his captivity had no one to teach them the Christian faith. So he trained as a missionary in France and returned to Ireland, where he spent the rest of his life, dying in about 468. He is, however, said to have visited Glastonbury somewhere around 460 and reorganized there the oldest religious settlement in England.

The Irish out of reverence avoided using Patrick's name until comparatively recent times. Patrick Sarsfield, Lord Lucan, regarded as a hero by his countrymen, is one of the earliest Irish bearers of note; he died in 1693. Nowadays in Ireland the name is usually spelt *Padraic*: Padraic Colum the poet, born in 1881, is remembered by his poem *The Old Soldier*; he was one of the leaders in the modern revival of Irish literature.

In Scotland Patrick was far more common. The ballad *Sir Patrick Spens* shows one example from the late Middle Ages; it tells of his mission to Norroway (Norway), to fetch back a princess to marry the king.

The name seems to have spread from Scotland to England, as its earliest English bearers recorded are Northerners; they occur from the twelfth century onwards. Between the thirteenth and fourteenth century a number of variations are found, and the surnames beginning with Pat- suggest that the short form has a longer ancestry than might be suspected; but until quite recently there were no outstanding examples.

Patrick Henry was the greatest orator of the American Revolution. Sir Patrick Manson, in the nineteenth century, was known as "Mosquito Manson," from his pioneer work on malarial research. *Patsy* Hendren, one of the greatest showmen in cricket earlier in the present century, scored 170 centuries; he is known by a common pet form, but his real name was *Elias*. Professor Patrick Blackett was awarded the Nobel Prize in 1948 for his work on atomic physics.

A paddy, which shows a third short form, and means a fit of rage, is derived from the quick temper of the Irish; a paddy-whack is a nursery word for a slap, such as might be given by a strong Irish hand. It goes without saying that *Pat* and *Paddy* are the common terms for an Irishman.

Padrig is the Welsh native form.

PAUL *Paulus* was a normal Roman name, more correctly spelt *Paullus*; it means 'little.'

Saul of Tarsus, besides being a Jew, was also a Roman citizen and so obliged to take a Roman name. He probably took Paul because it was nearest in sound to Saul; his choice does not mean that he was physically a little man. *Saul* means 'he who is asked for.' At first a violent persecutor of Christians, he was converted by a vision while on his way, "full of threatenings and slaughter," from Jerusalem to Damascus. The Acts are chiefly concerned with his missionary work, and his letters to his converts make up a large part of the New Testament.

Only six Popes have taken Paul as their official name, as against twenty-three Johns. Though, as *Pavel*, it was a favourite in Russia, there was only one Russian Emperor of the name. In Spain Paul becomes *Pablo:* Pablo Casals, the 'cellist, and Pablo Picasso, the painter, are celebrated present-day examples.

The Italian form of the name is *Paolo*; the tragic story of Paolo and Francesca, the lovers of Rimini, has been made the subject of poems, plays, and novels ever since Dante told it.

In England Paul has never been a popular name, even in the dedication of churches; St Paul's Cathedral is the notable exception. The bell in its bell-tower, known as "Great Paul," is the heaviest in Britain. "By St Paul!" was the favourite oath of Richard III.

The reason for the scarcity of Pauls in this country was originally due to the saint's association, always in the second place, with St *Peter.* They share a common feast-day, so that many old churches, though dedicated to both, were known only as St Peter's. Peter and Paul were also a common combination of personal names, as with Sir Peter Paul Rubens, the Flemish artist who became Court painter to James I. After the Reformation, when Peter became associated with Roman Catholicism, Paul gained in favour; before that time it had been pronounced (and spelt) *Powle*, actually more correctly; similarly, the Welsh form is *Pawl.*

Most famous Pauls must be looked for outside the British Isles; though Admiral Paul Jones was a Scotsman who served in the American fleet during the War of Independence. The "Paul Jones" type of dance may owe its name to his numerous captures of enemy ships. Longfellow's stirring poem *The Ride of Paul Revere* describes the midnight race of a patriot American to spread the warning of a British raid. Paul Harris, in our century, founded the Rotarians, an association of groups of businessmen. Paul Hindemith, a German by birth, is the most versatile musician of to-day; he plays a dozen different instruments and composes for all of them; since 1933 he has lived in the United States. Paul Robeson is the most celebrated of coloured actors and singers. Paul Riley, a schoolboy of fifteen, is, except Landseer (at twelve), the youngest artist to have had a picture accepted for a Royal Academy Exhibition. Paul Getty, an American, is reputed to be the richest man at present living.

A Paul Pry is an over-inquisitive man. The original was a character in a pre-Victorian comedy of that name; always interfering in other people's affairs, Paul invariably introduces himself with the words "I hope I don't intrude."

PERCIVAL *Percevale* was the name given by the French romance-writer Chrétien de Troyes in the twelfth century to a favourite medieval hero, using the French 'perce-val,' 'pierce-valley.' This character was based on a Welsh legendary hero, *Peredur*, whose name means 'warrior of the cauldron.' A seventh son, after his brothers had been killed his mother tried to keep him away from all knowledge of knightly adventure. But blood will out, and when he met armed men in the forest where he lived he followed them, to meet the usual series of monsters and maidens; he is specially connected with a mysterious castle where a magical spear and bowl were kept.

This story seems to be the early version of the 'Quest for the Holy Grail'; it is at least an odd coincidence that, in Old Welsh, 'pair cyfall' means 'warrior of the chalice.' At any rate, in later stories *Perceval*, or *Parsifal*, is the Knight of the Grail, hero of Wagner's opera *Parzifal*.

A more down-to-earth claim is that Percival was originally a surname, from *Percheval*, in Normandy, which is true in some cases, but probably only among connexions of the Percival family.

The first recorded English bearer seems to be a *Percevale* in the fourteenth century. The last known example before romantic names became popular in the eighteenth century was a Londoner in the year of the Great Fire, recorded as *Persefall*.

Alfred Perceval Graves, who wrote the words of the famous song *Father O'Flynn*, shows the old form of the name. Perceval Lowell, an American observer of the planet Mars, insisted that it was inhabited.

PERCY The village of *Perci* is near Saint-Lô, in Normandy, whence came William de Perci with the Conqueror to England, and founded the famous Northern family: the derivation from 'pierce-eye' is fanciful.

There is to-day a French surname *Percie* which, it is claimed, was the first name of a Scottish archer who settled in France in the fifteenth century. If this is true *Percy* as a Christian name may be earlier than is commonly thought. But there is no doubt that in most cases Percy was given to connexions of the Northumbrian family. Lord Percy Seymour, for instance, was the son of an eighteenth-century Lady Percy. From him the name was passed on to the distantly related Shelley family; hence Percy Bysshe Shelley, the poet. The memory of his romantic life may well have spread the name throughout this country.

The best-known bearers before 1939—at any rate, to boys—were Percy F. Westerman, whose books of adventure are still read, and the fictional Sir Percy Blakeney, Baroness Orczy's daring and debonair hero who, before each new rescue of French aristocrats from the Terror, signs his warning letters with a drawing of the Scarlet Pimpernel flower. Sir Percy Sillitoe was until recently head of the British counter-espionage organization known as M.I.5, and so chief of our modern Pimpernels. To-day Percy Grainger, born in Australia but working in America, is a lively composer, remarkable for his individualistic directions: for 'crescendo' he writes 'louden lots.'

The short form of Percy is *Perce.*

PETER is our version of the Greek *Petros*, the masculine form of 'petra,' which is the Greek word for 'rock.' Jesus gave the nickname *Cephas*, which is 'rock' in Aramaic, to Simon bar Jonah, as a symbol of the firmness of his faith. "Thou art Peter," Christ said, "and upon this rock I will build my Church." But in English the play on words is lost; not so in French, where *Pierre* is used for both 'stone' and Peter. The Latin form is *Petrus.*

Chief of the Apostles, Peter became first Bishop of Rome. None of his successors has presumed to take his name, and a fanciful belief has grown up that Peter II will be the last Pope of all. St Peter's Church in Rome, built over the Apostle's tomb, is the largest in the world. The Abbey Church of Westminster is also dedicated to St Peter.

Several saints have borne the name; the most appealing, St Peter Claver, in the seventeenth century devoted his life to helping negro slaves. Of rulers of this name, the best known is the Russian Peter the Great, who made his country a modern nation in the late seventeenth century, and studied shipbuilding at Deptford.

The Welsh soften the t into a d in their form of the name, *Pedr*, similar to the Spanish *Pedro.*

Peter is first recorded in England in Latin, as found in Domesday Book. But the normal form became *Piers*, an early form of the French *Pierre. Piers Plowman*, the great allegorical poem, giving a vivid picture of peasant life in the late fourteenth century, was the last masterpiece of verse written in the old English unrhymed metre. Piers is sometimes used to-day.

The name became so popular that we have such different medieval versions as *Petur*, *Petyr*, *Pierce*, *Pers*, and *Pearse*: *Perry* and *Perkin* were pet forms: Peter, as it is spelt to-day, is, however, not found before the fourteenth century.

When Henry VIII broke with the Pope the name fell out of favour, and was generally looked upon as old-fashioned and rustic throughout the seventeenth century and even the eighteenth. Sheridan's Sir Peter Teazle was a country squire who brought his wife to town, with the humorous results shown in *The School for Scandal*. Wordsworth's poem *Peter Bell* (1798) and Marryat's *Peter Simple* (1834) show that the name was still regarded as typical of the humbler classes. It was not until the present century that it became generally accepted.

This was probably due to J. M. Barrie's immensely successful play *Peter Pan*. Peter Scott, the bird-painter, and Peter May, England's cricket captain, are contemporary bearers. The golf prodigy Peter Toogood lived up to his surname by holing out in one at the age of eight.

'Peter Pence' are contributions to the papal treasury; they caused much complaint in the Middle Ages, when they were a compulsory exaction. 'To rob Peter to pay Paul' is an old expression, supposed to be an allusion to the rivalry between Westminster Abbey and St Paul's; it means to pay a debt with borrowed money. The Blue Peter is a blue flag with a white square in the centre, hoisted by vessels about to sail: Peter is here a corruption of the French 'partir,' 'to leave.' In contemporary thieves' slang a peter is a safe, a peterman is a safebreaker.

Pierre Curie, the co-discoverer of radium, is a notable bearer of the French form, which has the diminutive *Pierrot*—the name for a clown or comic singer at seaside resorts, etc., originally the lover of Columbine in the Harlequinade.

The only generally accepted short form of the name is *Pete*.

PHILIP is from the Greek 'phil-hippos,' 'lover of horses.' There were several other Greek names including one or other of these two words: *Hippolytus*, 'horse-destruction,' is one of the most common.

Philip of Macedon, father of Alexander the Great, the first famous example, spread the name throughout Greece and Asia Minor. Hence the two Philips in the New Testament: Philip the deacon, who converted the chamberlain of the Queen of Ethiopia, as told in the seventh chapter of the Acts, and Philip the Apostle. Philip the Arabian was Emperor of Rome in the third century, and later six kings of France bore the name, and five of Spain: the Philippine Islands were named after the Spanish Philip II. Philip the Good, Duke of Burgundy in the fourteenth century, was a ruler as powerful as any king of the age.

The name came to England in the twelfth century, at first, it seems, in the contemporary French form *Phelippe*.

Its use was widespread; *Philpot* was a common diminutive, and Philip became the nickname for a sparrow, as *Robin* did for a redbreast. The poet Skelton, in the reign of Henry VIII, wrote a delightful set of verses lamenting the death of a *Phylyp* (or *Phip*) Sparrow, killed by a cat.

After the reign of Mary Tudor, her widower, Philip of Spain, became the most hated enemy of England, so that the name fell largely out of use. Sir Philip Sidney was the last prominent English bearer; born while Philip of Spain was King Consort of England, he was the Spaniard's godson.

In the nineteenth century the name was revived. Philip Astley owned eleven riding-schools and founded a famous circus: perhaps his name influenced his career. A little later Philip Cowell discovered the gradual lengthening of the days. Sir Philip Joubert was an Air Chief Marshal of the Royal Air Force. And no list of famous bearers would be complete without mentioning Prince Philip, Duke of Edinburgh, husband of our present Queen.

From the old pet form *Phip* came the later *Pip*. The narrator in Dickens's *Great Expectations* is Pip Pirrip. Ian Hay, earlier in this century, wrote a novel with what is probably the shortest title ever chosen, *Pip*, about a doctor's twins, whom he calls Pip and Pipette. *Phil* is now the more usual short form.

The expression 'to appeal from Philip drunk to Philip sober' originated in the story of a woman condemned to death by Philip of Macedon. She declared that he was drunk, and insisted on a retrial when he had recovered.

QUENTIN is derived from the name of an Italian clan, the Quinctii, or Quintii, settled at Rome by King Tullius Hostilius, who, admiring their simple way of life, hoped they would counteract his subjects' love of luxury. But the Latin word for 'fifth' was 'quintus,' so that the personal name *Quintus* or *Quinctius* also came to be used for a fifth son, as *Septimus* and *Octavius* (p. 244) were for a seventh and an eighth.

Quinctius Cincinnatus was the most famous member of the Quintian clan. Summoned to take the supreme command of the Roman army, he was found cooking his own dinner. A descendant of one of the Quinctian families, *Quinctianus*, sometimes known as *Quintinus*, was martyred in A.D. 278, in the town in Northern France still named Saint-*Quentin*, after him.

The use of this name in Great Britain started with the Normans; there is a *Quintin* in Domesday Book, and it occurs occasionally until the thirteenth century. In Scotland, however, it continued in favour for some four hundred years longer. This was probably due, not so much to the close connexion between Scotland and France (England's chief enemies in the Middle Ages), as to its use as a substitute for the old Celtic *Cumhaighe* (pronounced 'cooley'), meaning 'hound of the plain.' Scott's historical novel *Quentin Durward* probably helped to spread the name in England during the nineteenth century. Quintin Hogg, Lord Hailsham, is the most prominent example to-day.

RALPH In Old Norse *Rathulfr*, in Anglo-Saxon *Raedwulf*, this name means 'counsel-wolf.' Even before the Norman Conquest it had become *Radulf*, a name borne by three recorded landholders in England at the time of Edward the Confessor. The Normans spread the name further in several forms.

By the end of the thirteenth century *Raffe* and *Rauf* were accepted spellings, but both were already probably pronounced as *Rafe*, which had become the common spelling two hundred years later, though Rauf persisted in East Anglia. All these go to show that the l was no longer sounded. It was not until the seventeenth century that *Ralph* was adopted as the normal spelling—an attempt to go back to some earlier form of the name. Nevertheless, the l remained mute till recently, and though the Scots and Americans tend to sound it, 'Rafe' is still the generally preferred pronunciation in England.

In France the old name became *Raoul*. As *Rowl* or *Rawl* it had been known in medieval England, and gave such surnames as Rawlings and Rowlett; but this personal name faded out with the decline of French-speaking in the time of the first three Edwards. Raoul is sometimes found to-day in this country, imported from France.

Ralph Roister Doister is the title of the earliest known English comedy, written by Nicholas Udall for his pupils at Eton in the 1550's. The name-part is that of a harum-scarum youth foiled in his pursuit of a rich widow. Shakespeare calls one of Falstaff's recruits, in *Henry IV, Part II*, Ralph Mouldy: the Elizabethan Ralph Lane was the first Governor of Virginia. Sir Ralph the Rover is the pirate who sinks the Inchcape Bell, and lives to regret it, in Southey's ballad *The Inchcape Rock.*

Ralph Hodgson is best remembered for his sad poem *The Bull*, written early in the present century. Ralph Vaughan Williams was one of the chief restorers of the English tradition in music. Sir Ralph Richardson to-day is one of our leading actors.

Rolf, from the Old German *Hrodulf*, 'fame-wolf,' was introduced by the early Normans into France, where it became *Rollo*. Rollo the Ganger ('Walker') was too long-legged to ride the small horses of the ninth century. Exiled from Norway for illegally requisitioning supplies from his neighbours, he took his followers off, to found the most dynamic nation of the early Middle Ages, the Normans. Rolf's likeness to Ralph caused its disappearance in England; though the Scottish pronunciation of Ralph with l suggests that *Rolph* was once the commoner name there. Both Rolf and Rollo have been revived since the beginning of this century. "Saki" used Rollo for one of the wicked and witty young men he was so fond of putting in his stories. The "Rollo" books were a popular series of American children's stories written by Jacob Abbot.

Americans use the pet form *Rod*, more commonly short for *Roderick* (p. 234). *Rudolf*, a German form of *Rolph*, is treated separately on p. 239.

RANDOLPH Though *Rudolph* is perhaps commoner to-day, *Randal* or *Randall* are more natural English forms of this name, which began in England as *Randwulf*, meaning 'shield-wolf.'

In use before 1066, it was spread by Norman bearers, who seem to have preferred the form *Ranulf*. By the end of the thirteenth century the name had settled down in normal usage into *Randal*, often written *Randle*. Earl Randal of Chester was a Crusader; he is mentioned in *Piers Plowman*, as a popular ballad-hero. The Border ballad of Lord Randal, poisoned by his lady-love, is one of the gloomiest examples of an often melancholy type of poetry.

Purely historical characters were *Rannulf* Flambard, William Rufus's minister, Bishop of Durham and a great castle-builder, and the seventeenth-century *Randle* Cotgrave, author of the first French-English dictionary in England. Among more modern bearers, *Randall* Davidson was the Archbishop of Canterbury who crowned George V.

Sir Winston Churchill's father, and his son, were both christened *Randolph*, which is a 'revived' ancient form. Randolph Turpin, the boxer, is known as *Randy*, a short form; *Dolph* is another abbreviation.

RAPHAEL was the name of the angel sent to guide the young Tobias on his journey to recover a debt owed to his blind and ruined father. By means of the gall of a monstrous fish caught in the Tigris, Raphael shows the boy how to get rid of a demon who torments his betrothed, and cure his father. This accounts for the name, which means 'healing of God.' The story is told in the Book of Tobit, part of the Apocrypha (books rejected from the Scriptures because they were not written in Hebrew), and racily retold in James Bridie's play *Tobias and the Angel*. St Raphael is one of the patrons of doctors and travellers. Milton describes him as "the affable Archangel."

As a personal name Raphael is most used, in England, by Jews. It is, however, more widespread in Italy, where *Raffaelo* Sanzio of Urbino was among the greatest masters of painting: he excelled with his sweet-faced Madonnas. Sir Thomas More, in his *Utopia*—a description of an ideal country, written in the reign of Henry VIII as a plea for toleration—puts the narrative in the mouth of the traveller Raphael Hythloday. The most popular historical novelist of the 1920's was *Rafael* Sabatini, who was of Italian extraction.

The short forms are *Raff* and *Rafe*, the latter shared with *Ralph* (p. 223).

RAYMOND *Raginmund* was an Old German name, made up of 'ragin,' 'counsel,' and 'mund,' 'protection,' parallel with the Anglo-Saxon *Raedmund*, which has become the surname Redmond.

Raymond was introduced into England by the Normans, and was a favourite in the times of the Crusades, particularly as the family name of the Counts of Toulouse. It was also much used in Northern Spain, where it was borne by two saints in the thirteenth century. St Raymond of Toulouse, a Dominican, was said to have sailed the Mediterranean using his cloak as a boat: more probably he used it as a sail. The second St Raymond, called Nonnatus, was a Trinitarian friar. On one occasion, having no funds to ransom a prisoner of the Moors (the principal work of his Order), he insisted on changing places with the captive. *Ramon* Lull of Majorca was an alchemist and mystic, who ended his life as a Christian missionary in Tunis, where he was stoned to death. In his native island he is regarded as a saint; as an alchemist he is introduced into John Masefield's strange story *The Box of Delights*. *Raymund* is another alternative form.

The name was never popular in England until the present century. To-day it is much favoured. Raymond Massey, the film and stage actor, is of Canadian origin; Raymond Chandler is one of our most popular writers of thrillers.

The short form *Ray* has for some time been used as a separate name. Sir Ray Lankester, the biologist, is one of the earliest examples.

REGINALD, from the Old English 'regen' and 'weald,' a pair of words with much the same meaning, 'power' and 'force,' was a little-used Anglo-Saxon name. The Normans, who changed the Old Norse *Raganwald* to *Reinald*, reinforced its use in England, where it had several forms, the most popular being *Reynold*, from the French *Reynault*, or *Regnault*. This, italianized as *Rinaldo*, was the name of one of the great heroes of romance, one of Charlemagne's champions, and cousin of Orlando; he owned a famous horse, Bayardo. Reginald Pecock, a fifteenth-century Bishop of Chichester, wrote the first Latin grammar for English schools; he died in disgrace, but for religious, not grammatical, reasons. He is often referred to as *Reynold*; and so was Mary Tudor's Archbishop of Canterbury, Reginald Pole. It is clear that Reginald was for some time a purely official version, generally written as *Reginaldus*, Reynold being used in daily life. In Scotland the popular version became *Ronald*, which is so common a name there (and in England) that it has been given a separate section, on p. 237; it is the only form of the name which has given a saint to the Calendar. After the sixteenth century, if not earlier, Reginald became normal in both official and popular use, being regarded as a more scholarly version. Even so, it became rare in this country, until the late eighteenth century. Scott uses it for the ruthless Sir Reginald Front-de-Bœuf in *Ivanhoe*, published in

1820, showing that at that time it was regarded as an aristocratic name.

This can hardly be said of Dickens's Reginald Wilfer, a clerk so poor that he could never realize his ambition to have a complete set of new clothes at one time. He is known to his fellow-clerks as *Rumty*, a pet form unlikely to be used again. *Reggie* is probably later, dating from the period of the real popularity of the name, after the middle of last century. It was in the early years of the present century that "Saki" (Hector Munro) wrote his *Reginald* and *Reginald in Russia*, two of the best collections of witty stories of the last fifty years or so. *Reg* is comparatively modern; Reg Butler is one of the most notable sculptors of to-day.

Rex is probably an older short form of Reginald than either Reggie or Reg. It was not known as a separate name to Charlotte M. Yonge, who first published her *History of Christian Names* in 1863. It may have been given as a Christian name in the last century; but its three best-known bearers have been Rex Whistler, the artist, and Rex Warner, the novelist, both born in 1905, and Rex Harrison, the actor, born in 1908. It looks, therefore, as if the accession of Edward VII as King in 1901, after the long reign of Queen Victoria, was responsible for Rex (the Latin word for 'king') becoming a favourite name. Rex is also popular for dogs—probably because it is so easy to shout.

RHYS, meaning 'rashness,' is a popular Welsh name, which has also become a surname as Rees, Reece (both giving the correct pronunciation), and Rice: Price is Ap Rhys, 'son of Rhys.'

An ancient form of the name is *Rhitta*, borne by a legendary British king, who became in Arthurian romance King *Rhyence* of North Wales. His hobby of collecting the beards of his rivals to trim his cloak proved his undoing when he attempted to complete his collection with King Arthur's. *Rieuk*, a Breton diminutive, was the name of a saint who lived for forty-one years on a rock by the sea, dressed in nothing but moss.

Neither of these odd characters, however, spread the name. Its popularity comes from the family of Prince Rhys, who checked the Normans' advance into South Wales; his grandson, known as "the Lord Rhys," was appointed by Henry II as his Welsh deputy. Later, in the fifteenth century, Rhys ap Thomas was so powerful that it was said:

> The King has all this isle as his
> Except the part possessed by Rhys.

It was, in fact, largely thanks to him that Henry VII had "all this isle"; Rhys was one of his chief supporters in his bid for the Crown.

RICHARD There was a rare Anglo-Saxon name *Ricehard*, meaning 'rule-hard.' An eighth-century English kinglet of this name died at Lucca, in Italy, on his way to Rome, and is there still venerated as St *Ricardo*. But it was the Old German *Ricohard* that was spread by two pre-Conquest Dukes among the Normans, and brought by them to this country.

A *Ricard* is recorded in Domesday Book; but the softer French *Richard* prevailed, with several short forms, such as the obvious *Rich*; though *Rick* shows that the native form was not forgotten. Richard Cœur de Lion's crusading exploits helped greatly in the spread of the name in all its forms. A *Dickë* Smith is mentioned as early as 1220; *Dick* had the rhymed form *Hick* and the diminutive *Dickon*, so much favoured by writers of historical romances. The thirteenth-century St Richard Wych was Bishop of Chichester, where he is still remembered for his charity.

The second and third kings of the name, both of them defeated by rivals for the Crown, have been given a bad reputation. This is due more to their failure than to their real character: Richard II, called by his opponents "Hick Heavyhead," was opposed in his policy of peace and prosperity by his warlike relatives; and it was in the interest of Henry VII to blacken his predecessor's reputation, to bolster up his own questionable claim to the throne. This slur on the name seems to have lasted till well into the nineteenth century; Jane Austen tells us that Katherine Morland's father, in *Northanger Abbey*, "was a very respectable man, though his name was Richard." There is, however, a brighter side to the picture; Richard Whittington, who died in 1423, can be mentioned without further details; Sir Richard Grenville's gallant fight with his single craft against fifty-three Spanish vessels off Flores, in the Azores, has been immortalized, if that were needed, by Tennyson's poem *The Revenge*; Richard Arkwright, in the eighteenth century, invented the spinning jenny, which enormously increased the speed of cotton manufacture. Richard Brinsley Sheridan was one of our greatest eighteenth-century writers of comedies, such as *The Rivals* and *School for Scandal*. Sir Richard Burton, the Victorian explorer, discovered Lake Tanganyika. Prince Richard to-day is the second son of the Duke of Gloucester. Dick Turpin, who rode Black Bess, is our most famous highwayman. The American Admiral Richard Byrd, in 1926, first flew over the North Pole, and over the South Pole in 1929.

Dickie is a nineteenth-century pet form. In E. Nesbit's *Harding's Luck*, published early in this century, Dickie Harding is the little tramp who turns out to be Lord Arden. Other modern diminutives are *Richie* and *Ricky*. *Dick*, once used, like *Jack*, to mean any ordinary man, is now only applied to detectives. A dickey is a detachable shirt-front. The dickey seat of a car probably took its name from the seat on which footmen, so often called *Dickey*, perched behind a carriage. *Dicky* is the more usual spelling of this short form when used as a personal name. 'Dicky bird' is a modern nursery term modelled on such expressions as *Robin* redbreast and *Tom* tit.

The Welsh have their own form, *Rhisiart*, or *Rhicert*, which is derived from the French pronunciation of the name. The 'ch,' having a different sound in Welsh, is here rendered by 'si' or 'c.'

ROBERT comes from the Old German *Hrodebert*, originally a combination of 'hrothi' and 'berhta,' 'fame-bright.' There was an Anglo-Saxon *Hreodbeorht*; but 'hreod' means 'reed' or 'rod.' *Robertus* appears in Domesday Book, and it was the Norman-French form *Robert* that prevailed over *Rodbert* and *Rotbert*. In Germany Hrodebert developed into *Rupprecht*, which is dealt with on p. 240 under *Rupert*.

The name had spread among the Normans before the Conquest through two Dukes of Normandy, Robert the Devil and Robert Curthose; but it became so popular in England after 1066 that it developed not less than six short forms, and in Scotland two further dialect versions.

There are too many notable bearers for more than a few to be mentioned, but some British examples may be of interest. St Robert's Cave can be visited at Knaresborough, though his hermit's retreat is more often connected with the name of Eugene Aram, a murderer who hid there. Robert Grosseteste ('big-head') was a great thirteenth-century scientist who became

Bishop of Lincoln. Robert Bruce, the Scottish national hero, popularized the name north of the Border.

The seventeenth-century Robert Boyle may be called the founder of modern chemistry; Boyle's Law, concerned with the elasticity of air, is named after him. Robert Blake was the admiral who destroyed the Spanish at Cadiz, "without one ship lost," in 1657, but was himself fatally wounded. Nearer our own time lived Robert Louis Stevenson, celebrated both for his stories and his verses; it was he who suggested one of the main themes of this book, for his *Essay on Nomenclature* tells of the thrill he felt as a boy on learning of his famous namesakes. Robert Baden-Powell, in 1908, founded the Boy Scout movement. Captain Robert Scott, hero of the Antarctic, added new and tragic glory to the name. Robert Wadlow, who died in 1940, was the tallest man so far officially measured: he was 8 ft. 10.3 in. high. General Robert E. Lee was Commander-in-Chief of the Confederate armies in the American Civil War.

Robin is a pet form that came originally from France; it is particularly associated with folklore. Robin Goodfellow is another name for Puck, whose mischievous tricks are described in Shakespeare's *Midsummer Night's Dream.* Robin Hood, though he is said to have been an Earl of Huntingdon, is a legendary rather than an historical figure. The robin redbreast was probably called by this name because of the alliteration of the two r's.

Rob recalls the Scottish freebooter Rob Roy, and Scott's novel of that name; also a type of canoe. *Rab* and *Rabbie* are Scottish dialect forms of *Rob* and its diminutive *Robbie*; the poet Burns is affectionately known as *Rabbie. Rab and his Friends*, by John Brown, is the story of a faithful dog.

Hob was used for Robert Bruce, and also occurs in Hobgoblin, another name for Puck, in his more frightening form:

he is also known as *Lob-lie-by-the-fire*, from his supposed habit of taking a nap on the hearth after doing the housework for well-behaved maids during the night. Shakespeare uses *Nob* as the nickname by which the elder Faulconbridge in *King John* addresses his younger brother. *Dob* gave us the name *Dobbin* for a horse.

Bob is yet another short form. Bob Acres, the pretentious bumpkin in Sheridan's play *The Rivals*, is full of strange oaths such as "odd's triggers and flints." A 'bob,' for a shilling, is first noted in 1812, for no known reason. *Bobby Shajtoe*, the folk song, shows another version of Bob. A policeman gets his name 'bobby' from Sir Robert Peel, who was responsible for the organization of the Metropolitan police force in 1828. A modern use of this form comes from America in 'bobbysox,' used for ankle-length socks. *Bobbie* is another spelling.

The written abbreviation of Robert is *Robt.*

RODERICK The Old German *Hrodric* was a compound of 'hrothi,' 'fame,' and 'ricja,' 'rule.' It was taken to Russia by the Vikings, and there took the form *Rurik*; and to Spain by the Goths, who turned it into *Rodrigo*, or *Ruy*. *Roderic* was the last Gothic King of Spain, whose misfortunes made him a popular character in English Romantic verse, such as Scott's *Vision of Don Roderick*. *Rodrigo* (or *Ruy*) the Cid (from the Arabic 'Said,' meaning 'my lord'), was also known as El Campeador ('the champion'). He fought the Moors in the eleventh century, and his courage and cunning made him a hero of romance.

The Gaelic *Ruaridh*, meaning 'red,' was a different name altogether; but it was turned into *Roderigh* by the Scots, and then confused with the similar-sounding Germanic name; *Rhuadrhi*, the Irish version, became *Rory*. Three high kings of

Ireland bore the name, the most famous being Rory O'Connor in the twelfth century. Later descendants, following the fashion of substituting English names for native names, used *Roger* instead. But Rory persisted among the people; "Rory of the Hill" in the nineteenth century was used as the signature on threatening letters sent to landlords who turned out their tenants for not paying rent. *Roddy* is another form, which is now used as a surname in Ireland, and as a pet form in England. The Americans prefer *Rod.*

There are yet two more names that have also been turned into Roderick, both Welsh: *Rhodri* is one, meaning 'circle-ruler'—the 'circle' ('rhod') referring to a crown or bracelet (bracelets are part of our coronation regalia). Rhodri the Great, King of North Wales in the eighth century, mastered most of the south and called himself King of the Britons. The other name is *Rhydderch*, pronounced 'Ruthergh,' 'exalted ruler.' Rhydderch the Generous, a sixth-century chieftain, claimed descent from Coel, the legendary Old King Cole.

Shakespeare, in *Othello*, calls Desdemona's first lover *Roderigo*. Roderick Random is the adventurer who gives his name as the title of Smollett's best-known novel, showing that the name was accepted in eighteenth-century England.

RODNEY, meaning 'reed island,' is by origin a Somerset surname, taken from the village of Rodney Stoke. Its appearance as a personal name is due to Admiral George Rodney, who captured seven French ships out of thirty-three in a battle off Dominica in 1782. For his naval exploits he was created first Baron Rodney.

Conan Doyle chose *Rodney Stone* as the title of his novel of early nineteenth-century prize-fighting.

Rod, the pet form, is shared by *Roderick*, *Ralph*, and *Rudolph*.

ROGER *Hrothgar* was a name used by the Anglo-Saxons even before they reached this country. 'Hroth,' also found in the first part of *Roderick*, means 'fame'; 'gar' means 'spear.' The oldest example of English literature surviving, known as *Beowulf*, tells the tale of King Hrothgar, who is delivered by the hero Beowulf from a monster that carries off his retainers. The present Chichele Professor of Economic History at Oxford is Dr Hrothgar Habbakuk.

The name was reinforced, or replaced, at the Norman invasion by a later form, *Roger*, a favourite from the time of Domesday Book onward. Three bearers were Earls of Norfolk, belonging to the Bigod family, the second of whom helped to secure the signing of Magna Carta. Roger de Kilpatrick, who took the oath of fealty to Edward I in 1296, shows the use of the name in Scotland. Roger Bacon was a learned Franciscan of the thirteenth century, who may have invented a microscope—he was regarded by his contemporaries as a magician. Roger Ascham was Queen Elizabeth's tutor and secretary; he wrote both on education and archery.

During the Middle Ages Roger produced short forms. Chaucer's Cook in the *Canterbury Tales* is called both *Roger* and *Hodge*. *Dodge* was another.

After the sixteenth century the name in all its forms died out, except among country people. Even Sir Roger de Coverley, portrayed so affectionately by Steele and Addison in the early eighteenth century, is an old-fashioned rustic squire: he is made to claim that the country dance of his name was invented by his grandmother. Sir Walter Scott quotes an old verse:

> What though thy name be Roger
> Who drives the plough and cart?

Hodge was a frequent name for rustics in the captions of old

Punch pictures. An eighteenth-century Hodge was Dr Johnson's cat; the great literary figure always insisted on buying its fish, to save his servants trouble.

The name only 'came to town' again somewhere about the end of the last century, with such bearers as Roger Quilter, a typically English composer and a collector of folk-music, and Roger Fry, the art critic. Roger Bannister, in 1954, was the first to run a mile in less than four minutes. Arthur Ransome, in *Swallowdale*, names the 'ship's boy' Roger.

Rosser is the Welsh form of Roger. In Ireland it is used as a substitute for *Rory* (see *Roderick*, p. 233). *Rodge* is now used as the pet form; the older diminutives have died out.

The Jolly Roger was the name given to the pirate flag, with its skull and crossbones.

ROLAND The Old German *Hrodland* was a combination of 'hrothi' and 'landa,' 'fame' and 'land.'

Roland was the most celebrated champion of the Court of Charlemagne. The *Chanson de Roland*, greatest of French epics, describes his death at the hands of the Spanish Saracens in an ambush as he crossed the Pyrenees. His famous horn could not help him; it cracked in two as he sounded it to summon aid. His sword, Durandal, was unbreakable; to save it from the Moors he hurled it into a mountain torrent.

Childe *Rowland*, with a later spelling of the name, was a very early legend. In the ballad *Burd Helen* he rescues his sister from the power of the elfin king. Shakespeare quotes from it in *King Lear*, giving a verse which contains familiar nursery words:

> Childe Rowland to the dark tower came.
> His word was still "fie, foh and fum,
> I smell the blood of a British man."

Such associations made Roland a popular name. *Rolland* occurs in Domesday Book, but the usual English spelling was *Rouland* at first; the later *Rowland* was the normal form until modern times, when the French *Roland* became fashionable.

Rowland was a favourite name with the Hill family. One Rowland Hill, a knight, was Lord Mayor of London in the sixteenth century; a second, a viscount, was an eighteenth-century general. To Sir Rowland Hill, a Victorian bearer, we owe the introduction of cheap postage. Rowland Biffin is the first Professor of Agricultural Botany appointed at Cambridge.

Orlando is the Italian version. Shakespeare hints at its introduction as a fashionable name in *As You like It*, where he makes the young Orlando the son of the old-fashioned Sir Rowland de Bois. Orlando Gibbons is among the best known of Elizabethan musicians. More than one Italian epic poem is devoted to the exploits of Charlemagne's Roland, as Orlando.

The expression 'a Roland for an Oliver' refers to a friendly duel between Charlemagne's greatest champions, in which Roland and Oliver (see p. 209) fought for five days, to decide which of them was the better man; but the result was a draw. The saying means much the same as 'tit for tat.'

The older pet form of the name was *Rowly*; *Rolly* and *Roly* are also found.

RONALD is the Scottish version of *Reginald* (see p. 227), now regarded as a separate name. The older English *Reynold* shows the connexion more clearly.

The Scottish name comes almost directly from the Norse *Roegnvaldr*. There is another form, *Ranald*, found only in Scotland; Ronald, however, has become widespread in England.

Ranald Bannerman's Boyhood is the story of a Scottish country boy by George Macdonald.

Ronald Searle is well-known for his terrifying drawings of the schoolboys at St Custard's, and of the schoolgirls of St Trinians. Ronald Knox, in 1945, published his new translation of the Bible; a versatile writer, who also wrote satires and detective stories, he was usually known by the short form *Ronnie*; *Ronny* is an alternative form, but nowadays the shorter *Ron* is more popular.

ROY is commonly taken to mean 'king' because of its resemblance to the French 'roi' (in Norman French this word was actually spelt 'roy'), and this probably accounts for its popularity (see also *Rex*, p. 228). It is in fact derived from the Gaelic 'rhu,' meaning 'red.' The Celts were fond of giving names that described colour or complexion: *Finn* and the Welsh *Gwyn* or *Wynn*, mean 'fair'; *Duncan* (p. 99) and *Dougal* (p. 99) are other 'colour' names. Rob Roy, the Scottish brigand, was 'Robert the Red.'

With our modern preference for short words and names, Roy has become extraordinarily popular, being one of the few which cannot be shortened; it is also widespread geographically; Sir Roy Welensky, who has no British blood at all, is Prime Minister of the Central African Federation; Roy Agnew was the first Australian musician to win world-wide recognition; Roy Salvadori, the racing-motorist, shows by his surname that he is of Latin extraction; Roy Campbell, the South African poet, wrote *Horses on the Camargue*.

Rufus, a Latin name, also means 'red.' Simon of Cyrene, who helped Jesus carry His cross, is referred to by St Mark as the father of Alexander and Rufus; the sons must have been well known to be so mentioned. Probably even then the

Roman name was a substitute for *Reuben*, as it is among Jews to-day: Sir Rufus Isaacs, a celebrated barrister and judge earlier this century, is a case in point.

King William Rufus was so called because of his red hair; 'rufous' is to be found in our dictionaries with this meaning.

The French 'rousse' also means 'red-haired.' From it comes the English surname *Russell*, sometimes given as a Christian name, as with Russell Flint, the artist. *Cadet Roussel* is one of the best-known French nursery songs.

Red is a common nickname to-day in America.

RUDOLPH, or *Rudolf*, is the modern German form of *Hrodulf*, meaning 'fame-wolf' (see *Rolf*, p. 224), but has been used in this country during the past century as a separate name. When found earlier it implies a German origin.

Rudolph Agas, for instance, was a German sixteenth-century immigrant who engraved maps and plans of great interest to historians. Rudolph Ackerman, again of German origin, was also an engraver. His prints of famous London buildings give an excellent idea of the city in the early nineteenth century. Rudolf Diesel invented the engine named after him, as early as 1897.

The spread of the name in England was no doubt much helped by Anthony Hope's *Prisoner of Zenda*, a novel that set the fashion for stories of romantic adventures in imaginary Balkan countries, during the early years of this century. In this story, and its sequel, *Rupert of Hentzau*, the gallant Englishman Rudolph Rassendyl is involved in political plots of the kingdom of Ruritania, and impersonates the captive king, his double in appearance.

A second, and stronger, popularizing of the name was due to the American film-star Rudolf Valentino, best known in his part of 'The Sheik.' His funeral, in 1926, nearly caused a street riot. Another popular film-star, a little later, was *Rudy* Vallee, known by the commonest short form of the name.

Rodolphe, the French version, is sometimes used in English-speaking countries, as also is *Rodolph*.

RUPERT, like *Robert* (see p. 231), is derived from the Old German *Hrodebert*, 'fame-bright'; the usual German version is *Rupprecht*.

As a separate name it was introduced into England by Prince Rupert of the Rhine, nephew and champion of Charles I. His gallantry during the Civil War has made his name popular in modern times; though to his English contemporaries he was always known as Prince Robert. He was not only a soldier but also a scientist, experimenting with explosives and improving methods of engraving, particularly with the 'mezzotint' process.

Rupert, the little brown bear, has long been a favourite with young children, as has Rupert of Hentzau among their elders. He is the unscrupulous but gallant Ruritanian who gives the title to Anthony Hope's novel named after him. An equally gallant bearer in real life was the poet Rupert Brooke, chief of the school of poets who flourished before and during the First World War. *Grantchester* and *The Fish* are two of his most celebrated poems.

SAMUEL is a combination in Hebrew of 'schama' and 'El,' 'hear' and 'God,' probably to give the meaning 'heard by God'; the mother of the prophet Samuel regarded his birth as the answer to her prayers.

The prophet became the virtual ruler of Israel, until the people insisted on having a king; he unwillingly appointed

Saul, but when he proved unsatisfactory Samuel prepared David to be his successor. The two Old Testament Books of Samuel tell the full story.

An Irish Samuel who was Bishop of Dublin in the twelfth century was probably originally a *Sombairlie* ('summer sailor'—now found as the surname Summerlee). *Sombairlie* was the Gaelic name of *Somerled*, the twelfth-century Scottish chieftain and Lord of the Isles. In England and Scotland Samuel was a rare name, except for a few examples in the thirteenth century, and most bearers seem to have been Jews.

It was after the Reformation had aroused interest in the Old Testament that Samuel came into its own. Samuel Daniel, an Elizabethan poet, was so careful in his choice of words that he was known as "well-languaged Daniel." Better known is Samuel Butler, who laughed at the Puritans in his satire *Hudibras*. Oddly enough, the greatest Victorian satirist was another Samuel Butler, author of *Erewhon*, which describes a visit to that country, where crime is given hospital treatment and the sick are sent to prison; his serious novel, *The Way of All Flesh*, is one of the masterpieces of English literature. Samuel Johnson is the best-known English Samuel of all, through Boswell's accounts of his habits and conversation. Samuel Beckett is a modern playwright, author of that strange play *Waiting for Godot*.

But not all Samuels have been men of letters. The Frenchman Samuel Champlain discovered the lake in the United States that bears his name, and founded the city of Quebec; Samuel Romilly, in the eighteenth century, was a pioneer of English prison reform; Samuel Palmer was the most imaginative of Victorian artists; Samuel Wesley was, after Handel, the leading composer of Church music in this country until his death in 1837.

Sam Weller (known to his father as *Samivel*) shows the most usual short form; he was Mr Pickwick's eccentric but endearing manservant in *The Pickwick Papers*, and Mr Pickwick was himself a Samuel. Samuel Weller Widdowson, a Nottingham Forest footballer, invented shin-guards. His names are interesting, as Sam Weller's father, owing to his own unfortunate experiences, advised his son to "beware of widders!" The alternative short form is *Sammy*, and the name is often pronounced 'Sammle.'

American Samuels include Samuel Morse, inventor of the Morse Code, and Samuel Lind, who, in our own century, invented the electroscope. But best known of all is the type-figure, Uncle Sam. This name for the United States originated from the initials U.S.AM.; the old expression 'to stand Sam,' meaning to pay for a treat, came from the same initials stamped on the knapsacks containing army rations.

In England the Sam Browne, a military officers' belt, was designed by General Sir Samuel Browne.

SEBASTIAN is derived from the Greek 'sebastos,' used in the Eastern Roman Empire as the equivalent of *Augustus* (p. 58), and so meaning 'majestic.'

As a personal name, we owe Sebastian to a soldier-saint of third-century Rome. Though he was probably a grizzled legionary, Italian artists preferred to paint him as an athletic young man; his martyrdom—by shooting to death with arrows—gave them an opportunity for anatomical studies, both of the victim and of his executioners.

The name became particularly popular in Spain, Portugal, and France. King Sebastian of Portugal lost his life fighting the Moors in North Africa in the sixteenth century; but his gallantry so much impressed his people that they refused to believe he was dead, and long awaited his reappearance to lead them to victory. In France *Sébastien* Lenormand made the first parachute jump, in 1783.

The close ties between Brittany and Cornwall—the inhabitants of both were British by origin, and mostly fishermen by occupation—led to the adoption of the French short form *Bastien* in the West Country, as *Bastian*, with the short form *Basty*. Elsewhere in England the name seems unrecorded until recent times, though Shakespeare used it for two characters—neither of them English, however: Viola's brother in *Twelfth Night*, and the brother of the King of Naples in *The Tempest*. The seaman we know as Sebastian Cabot, who claimed Newfoundland for England in the reign of Henry VII, was of Italian origin. He may be regarded as the founder of the British Commonwealth; but the only official record of this great event runs: "to him that discovered the New Isle, £10."

SEPTIMUS The Romans were an unimaginative people; even their poets derived their inspiration from Greece. They excelled in engineering and organization, and their names show their matter-of-fact outlook. *Cicero* means 'chick-pea,' *Scipio* is 'walking-stick.' But most uninspired of all were their numeral names, which they employed from *Primus*, 'first,' to *Decimus*, 'tenth.' The unfortunate Roman girls had nothing to distinguish them except the feminine form of their family names and their number in order of birth.

Among men *Primus* was rare; *Secundus* likewise. St Patrick, it is true, had a companion called *Secundinus*, but this was a late and barbarous form. *Tertius*, 'third,' with alternatives *Tertullus* and *Tertullianus*, were used by early Christians. St Paul mentions a *Quartus*. *Quintus* was common (see *Quentin*, p. 222). *Sextus*, name of the objectionable son of King Tarquin, later became *Sixtus* (or *Xystus*), borne by several Popes; *Sextilius* may be the origin of the Welsh *Seissyllt* (see *Cecil*, p. 71).

The next two numeral names, *Septimus* and *Octavius*, have survived, largely because, by the time a seventh son was born parents had often run out of their favourite choices. And, of course, a seventh son was regarded as lucky; still more *his* seventh son. But Septimus has often been used in England and America, particularly in the nineteenth century, without regard to its meaning. In Wales it became *Seithenyn*, the name of the king whose neglect of the dykes is said to have caused the flooding of what is now Cardigan Bay. The Roman Emperor *Septimius* Severus, a successful general—he built a wall across Scotland north of Hadrian's Wall—and a patron of art and letters, helped to popularize the name.

Octavius was early taken by a Roman clan, and borne by the Emperor Augustus: there was an alternative form, *Octavian*. Both were used in England after the sixteenth century.

Nonus, 'ninth,' only spread in its feminine form, Nona. *Decimus* Mus was the name of three Romans, all of one family, each of whom deliberately sacrificed his life for his country. The Emperor *Decius* being a savage persecutor of Christians, his name was prevented from surviving; but *Decimus* had no such unpleasant associations. Decimus Burton, the early nineteenth-century English architect, tried before his time to introduce houses designed for convenience instead of for show; but he is best remembered by his triumphal arch at Hyde Park Corner in London.

SIDNEY The Sidney family came to England from Anjou in the reign of Henry II. When their name was recorded in official documents it always appeared as 'de Sancto Dionysio' (which proves it meant 'of Saint Denis,' probably referring to the name of their original home).

This contraction of saints' names is not uncommon: the surnames Seamark and Simper come from '*St Mark*' and '*St Peter*,' while Tobin is '*St Aubyn*.' The more common *St John*, a not unusual personal name, though written as it is here, shows by its accepted pronunciation, "Sinjun," how the pro-nunciation of a name can change before its spelling is altered. *St Clair* is also found spelt *Sinclair*, showing a half-way stage; Sinclair Lewis, best known for his novel *Babbitt*, is an example from America.

Two important characters in English history have been responsible for the spread of Sidney, or *Sydney*, as a personal name: Sir Philip Sidney, the gallant Elizabethan poet and soldier, who gave his precious cup of water to a dying soldier at Zutphen, and Algernon Sidney, who for his republican ideals in the seventeenth century became the hero of the Whigs. But the name was also spread through family connexions.

Sidney Smith, though a clergyman, was the finest wit of the early nineteenth century. Dickens created one of his greatest tragic characters in Sidney Carton, the wastrel lawyer in *A Tale of Two Cities* who gave his life under the guillotine for the happiness of the woman he loved. Sydney Dobell, the poet, shows that this spelling of the name was used as early as 1824. The Australian city of Sydney was named after Viscount Sydney, Secretary of State at the time of its foundation. Sidney Nolan was the first Australian sculptor to win an international reputation.

To-day the name is as well known from users of its short forms—*Sid* being more common than *Syd*—as from those who prefer to use it in full. Sid Barnes was an England bowler who mastered great batsmen on batsmen's wickets.

SIMON is the Greek substitute for the Hebrew *Simeon*, originally *Schimeon*, meaning 'hearkening' or 'he who hears.' 'Schama,' the Hebrew for 'to hear,' is also the origin of the name *Samuel* (see p. 240); though Simeon can also mean 'hyena.' The literal meaning of the Greek word 'simon' is 'snub-nose.'

The first known Simeon was Jacob's son, who gave his name to one of the tribes of Israel. In the New Testament the aged Simeon hailed the child Jesus with the song known from its first words in Latin as the *Nunc Dimittis*. Other biblical bearers are called by their Greek form—for instance, Simon Peter, the other Apostle Simon the Zealot, and Simon Magus, who tried to buy the power of working miracles: hence the word 'simony' for attempting to obtain a position in the Church by bribery.

Simon and Simeon were both popular names for saints. St Simeon Stylites lived for many years on the top of a column. The Englishman, St Simon Stock, re-created the Carmelite Order, or Whitefriars, in the thirteenth century.

Simon and Simeon were regarded in medieval England as separate names, and were spelt with an i or an e in the first syllable. Simon de Montfort by his resistance to royal claims probably did most to spread the name; he organized the first Parliament, in 1264. Chaucer, in *The Reeve's Tale*, calls his miller both *Symond* and *Symkyn*. Beatrix Potter, in her *Tailor of Gloucester*, published early in this century, makes *Simpkin*, the tailor's cat, her hero: these are the oldest pet forms. Simon Eyre, a fifteenth-century London master shoemaker, built Leadenhall, and gave it to the City.

After the Reformation, Simon, as a name of St Peter, lost favour, except among the common people. *Simple Simon*, the nursery rhyme, suggests this. So does Dickens's *Sim* Tappertit (showing another short form), the obstreperous apprentice in *Barnaby Rudge*. Other short forms are *Si* (used also for *Silas*), *Simmie*, and *Simie*.

'Simon Pure,' meaning 'genuine,' comes from an eighteenth-century play, *A Bold Stroke for a Wife*, by a Mrs Centlivre.

Simon is a particularly popular name in South America, from Simon Bolivar, known as "the Liberator," who won independence from Spain for Venezuela, Colombia, and Bolivia.

SPENCER shows its origin more clearly in the surname of Edmund Spenser, the poet of the *Faërie Queene*; it is a short form of 'dispenser,' that is, the dispenser of food and supplies to a feudal household; 'spence,' at least until recently, was a North Country word for a pantry.

The Le Despenser family came into prominence in England during the thirteenth century, especially with Hugh le Despenser, Henry III's Chief Justice. Spenser, without the 'le,' was the surname of a fighting Bishop of Norwich in the 1400's.

By the seventeenth century Spencer had become the commoner spelling. Robert Spencer, who died in 1627, was reputed the richest man in England. Charles Spencer became the second Duke of Marlborough, succeeding John Churchill, the great general. Through him Sir Winston Churchill eventually inherited Spencer as his third name.

Spencer, in fact, was often used as a personal name for connexions of the Spencer family, one of whom, Spencer Perceval, in 1812 had the unfortunate distinction of being our only Prime Minister to be assassinated.

The original type of knitted waistcoat was called a spencer, from the second Earl, who first wore one; yachtsmen call the trysail by the same name, because its shape resembles that of the garment.

STANLEY, a surname derived from the common Saxon place-name Stane-leah, means 'stony field.' Its popularity to-day as a personal name is no doubt due partly to its being the family name of the Earls of Derby, which gave it an aristocratic flavour; partly to the famous meeting between Stanley the journalist and Livingstone. Stanley's original name was John Rowlands: he adopted the surname Stanley from one of his early employers. The extraordinarily down-to-earth greeting, "Dr Livingstone, I presume," when he first met the great missionary, after months of search through Central Africa, impressed the speaker's name on the public imagination, and became a proverbial saying.

The stamp-dealing firm of Stanley Gibbons was begun just over a century ago. The founder's name shows that Stanley was in use before 1850. Kipling's Stanley Ortheris is the principal character of *Soldiers Three* and other tales of soldiering in India, written about the turn of the present century.

The name is now popular, with the pet form *Stan*. Stanley Matthews, for instance, has had the distinction of playing in seventy-three international matches; Stanley Holloway, for his talent as a comedian, was awarded the C.B.E. in 1960.

Stanley is also used, by Poles who have been naturalized in England and America, for *Stanislaus*, or *Stanislas*, a particularly Polish name (from 'stan,' 'to stand,' and 'slav,' 'glory'), with two saints to its credit.

STEPHEN The Greek 'stephanos' means 'crown,' or rather 'wreath'—the Greeks in their great days had no liking for kings, but the wreath of leaves awarded to athletic champions was looked upon as the greatest award obtainable. And, no doubt, athletes would give their sons the name *Stephanos* to commemorate their victories.

There were, however, no outstanding bearers in Ancient Greece; it was St Stephen, the first martyr, who made the name famous. The story of his death is told in the seventh chapter of Acts. And as martyrdom was regarded by Christians as a victory, the name was particularly appropriate. Several Popes chose to be officially known as Stephen; and there were five kings of Hungary named Stephen, the first of whom, a saint, was virtual founder of the Hungarian monarchy: only the wearer of his famous crown was regarded as the rightful ruler.

The only English king of the name was the ineffective Stephen of Blois; more admirable was Stephen Langton, Archbishop of Canterbury, who led the barons in their opposition to King John.

Though widespread on the Continent, Stephen was not used in England before the Conquest: it is first recorded in Domesday Book, as *Stefanus*. But by the fourteenth century it was generally written in such forms as *Stevyn* or *Steven*, which explains why most surnames to-day are spelt with a v. *Steb* and *Steen*, not forgetting *Steve*, were old diminutives. James I called his favourite, George Villiers, Duke of Buckingham, *Steenie*, a Scottish pet version, in allusion to the young man's good looks (at the martyrdom of the first St Stephen, we are told that "his face was as the face of an angel"). The Irish form is *Stiobhan*; the Welsh use *Steffan* and *Ystffan*.

The drunken butler in Shakespeare's *The Tempest* is called *Stephano*. This is the Italian version; *Etienne* is the French. In Bohemia *Waclaf*, the Slavonic word for 'crown,' was used as a name and latinized into *Wenceslaus*. It will be remembered that:

Good King *Wenceslas* looked out
On the feast of Stephen.

As this falls on December 26, Stephen is a particularly appropriate name for boys born on Boxing Day.

After the Reformation Stephen was still used, probably rather as a classical name than in memory of a saint. Stephen Daye printed the first book in English to appear in America, in 1640. Stephen Foster composed such well-known songs as *Old Folks at Home*, and *Oh! Susannah*, in the nineteenth century. The Canadian Stephen Leacock, who died in 1944, was, like Lewis Carroll, both a university lecturer and a great humorous writer. Stephen Donaghue, the Irish jockey, was six times Derby winner; "Come on, Steve!" was a catchword in the 1920's. To-day Stephen Spender is one of our more important modern poets.

Stephan and *Stepan* are imported modern forms.

STUART is the more generally accepted spelling of the Scottish royal family name; but *Steuart* and *Stewart* are commonly found too, both as surnames and as Christian names. 'Steward' is now used to describe a manager of property or a responsible official; originally it was a 'sty ward,' who looked after animals intended for meat—not necessarily pigs. Walter, the High Steward of Scotland, in 1315 married Marjorie Bruce, and from them the Scottish Royal House was descended.

Stewart and Stuart are common personal names to-day, and by no means only among those of Scottish origin. They have been used since before the beginning of the present century, probably on account of their romantic flavour, as connected with the Stuart kings of the seventeenth century, and the two Pretenders, James and Charles Stuart.

Stuart Hibbert, the radio announcer, was known as "the man with the golden voice"; Stuart Surridge was captain of the Surrey cricket team that during his captaincy won the championship five years in succession; he retired in 1956.

The pet forms are *Stew* and *Stewy*.

SYLVESTER When used as a Christian name to-day Sylvester seems to be more usual than the more correct spelling, *Silvester*, the Latin for 'wood-dweller,' one of a group of names including *Silvanus*, *Silvius*, and *Silas*.

Silvanus was the Roman woodland god, represented as an old man carrying a cypress branch. St Paul had a companion who is named *Sylvanus* in the Epistles, but in the Acts "Silas, a leading man among the brethren" (Acts xv, 22). Aeneas Silvius, according to Virgil, was the son of Aeneas and Lavinia, from whom the first kings of Rome were descended, and Silvius seems to have been almost a family name among them; the feminine, Sylvia, is a popular name to-day.

There are two saints Silvester; one was Pope in the reign of Constantine the Great. In Germany New Year's Eve is celebrated as *Silvesterabend* ('Sylvester Eve') as St Silvester's feast-day is December 31. Pope Silvester II, a tenth-century Pope and scientist, invented the pendulum clock.

In England the name is first recorded in 1200. After the Reformation it did not die out, though it became less common than Silas: George Eliot's Silas Marner, the lonely weaver who takes charge of the orphaned Eppie, shows the rustic use of Silas in the nineteenth century. Sylvester is, however, the more common to-day.

Sylvester and Tweetie Pie are the cat and canary of a celebrated series of American cartoon-films.

Sil and *Syl* are pet forms.

TERENCE is a Roman clan name of uncertain meaning, perhaps from 'terere,' meaning 'to rub' or 'thresh.'

The Roman comic playwright of the second century B.C., whom we call Terence, was actually Publius *Terentius* Afer, and, as his third name suggests, a North African. A slave, he took his master's name on becoming a free man. A fellow-countryman of his, in the third century A.D., became a Christian martyr.

In England Terence seems never to have been used until recently. Modern bearers are generally indebted to Ireland for their name; for there it was used to replace *Turlough*, introduced by the Vikings, and meaning 'like Thor'—hardly a suitable name for use in baptism: Thor was the Norse god of thunder.

Terence McSwiney was Lord Mayor of Cork. A determined opponent of British rule in Ireland, he finally starved himself to death in Brixton prison in 1920, during the final struggle of the Irish for independence. Major Terence Otway led the paratroops in the invasion of France on D-Day, 1944. Terence Rattigan, the playwright, has written *The Winslow Boy* and *French Without Tears*.

Terry is now regarded as the pet form of Terence. It was in fact in the first place an independent name, a version of *Derek* (see p. 95); there is one example of *Terye* as a personal name in 1629.

THEOBALD is the Old German *Theudobald*, made up of 'theuda,' 'people,' and 'bald,' 'bold.' There was an Old English *Theodbald*, but whether the numerous entries in Domesday Book of *Tedbaldus*, *Theodbald*, and *Tetbald* are forms of this name, or of the Norman *Theobald*, is uncertain.

By the thirteenth century the name had settled down, as *Theobaldus* in Latin documents and *Tebald* (resembling the modern Italian *Tebaldo*), *Tibald*, and *Tedbald* in common use, showing its pronunciation. It gave several surnames, including Tibbles.

St Theobald, an Italian, died in 1066. Theobald of Canterbury was the patron and predecessor as Primate of Thomas à Becket. The nineteenth-century Father Theobald Mathew, an Irishman, gained widespread support in his campaign against excessive drinking.

In the great beast-epic of the Middle Ages, *Reynard the Fox*, *Tibert* or *Tybalt* is the name of the cunning cat. The Tybalt in Shakespeare's *Romeo and Juliet* is called "ratcatcher" by Mercutio, in allusion to this. And, of course, our 'Tibbies' to-day trace their name to their epic ancestor.

Theo is used as the short form of Theobald, and of several other names (see *Theodore*, below).

THEODORE is the Greek *Theodoros*, 'God's gift.' It is hardly surprising that so religious a name has provided twenty-eight saints for the Calendar.

St Theodore of Heraclea was, not without some justification, put to death in 306 for setting fire to a temple. Another St Theodore, like St Paul, from Tarsus in Asia Minor, was appointed Archbishop of Canterbury in the seventh century. Our system of parishes was originated by him.

Nevertheless Theodore was not adopted in England until the nineteenth century. In Wales, however, it has long been favoured, taking the forms *Tewdwr*, *Tudyr*, and *Tudor*. There was a seventh-century Welsh St Tudyr; Tewdwr Aled was a fifteenth-century bard and patriot. As Tudor, it became the surname of the dynasty founded by Henry VII.

There have been many famous bearers on the Continent. In Russia *Fyodor* was among the commonest names; Fyodor Dostoevsky, the novelist, in the nineteenth century, in *Crime and Punishment*, wrote one of the world's greatest crime novels. *Theodor* is the German spelling; during his double term as President of Western Germany Professor Theodor Heuss became godfather to some 16,000 children, most of them called Theodor in compliment to him.

In America Theodore Roosevelt was President from 1901 to 1909. He was an enthusiastic big-game hunter, and the teddy bear was named after him—in the United States *Teddy* is the pet form of Theodore, not of Edward. Theodore Dreiser, the writer, is best known for his book *An American Tragedy*, which set a fashion for turning stories in the news into novels.

A unique English bearer deserves mention: the Reverend Theodore Bayley Hardy, an Army chaplain, killed in action in 1918, and awarded the V.C., the D.S.O., and the Military Cross.

Theo is the short form of Theodore, as it is of Theobald. But it may stand for other names, such as *Theophrastus*, a Latin-Greek name meaning 'divine (or inspired) speaker,' *Theotimus*, meaning 'honouring God,' or the more common *Theophilus*, meaning 'lover of God.' St Luke's Gospel, and the Acts, which are also his work, are both dedicated to a Theophilus.

THOMAS in Aramaic means 'twin.' It seems first to have been given as a name to one of the Apostles, originally a *Judas,* to distinguish him from Jude and Judas Iscariot (see p. 165). Thomas was also known by the Greek translation of his name, *Didymus*. The twin, according to tradition, was his sister Lysia.

The Apostle is said to have preached in India, where a body of native Christians in the Malabar district claims to be descended from his converts.

Thomas is not recorded as an English baptismal name before the Norman Conquest, but occurs in Domesday Book. A *Thome* (the first written version of *Tom* and *Tommy*) is recorded in the thirteenth century; an actual Tom occurs in Yorkshire during the 1400's. Other old pet forms are *Thomasin* and *Thomelin*.

The expression 'every Tom, Dick and Harry' shows the popularity the name owed to St Thomas of Canterbury, or Thomas à Becket, the Archbishop murdered in his own cathedral in 1170. So universal was the habit of making pilgrimages to the site of his martyrdom that we have the word 'canter,' meaning originally the gentle pace at which the pilgrims rode to Canterbury. In order to discredit St Thomas, Henry VIII held a mock trial, some four hundred years after the saint's death, in which he was convicted of high treason, for opposing Henry II. Two other Englishmen of the name have been canonized; the thirteenth-century St Thomas of Hereford, and Sir Thomas More, Henry VIII's Chancellor, scholar and wit, beheaded for refusing, like his archbishop namesake, to admit royal interference in Church affairs. St Thomas Aquinas, a thirteenth-century Sicilian friar, was the greatest thinker of the Middle Ages.

Mention of other celebrated bearers, even if we confine ourselves to England, leaves us with an impressive list. Thomas Linacre founded the Royal College of Physicians; Cardinal Thomas Wolsey built Hampton Court and Christ Church, Oxford, in the sixteenth century. In the eighteenth century Thomas Arne composed *Rule, Britannia*, and turned the story of Tom Thumb into a comic opera; Thomas Gainsborough, the painter, was the rival of Sir Joshua Reynolds. The nineteenth-century Dr Thomas Arnold, of Rugby, revolutionized education, and Thomas Hardy, born in 1840, had become by his death in 1928 one of our greatest novelists.

In America Thomas Jefferson was elected third President, in 1801; Thomas Jackson, Confederate general in the Civil War, was known as Stonewall Jackson, from his ability to keep his troops standing in impenetrable ranks; Thomas Alva Edison patented over a thousand inventions, including the incandescent electric lamp and the earliest record-player. His death in 1931 brings us to our times, with Thomas Stearns (T. S.) Eliot, the Anglo-American poet and playwright; he is best known for his play *Murder in the Cathedral*, dealing with Becket's martyrdom.

Thomas has apparently no special Welsh form, but in Ireland it was used to take the place of *Tomaltach* (*Tumelty*), a native name meaning 'tall as a tower.' The Scottish Thomas the Rhymer was a real poet of the thirteenth century, supposed to have spent three years with the Fairy Queen, who gave him the gift of prophecy. Burns's poem *Tam o' Shanter* is an extravagant story of a man chased by witches, who escapes with the loss of his horse's tail; it shows another short form of the name.

Like Jack, *Tom*, with its diminutive *Tommy*, is frequent in folklore, literature, and life. Tom Tiddler, Tom the Piper's son, Tommy Tucker, are nursery figures; Peeping Tom of Coventry watched Lady Godiva ride naked round the town, and was blinded for his shamelessness. The anonymous Elizabethan poem *Tom o' Bedlam* has such fantastic power that it almost might have been written by Shakespeare. Fielding's *History of Tom Jones*, published in 1749, is among the most influential English novels, one of the first to have a hero with faults as well as good qualities. *Tom Brown's Schooldays*, by Thomas Hughes, which appeared in 1857, was the first great school story. *Uncle Tom's Cabin*, by the American Harriet Beecher Stowe, was a powerful influence in the abolition of negro slavery. *The Adventures of Tom Sawyer* is Mark Twain's best-known novel.

To-day *Tommy* Steele, in entertainment, and *Tom* Graveney, the England cricketer in sport, are always known by these short forms. The written abbreviation of the full name is *Thos.*

Tom-tit and tom-cat are examples of Tom used for animals; the expressions tomfoolery, tomboy and tommy rot are too well known to need explaining. "Thomas Atkins" was the specimen signature on the model forms given to soldiers to sign on their enlistment: it dates from 1815; thus, a Tommy came to mean a private soldier. A Long Tom was a naval gun; the tommy-gun was invented by S. T. Thompson. Tommy was also used for a wrench, and for the food once given to workers instead of wages (alluding to Tommy Tucker, who sang for his supper). A doubting Thomas refers to the Apostle, who refused to believe in Christ's Resurrection until he had touched His wounds. St Thomas's Day, December 21, is the shortest day of the year; as the old rhyme puts it:

St Thomas grey, St Thomas grey,
The longest night and the shortest day.

The weather on that date was supposed to predict the price of corn. If it froze prices would fall; if it was mild they would rise.

TIMOTHY is the Greek *Timotheos*, which means 'honouring God.' It was the name of St Paul's convert and companion, to whom he addressed two Epistles, both full of commonsense advice. The name had, however, been in use among the Greeks, at least since the time of Alexander the Great, whose musician

Timotheus, placed on high,
With flying fingers touched the lyre,

as Dryden puts it in *Alexander's Feast*.

Neither Timotheus, the Latin form, nor Timothy, the English, was often used in Europe until the sixteenth century, when the revival of classical learning led to the use of classical names, and the Reformation popularized many Bible names neglected in Catholic times.

One of the earliest known English bearers was Timothy Bright, Elizabethan inventor of a system of shorthand. In the nineteenth century Timothy Hanson introduced timothy grass into the United States. The first and only Governor-General of Ireland was always known as Tim Healey.

Tiger *Tim*, which shows the usual short form, was used for page-boys in Georgian and Victorian times, because striped waistcoats were part of their uniform. In Richard Barham's *Ingoldsby Legends*,

> Tiger Tim, come tell me true,
> What may a nobleman find to do?

occurs in "The Honourable Mr Sucklethumbkin's Story." The Tiger Tim in 'comics' got his name from this expression.

Timothy has become so popular in England to-day that at any moment a crop of famous bearers may be expected. Beatrix Potter's mouse *Timmy Tiptoes* not only gives a second pet form, but, dating from the early years of this century, shows its common use in nurseries of the time.

TOBY is the traditional English form of the Hebrew *Tobiah*, in Greek *Tobias*, meaning 'the Lord is good.'

The Book of *Tobit* ('son of Tobias') in the Apocrypha was excluded from the Authorized Version of the Bible by the Reformers. The story is briefly sketched under the heading *Raphael* (see p. 225), and was turned into a play, *Tobias and the Angel*, by James Bridie.

Although the story of '*Tobye*' was popular in the Middle Ages, and is mentioned in *Piers Plowman*, there seems to have been no well-known Tobit or Tobias; but as they have given us surnames, such as *Tobin* (a pet form), there must have been Tobys before the thirteenth century, when surnames became established.

Shakespeare's old reprobate Sir Toby Belch, in *Twelfth Night*, shows that the name was used in the reign of Queen Elizabeth. Tobias Matthew was Archbishop of York; he had an eccentric son, always known as *Tobie*, a picturesque figure at the Court of James I. The eighteenth-century novelist Tobias Smollett, writer of such racy stories as *Roderick Random* and *Peregrine Pickle*, was a Scotsman. Laurence Sterne, in *Tristram Shandy*, introduces a delightful old campaigner, Uncle Toby Shandy.

Punch's dog Toby is so called from the dog who went with the original Tobias on his travels—the only dog who plays a part in ancient Jewish literature. A Toby jug, in the form of a fat old man in a three-cornered hat, either represents Uncle Toby, or a great drinker of the eighteenth century, Toby Philpot.

TREVOR This name is the English version of the Welsh *Trefor*, probably a combination of the native 'tref,' 'homestead,' and 'mawr,' 'great,' the name of several Welsh villages.

Three early bearers had Trefor as a second name: Tudor Trefor ap Ynyr, a tenth-century chieftain, and two successive medieval Bishops of Llandaff.

Trevor Howard, the film-star, is a modern example; and the name has become popular, both in Wales and in England, with *Trev* as a pet form.

TRISTRAM comes from *Drystan*, or *Drustens*, derived from the Old Welsh 'drust,' meaning 'din.'

The first recorded bearer of the name was a king of the Picts, known as "*Drwst* of the hundred battles"; one of his descendants was Drwst ap Taran: 'din, son of thunder.'

Another bearer was the Tristram of Arthurian romance, and if the tombstone near Fowey commemorating a Drustens of the sixth century is really his, he was also an historical character. But by the thirteenth century, when a Scottish version of his life was written, the real meaning of the name had been forgotten and it was connected with the French 'triste,' 'sad.' Sir Tristram's tragic entanglement with Iseult, destined bride of his uncle, King Mark, encouraged this interpretation; this story is the theme of Wagner's opera *Tristan and Isolde*. The Scottish St *Drostan* of Deer shows a northern version.

The form *Tristan* was continental, but *Tristram* was normal in England and common enough to have produced, as a surname, eleven entries in a recent London telephone directory. But it is probable that Tristram was sometimes confused with the Old English *Thurstan*, meaning 'Thor's stone,' occasionally found to-day.

Tristram Shandy is Laurence Sterne's great eighteenth-century novel, in which, though Tristram is the nominal hero, the story is almost entirely connected with events previous to his birth.

The group of islands named Tristan da Cunha, in the South Atlantic, was discovered by a Portuguese navigator of that name, and annexed by Great Britain in 1816.

ULYSSES, often written as *Ulixes*, was used by the Romans for the Greek *Odysseus*, meaning 'hater,' or possibly 'limping.' He was the cunning Greek leader at the siege of Troy, who devised the gigantic wooden horse, in which he and his companions hid, to emerge after the Trojans had dragged it into the town, and open the gates to the Greek army. His return home—the subject of Homer's *Odyssey*—took him ten years packed with adventures on land and sea.

Though rarely, if ever, used in England, Ulysses was taken in Ireland as a substitute for *Ulick*, meaning 'mind reward.' In America Ulysses S. Grant was a Northern general in the Civil War, and twice President, in 1868 and 1872.

James Joyce published his extraordinary novel *Ulysses* in 1922, in which he makes every incident in one day of a Dubliner's life correspond with an episode in the story of the Greek hero. Tennyson's poem of the same name makes the old Ulysses tell of his unquenched longing for adventure.

VALENTINE comes from the Latin 'valens,' meaning 'strong' or 'healthy,' itself used by the Romans as a personal name: our 'valiant' and 'valid' have the same derivation.

The spread of the name is due to a third-century Roman priest, *Valentinus*. The day of his martyrdom, February 14, happened to fall on the eve of a festival of the goddess Juno, when lots were drawn for the choice of lovers. This pagan celebration, transferred to the saint's day, has kept the name in use. Ophelia, in Shakespeare's *Hamlet*, refers to the traditional customs of St Valentine's Day in the verse:

To-morrow is Saint Valentine's day,
All in the morning betime,
And I a maid at your window,
To be your Valentine.

Birds were supposed to begin building their nests on St Valentine's Day, but the custom of sending Valentine Cards seems to date only from the nineteenth century, when Christmas cards were also invented.

Valentine appears to have been used in England since the thirteenth century, practically unaltered in spelling, apart from the Latin ending, which, if ever used in speech, had been dropped by the 1500's. Valentine has been used as a name for either sex.

Valentine and Orson, a medieval romance, tells the story of two brothers: Valentine was a courtly knight, the other, Orson, lost as a baby, became a wild man of the woods. *Orson*, meaning 'little bear,' is familiar from Orson Welles, most individual of film stars and producers.

Shakespeare uses Valentine for one of his *Two Gentlemen of Verona*. Valentine Carey was a bishop of Exeter in the seventeenth century; Valentine Greatrakes, his contemporary in Ireland, was known as "the touch doctor," for his curing the 'King's evil' (a disease known medically as scrofula), by laying his hands on his patients. To-day Valentine Dyall is known to his radio listeners as "The Man in Black"; his sinister tones introduce horror stories and plays. *Val* Gielgud, also a radio personality, is known by the only short form of the name.

VICTOR is a name needing no translation, being one of the few Latin words that have been taken into our own language unchanged. Most schoolboys would find their ambition fulfilled by being declared "Victor Ludorum," actually an ancient Roman title, meaning 'champion of the games.'

The name was favoured by early Christians, from its suggestion of victory over evil. One early Pope bore it, and won the victory of martyrdom.

In England the name is found by the early thirteenth century; but it remained uncommon until after 1800, when it became popular from its resemblance to Victoria. It is possible, at the same time, that supporters of Italian independence chose it for their sons in compliment to Victor Emmanuel II of Sardinia, first king of a united Italy: Victor Emmanuel and Victor Amadeus were the favourite combinations of names in his family. The French used the Latin form unchanged: Victor Hugo is an example; he wrote not only the novels *The Hunchback of Notre-Dame* and *Les Misérables*, but also great poetry. Mary Shelley took Victor for the first name of the unfortunate Frankenstein, the German who created a monster that killed him: Frankenstein was *not* the name of the monster.

During this century *Viktor* Barna was five times world table-tennis champion; Victor Trumper, who died in 1915, aged thirty-eight, is still a legendary hero of Australian cricket. Victor Sylvester's orchestra has for long been among the best known in England. *Vic* Oliver, the Austrian-born comedian, always uses this short form: others are *Vick* and *Vicky*.

The Welsh turned Victor into *Gwythyr*, the name of a hero in the ancient legends of the *Mabinogion*. It is extraordinary how many Roman names are preserved by the Welsh, though few are easily recognized.

VINCENT, like *Victor*, is a name of victory; 'vincens,' in Latin, means 'conquering.' As a personal name, the usual Latin form was *Vincentius*.

With St Stephen and St Lawrence, St Vincent was one of the three great martyr deacons; he was put to death at Saragossa, in Spain, where the spread of the name began. Best known to-day is St Vincent de Paul, the seventeenth-century French priest who organized the care of waifs and strays, and founded the well-known Order of Sisters of Charity.

In medieval England—nearly always friendly with Spain—Vincent occurs in documents from 1200 onwards. After the fifteenth century it seems to have practically died out until the Victorian age; though Shakespeare uses the Italian form *Vincentio* for the Duke of Vienna who wanders about the city in disguise, to discover the true characters of his officers.

Vincent Novello, whose father was an Italian, became organist at the Portuguese Chapel in London, in the early nineteenth century; he arranged the famous setting for *O Come, All Ye Faithful.* It is chiefly among Catholics that the name is found, but not exclusively. Vincent van Gogh, best known of Dutch painters in recent times, began his career as a Protestant missionary in Belgium. Sir Vincent Tewson was formerly General Secretary of the Trades Union Congress.

Cape St Vincent, named after the Spanish martyr, was the scene of the battle won by Admiral Jervis, created Earl St Vincent.

Short forms used to-day are *Vince*, *Vinnie*, *Vinny*, and *Vin.*

VIVIAN is from the Latin *Vivianus*, connected with 'vivus,' meaning 'alive.' St Vivianus was a fifth-century martyr.

The name is not recorded in England before the end of the twelfth century, when, as usual in documents, it appears in its Latin form, with a feminine version Viviana, which, as Vivien and Vivienne, is now more popular than the masculine.

Most of its English medieval bearers appear to have lived near the Celtic districts in the west. This suggests that it was another old Roman-British name that persisted in Wales. The Welsh have, in fact, three forms of it: *Vyvyan*, *Vivian*, and *Fithian*; even a *Phytheon* has been noted. The name is found in other parts of the country, however, and though never common, has never died out. St Vivian of Fife, a seventh-century

Churchman, shows that Scottish Celts also used the name.

Vivian has at least one famous bearer to-day, Sir Vivian Fuchs, the Antarctic explorer; the short form, *Viv*, shows that it is not uncommon.

WALLACE, as a given name, is of Victorian origin. It may first have been given to connexions of the Wallace family, or in honour of the thirteenth-century Scottish patriot Sir William Wallace, "hammer and scourge of England." Perhaps the best-known lines in all Burns's poetry are:

> Scots, wha hae wi' Wallace bled,
> Scots, wham Bruce has often led.

In any case, the surname has given the Christian name.

But, like all names, Wallace has a meaning; it was originally the Saxons' word for 'foreign': 'waelisc' (pronounced almost like our word 'Welsh,' which has the same meaning).

Another form of the name is *Wallis*, much used in America for both boys and girls.

An early English bearer was Sir Wallis Budge, keeper of the Egyptian and Assyrian antiquities of the British Museum, knighted in 1920. Wallace Beery was a leading 'tough guy' of the screen in the years following the First World War.

Wally, the usual short form, is shared with Walter; there is also *Wal*. An extraordinary corruption of the name is *Belize*, an attempt of the natives of British Honduras to pronounce the name of the founder of their capital—a gentleman named Wallace.

WALTER is from the Old German *Waldhar*, from the words 'vald' and 'harja,' meaning 'rule-people.' Though there was an Anglo-Saxon name *Wealdhere.* it was displaced at the Conquest by the Norman Walter, fashionable in France from very early times. The Latin *Walterius* appears in Domesday Book.

By the time of Edward II *Wauter* appears, showing that the usual pronunciation had become 'water.' In Shakespeare's *Henry VI, Part II*, the Earl of Suffolk says to Walter Whitmore:

> A cunning man did calculate my birth
> And told me that by Water I should die.

The "cunning man" was an astrologer, and did not explain whether "Water" was the name or the element.

Walters have been famous in many callings. Walter Mapes was the earliest English gossip writer: he recorded the scandals of the Court of Henry II, wrote Arthurian stories, and composed comic songs in Latin. Walter Odington of Evesham, in the thirteenth century, wrote a book on musical theory. Sir Walter de Manny, a soldier of fortune, followed Queen Philippa of Hainault to England. His exploits are often mentioned in Froissart's *Chronicles*. Sir Walter Raleigh will always be remembered for his cloak, his popularizing tobacco in England, and his tragic death on the scaffold.

In modern times, Walter Sickert was the pioneer of impressionist painting in England; Walter de la Mare's poems are in every twentieth-century anthology of verse; Walter Hammond was England's cricket captain in the 'thirties.

In America Walter Gropius, of German origin, is the most celebrated architect; Walter Jess, born in Switzerland, won the Nobel Prize in 1949 for his work on brain surgery. These two examples show that the name is common to more than one European country. Walter Gieseking, the concert pianist, was born of German parents in France. The normal German form, however, is *Walther*.

The oldest short form is *Wat*: Wat Tyler led the peasants to London to seek redress from the boy-king Richard II. *Gwatcyn* was introduced into Wales by Flemish immigrants brought there by Henry I, and produced the surname Watkin(s).

Walt, another pet form, is used as a separate name in America. Walt Whitman, in the mid nineteenth century, wrote *Leaves of Grass*, poems praising everything under the sun. To-day Walt Disney, creator of Mickey Mouse, has produced film cartoons that rank as classics.

Wal and *Wally* are also pet forms.

WARREN is the present-day English form of the Old German *Varin*, probably meaning 'defender.' *Warin*, or *Garin*, de Monglane, was a hero of early French romance.

The name came to England with the Normans as *Warin* and *Guarin*, both recorded in Domesday Book, and both were still in use in the thirteenth century. During the next hundred years the name seems almost to have died out; though Warren is noted by William Lyford in a list drawn up as late as 1655. Waring and Garnet (from the diminutive *Guarinet*) are surnames derived from it. As there was no w in French, 'gu' was used to represent the letter in many old names, such as Walter and William. John Warenne, Edward I's general, was defeated by Wallace at the battle of Stirling Bridge.

Warren Hastings, Governor-General of India, who figured in one of the most sensational political trials in English history, bore his mother's maiden name. In 1924 Warren Harding was elected President of the United States; Warren Lewis to-day is a leading American chemist. Warren seems to be more popular across the Atlantic than it is in Britain.

General *Garnet* Wolesley, later a Viscount and Field Marshal, was so popular with the Army at the turn of the century that 'all Sir Garnet' was used by the troops as the equivalent of 'O.K.'

Warner, an elaboration of the name ('varin-harja,' meaning 'defender of the people'), was introduced by the Normans into England as *Garnier*; as Garner it has become a surname. *Wariner* also was used in the Middle Ages; but the surname Warriner is often derived from 'warrener'—the man in charge of the game preserve on an estate. Warner has been taken into use again as a personal name, but, like Warren, seems popular chiefly in America.

WASHINGTON is the name of the English village from which came the surname, which means 'home of the people of Wassa.' There Wassa's family must first have settled; though Sulgrave was the home of that branch of the family which produced the first American President.

Considering the fondness of Americans for surnames as personal names, it is not surprising that Washington soon became popular among them. Washington Irving, the best-known bearer outside his own country, was born in 1783. He wrote *Rip van Winkle*, an American legend, and *Old Christmas*, based on his pleasant recollections of a winter stay in England.

WILBUR is a name extraordinarily popular in America, but practically unknown in Britain. It presumably comes from the Old German 'wil' and 'burh,' 'will' and 'defence.'

There is an uncommon English surname Wilber, sometimes apparently mistakenly turned into Wildbore; but there was a similar Dutch surname with the same origin, also mistakenly changed into another form: Wildeboer ('wild farmer'). Dutch place and family names were brought to America by the settlers from Holland, but became altered in the course of time. Wilbur must be one of these. The 'ur' ending is clearly meant to give the pronunciation of the Dutch 'oer.' The only normal English name ending in 'ur' is *Arthur*, and that is of Welsh origin.

Wilbur Wright is the best-known bearer. Born in 1867, he was a pioneer airman who worked in partnership with his brother Orville; they made their first powered flight in 1903. Wilbur Voliva, an eccentric who died in 1942, owned the "City of Zion," near Chicago; he forbade doctors in his town, prohibited the eating of pork, and public entertainments, and maintained to his dying day that the earth was flat.

WILFRED, or more correctly, *Wilfrid*, is a combination of the Anglo-Saxon 'will' and 'frith,' 'will' and 'peace.' *Wilbrord* (*Willibrard*), 'will-javelin,' *Willibald* ('will-bold'), *Willihold* ('will-loyal'), were all Old English names.

St Wilfrid, who flourished in the seventh century, was the first prominent bearer. No less suitable name could have been chosen for a man who spent most of his life asserting his claims against rivals. Founder of the old sees of Ripon and Hexham, he also preached in Sussex, where he earned the gratitude of his converts by teaching them sea-fishing. It seems to have been in the Ripon district that his name chiefly found favour and was later corrupted into *Wilfroy*.

No prominent bearers are found before the nineteenth century. Wilfrid Scawen Blunt is an early example, born in 1840. He was a diplomat, and explorer in the East, where he was one of the first champions of national independence; he was also a poet, like Wilfred Owen, who, though his verses show his hatred of bloodshed, gained the Military Cross for bravery in the First World War. Another poet of the name is Wilfrid Gibson, who wrote *Breakfast* and *Luck*. Wilfred Hyde White, the actor, and Wilfred Rhodes, one of the great Yorkshire cricketers, made the name famous in other callings; Wilfred Pickles has been a popular broadcaster since 1927.

The short form of the name is *Wilf*.

WILLIAM. The Old German words 'vilja' and 'helma,' 'will' and 'helmet,' are the origin of our William; the modern German *Wilhelm* clearly shows this.

The name became a particular favourite with the Normans; the second Duke of Normandy was William "Long-sword." William the Conqueror brought the name to England; so did many of his numerous followers; his form of the name was *Willelm*, which is the version used in Domesday Book. By the time of Henry II there were so many Williams that when two who were court officials held a feast, to which they invited all their namesakes, no less than a hundred and twenty turned up. In fact, William is the commonest recorded English name until the thirteenth century, when it was ousted by *John*.

There were two English saints William: one an Archbishop of York, the other a boy, "Little St William" of Norwich. William of Wykeham, in the fourteenth century, founded Winchester College.

By the thirteenth century pet forms had come to be used, *Wylecoc* being among the earliest known. *Wylymot* appears later: *Wilmot* is found to-day as a Christian name. *Wilkin* survived in the surnames Wilkins and Wilkinson: Dickens's Micawber in *David Copperfield* had *Wilkins* as his first name. *Wyll* is found in the early sixteenth century. From the sixteenth to the nineteenth century William ties with John for the first place, amounting to twenty per cent of all names in use.

Best known of all English Williams is William Shakespeare; William Byrd, the great Elizabethan composer, was born twenty-one years before him, and died seven years after him, in 1623. William Harvey, in the reign of Charles I, discovered the circulation of the blood. William of Orange came from Holland to be King of England in 1689. William Wordsworth, the poet, was born in 1770. William Ellis, at Rugby, in 1823, picked up the football during a game and so inaugurated Rugby football. William Fox Talbot took the first surviving photograph in 1835. Also in the nineteenth century, William Freese-Greene gave the first film show, to an audience of one policeman, in 1889. William Gilbert (W. G.) Grace was the greatest of Victorian cricketers. William Booth, founder of the Salvation Army, born in 1829, lived till 1912.

Of foreign bearers, perhaps the most celebrated are *Wilhelm* Tell, the Swiss national hero, and William the Silent, who won independence for the Netherlands. Hyamson's *Dictionary of Universal Biography* lists over 190 Williams known to fame.

Will Scarlet, Robin Hood's companion, is an early example of the use of the short version by which Shakespeare was known to his friends. It occurs in folklore with the Will o' the Wisp. The American bird the whip-poor-will is so called because its cry sounds like 'whip poor Will'! Wandering *Willie*, which shows the usual Scottish pet form, is the name of the blind fiddler in Scott's *Redgauntlet*. Willie McTurk is one of Kipling's schoolboy gang in *Stalky & Co. Wee Willie Winkie*, the nursery rhyme, was written in the nineteenth century by William Miller. The first tank used in warfare was christened "Little Willie," in scorn of the German Crown Prince

Wilhelm. Willie Park, in 1860, was the winner of the first Open Golf Championship.

Bill, probably the most used English diminutive, recalls Bill Sikes, the burglar in Dickens's *Oliver Twist*, and Buffalo Bill (Colonel William Cody), a real American horseman, who has become a legendary figure in countless Wild West stories. The expression 'a silly billy' is supposed to originate from William IV, a king not remarkable for intelligence. Little *Billee* is the unfortunate cabin-boy in Thackeray's ballad, nearly eaten by his shipmates. A hill billy is an American term for a poor countryman. Australians call themselves Bill Jims, and boil tea in their billy cans. *Billy* Bunter dates from about 1909, when Frank Richards began his "Greyfriars" stories in the *Magnet*, a popular boys' paper. *Billie* is a less common diminutive. *Willy* and *Willi* are sometimes found: both probably imported from Germany.

The Welsh version is *Gwylim*, probably brought to Wales by Henry I's Flemish settlers, and clearly akin to the French *Guillaume*; a whole crop of French forms occurs in State documents of the fourteenth century: *Guilliame* and *Guillot* are two, *Gilow* another. The 'gu-' was the French attempt to give the sound of w, which does not occur in the Latin or early French alphabets.

The Irish have shortened William to *Liam*. Liam O'Flaherty, the author, for instance, is best known by *The Informer*, a novel dealing with the Dublin rising against British rule in 1916.

Wm. is a common written abbreviation of the name.

WINSTON is the name of a hamlet in Gloucestershire, presumably meaning 'Wine's settlement.' 'Wine,' however, if that was his name, meant 'friend.' But it is tempting to derive the name from 'wine' and 'stane,' which would mean 'friend' and 'stone.'

The first Duke of Marlborough was given Winston as his second name by his father, a seventeenth-century Sir Winston Churchill, who had inherited it from his mother's family, and it came into regular use among the Churchills. One of their connexions, the American writer Winston Churchill, was born in 1871.

Sir Winston Churchill's leadership during the Second World War spread the name through the English-speaking world. As a gesture of defiance, the Dutch also adopted it for boys born during the German occupation of Holland, where it has been more popular even than in this country. George Orwell chose Winston Smith to name the hero of his terrifying story *1984*.

Winnie is the popular short form.

ZACHARY is the traditional English version of the Hebrew *Zachariah*, or *Zechariah*, meaning 'the Lord is renowned.'

There was a King Zachariah of Israel, and the Book of the Prophet Zachariah is last but one of the books in the Old Testament. In the New Testament *Zacharias* is the name of the father of John the Baptist, and appears in the first chapter of St Luke.

In England Zachary was given often enough to produce a surname, though not recorded as such before the sixteenth century; a hundred years later it was well established among the Puritans, and has survived, though chiefly among country people, who long kept up the use of Old Testament names.

The Puritans took the name to America, where Zachary Taylor was President in 1849 and 1850.

The pet forms of Zachary are *Zack*, *Zacky*, and occasionally *Zaz*.

Zacchaeus, in the original Hebrew *Zakkai*, is a short form of Zachariah found in the New Testament as the name of the little man who climbed a sycamore-tree to see Jesus over the heads of the crowd that had followed Him into Jericho. He offered half of his property to the poor, and was praised by Jesus as a true son of Abraham.

MAIN INDEX

The names printed in italic are the head-names of the text

SUPPLEMENTARY INDEX

The following list contains only names not included in the Main Index, though some less common versions of names included in the main body of the text are given. With these a page reference to the original name is given.

To compile an exhaustive list of names in use is impossible, partly because it is difficult to know when a particular name has gone out of use, partly because a new name may be taken into use at any moment: names are as subject to fashion as anything else, and particularly nowadays.

A large number of the names in this supplementary index are surnames by origin. This use of surnames for individuals is a particularly English and American habit, dating from the sixteenth century at least. Those that are well established are dealt with in the text; those in this index are less commonly used, but have been noticed as occurring more than once in present-day records, such as the Press. But as any surname may be taken as a Christian name, either because it perpetuates the mother's family name, or compliments some respected relative, or in honour of a popular hero, far more such names have been omitted. There are books enough devoted to surnames, that can be consulted in any public library.

As far as possible, just as in the text, each name has been provided with an interpretation, but the authorities themselves often disagree; so if there are some blanks it is because we think it more prudent to confess ignorance than to make guesses. It is hoped that any corrections, or additional information, that can be supported with reasonable evidence will be sent to the compilers, who would welcome such constructive criticism.

AARON (*Egyptian*), high mountain

ABDIEL (*Hebrew*), servant of God

ABELOT (*French-Hebrew*), a diminutive of *Abel* (p. 33)

ABIAH (*Hebrew*), my father is the Lord

ABIATHAR (*Hebrew*), father of plenty

ABIEL (*Hebrew*), my father is God

ABIMELECH (*Hebrew*), father of the king

ABIUD (*Hebrew*), father of glory

ACHILLES (*Greek*), without lips

ADAIR (*Celtic*), oak ford

ADDIS (*English-Hebrew*), an old pet form of *Adam* (p. 35)

ADELGAR (*Germanic*), noble spear

ADELPHO (*Greek*), brother

ADIEL (*Hebrew*), an ornament is God

ADIN (*Hebrew*), voluptuous

ADLAI (*Hebrew*), my ornament

ADNA (*Hebrew*), pleasure

ADOLF
ADOLPH
ADOLPHE
ADOLPHUS } (*Germanic*), noble wolf

ADONIS (*Greek-Hebrew*), my Lord is exalted

ADRASTUS (*Latin-Greek*), inescapable

AELHAEARN (*Welsh*), iron brow

AGAMEMNON (*Greek*), resolute

AGATHENOR (*Greek*), good-brave

AGATHON (*Greek*), good, kind

AHE(A)RN (*Welsh*), iron

AIDAN (*Irish*), fire

AJAX (*Greek*), earthy

ALADDIN (*Arabic*), servant of Allah

ALARD (*Germanic*), noble-hard

ALARIC (*Germanic*), noble rule

ALASTOR (*Greek*), avenger

ALDEN (*Anglo-Saxon*), old friend

ALDHELM (*Anglo-Saxon*), old helmet

ALDIS (*Germanic*), a form of *Aldous* (p. 42)

ALDRIC(H) (*Anglo-Saxon*), old rule

ALDWIN (*Anglo-Saxon*), old friend

ALFO, a short form of *Alphonso*

ALFONSO (*Germanic*), noble-ready

ALGAR
ALGER } (*Germanic*), noble spear

ALI (*Arabic*), servant

ALMERIC
ALMERY } (*Germanic*), work rule

ALONSO
ALONZO } (*Italian-Germanic*), forms of *Alphonso*

ALPHONSE
ALPHONSO
ALPHONSUS } (*Germanic*), noble-ready

ALROY (*Spanish*), the king
ALSTON (*Anglo-Saxon*), noble stone
ALTON (*Anglo-Saxon*), old village
ALVA (*Spanish*), white
ALVAH, ALVAN (*Hebrew*), exalted
ALVAR (*Anglo-Saxon*), elf-army
ALVERY, a medieval English form of *Alfred* (p. 45)
ALVIN (*Germanic*), noble friend
ALVIS (*Scandinavian*), all-wise
ALY (*Arabic*), servant
AMADEUS (*Latin*), love-God
AMADIS (*French-Latin*), love-God
AMANDUS (*Latin*), worthy of love
AMBLER (*English*), stable-keeper
AMERY (*Germanic*), work rule
AMFRID (*Germanic*), ancestor peace
AMORY (*Germanic*), work rule
AMOS (*Hebrew*), bearer; *or* courageous
AMUND (*Scandinavian*), divine protection
AMYNTAS (*Greek*), protector
ANANIAS (*Hebrew*), the Lord has been gracious
ANARAWD (*Welsh*), eloquent
ANASTASIUS (*Greek*), rising again
ANATOLE (*Greek*), sunrise
ANCEL (*Germanic*), godlike; *or* (*Latin*) servant
ANCHITEL (*Scandinavian*), divine cauldron
ANDROCLES (*Greek*), man-glory
ANDRONICUS (*Greek*), man-victory
ANEW (*French*), lamb
ANGEL (*English-Greek*), messenger (angel)
ANGELO (*Italian-Greek*), messenger (angel)
ANGWYN (*Welsh*), very handsome
ANKETIL (*Scandinavian*), divine cauldron
ANNO, a variant of *Arnold* (p. 54)
ANSEL(M) (*Germanic*), divine helmet
ANSTEY, ANSTICE, ANSTIS (*English-Greek*), rising again
ANTINOUS (*Greek*), contradictory
ANTON, a German form of *Antony* (p. 52)
ANWYL (*Welsh*), dear
AODH (*Celtic*), fire
AQUILA (*Latin*), eagle
ARCHELAUS (*Greek*), ruler of the people
ARCHER (*English*), bowman
ARCHIMEDES (*Greek*), master mind

ARETAS (*Greek*), virtue
ARGUS (*Greek*), bright; vigilant
ARIEL (*Hebrew*), lion of God
ARISTARCHUS (*Greek*), best leader
ARISTIDES (*Greek*), son of the best
ARISTOCLES (*Greek*), perfect glory
ARISTOTLE (*Greek*), best thinker
ARMAND (*French-Old German*), army man
ARMIN, ARMYN (*Germanic*), army man
ARTEMAS, ARTEMUS (*Greek*), masculine forms of Artemis (moon-goddess)
ARTHFAEL (*Welsh*), bear strength (literally, bear metal)
ASA (*Hebrew*), healer, physician
ASAPH (*Hebrew*), gatherer
ASCELIN (*Germanic*), provisioner
ASHCROFT (*English*), small farm with ash-trees
ASHER (*Hebrew*), happy
ASHLEY (*Anglo-Saxon*), ash-field
ASKETIL (*Scandinavian*), divine cauldron
ASTROPHEL (*Greek*), star lover
ATHALARIC (*Germanic*), noble ruler
ATHANASIUS (*Greek*), immortal
ATHELSTAN (*Anglo-Saxon*), noble stone
ATHERTON (*Anglo-Saxon*), woodland dweller
ATHOL(E) (*Scottish*), place-name
ATLAS (*Greek*), sufferer
AULAY (*Gaelic-Scandinavian*), a form of *Olaf* (p. 208)
AURELIAN, AURELIUS (*Latin*), golden (-haired)
AURYN (*Welsh*), gold
AVENEL (*Old French*), hazel
AVERIL(L) (*Anglo-Saxon*), bear-battle
AXEL (*Scandinavian*), divine reward
AYLWARD (*Anglo-Saxon*), noble protection
AYMON (*Old French-Germanic*), home
AZAR, AZARIAH, AZARIAS (*Hebrew*), whom the Lord helps

BALDRED (*Anglo-Saxon*), bold counsel
BALDRIC (*Germanic*), bold rule
BANCROFT (*Anglo-Saxon*), bean farmstead
BANQUO (*Gaelic*), white
BAPTIST (*Greek*), baptizer

BARAK (*Hebrew*), flash of lightning

BARCLAY (*English-French*), place-name (Berchelai); *or* (*Anglo-Saxon*) birch-meadow

BARDELL (*Germanic*), bright wolf

BARDO (*Germanic*), giant

BARDOLF, BARDOLPH (*Germanic*), bright wolf

BARLOW (*Germanic*), boar's hill

BARON (*English*), title of rank; *or* (*Germanic*), warrior, hero

BARRET(T) (*Germanic*), bear strength

BARUCH (*Hebrew*), blessed

BAXTER (*English*), baker

BAYARD (*Old French*), reddish-brown; *or* a gentleman of courage and honour

BEAUREGARD (*French*), fair view, handsome

BEAVIS (*English-Frankish*), ox

BEDAWS (*Welsh*), birch-tree

BEDE (*Anglo-Saxon*), prayer

BEDEVERE (*English-Welsh*), birch-hero

BEDFORD (*English/American*), place-name

BEDIVERE: see *Bedevere*

BEDVER (*Welsh*): see *Bedevere*

BEDWIN (*Welsh*), birch-like

BEDWYR (*Welsh*): see *Bedevere*

BELI (*Welsh*), bright

BEL(L)AMY (*French*), fair friend

BENIAH (*Hebrew*), son of the Lord

BENNO, a form of *Bernard* (p. 67)

BENTLEY (*Anglo-Saxon*), grassy meadow

BERENGER (*Germanic*), bear-spear

BERGEN (*Germanic*), hill mountain

BERK(E)LEY (*English-French*), place-name (Berchelai); *or* (*Anglo-Saxon*) birch-meadow

BERNARDINO (*Italian*), a form of *Bernard* (p. 67)

BERRY (*English*), berry; *or* from French place-name (Berri)

BERTHELM (*Anglo-Saxon*), bright helmet

BERTHOLD (*Germanic*), ruling in splendour

BERTWIN (*Anglo-Saxon*), illustrious friend

BEVERLEY (*Anglo-Saxon*), beaver meadow

BEVIS (*English-Frankish*), ox

BEYNON (*Welsh*), son of Eynon

BIDDULPH (*Germanic*), commanding wolf

BING

BLADUD (*Welsh*), wolf tribe

BLAIN(E) (*Anglo-Saxon*), the flaming one

BLAIR (*Gaelic*), marshy plain

Blaise (*French-Latin*), stammering
Blake (*Anglo-Saxon*), black, dark-complexioned
Blanco (*Spanish-Latin*), white
Blase
Blasius } (*Latin*), stammering
Bleddian
Bleddyn } (*Welsh*), little wolf
Bledig (*Welsh*), wolf-like
Bledri (*Welsh*), wolf ruler
Bleduc (*Welsh*), wolf-like
Bleiddian (*Welsh*), little wolf
Bleiddud (*Welsh*), wolf tribe
Bleiddyn (*Welsh*), little wolf
Blyth(e) (*Anglo-Saxon*), happy
Boaz (*Hebrew*), swiftness
Bobo (*Frankish*), ox
Boleslav (*Slavonic*), great glory
Bonamy (*French*), good friend
Bonar (*Old French*), gentle, courteous
Bonaventure (*French-Latin*), good fortune
Boniface (*Latin*), doing good
Boon(e) (*Scandinavian*), prayer; *or* (*Anglo-Saxon*) favour
Booth (*Anglo-Saxon*), cowman, herdsman
Botolph (*Germanic*), commanding wolf
Boyce (*French*), woodland
Boyd (*Scottish*), from the place-name Bute (found in Wales because of great estates of Marquis of Bute there)
Braden (*Anglo-Saxon*), broad valley
Bradley (*Anglo-Saxon*), broad meadow
Brady (*Anglo-Saxon*), broad island
Bransby (*Scandinavian*), Bran's settlement
Brent (*Anglo-Saxon*), steep hill
Bret(t) (*English-French*), Breton
Brewster (*English*), brewer
Brice (*Celtic*), son of *Rhys* (p. 228)
Brinsley (*Anglo-Saxon*), Brin's meadow
Britius (*Latin*), man of Brittium (not Britain)
Brocard (*Germanic*), badger's earth
Brocas (*Germanic*), badger's wood
Brock (*English*), badger
Broderick (*English-Welsh*) = ap Roderick, 'son of Roderick' (p. 233)
Bruin (*Dutch*), brown
Bruno (*Germanic*), brown
Brutus (*Latin*),heavy
Bryce (*Celtic*), son of *Rhys* (p. 228)

BRYCHAN (*Welsh*), speckled, freckled

BRYN (*Welsh*), hill (usually short for a place-name such as *Bryn-mor*, 'hill-sea' or 'great hill')

BUCKLEY (*Anglo-Saxon*), beech meadow

BUD, nickname—short for *buddy*, 'friend'

BURL (*Anglo-Saxon*), a short form of *Burleigh*, 'town meadow'

BURT (*Anglo-Saxon*), bright

BUSTER, BUTCH } nicknames (common in U.S.A.)

BYRNE (*Anglo-Saxon*), coat of armour

BYRON (*French*), place-name (Biron); (*Anglo-Saxon*), cow-man

BYSS(H)E (*Anglo-Saxon*), thicket

CADEL(L) (*Welsh*), battle

CADEYRN (*Welsh*), battle-king

CADFAEL (*Welsh*), battle-metal

CADFAN (*Welsh*), battle-peak

CADFARCH (*Welsh*), battle-steed

CADFER (*Welsh*), war-lord; *or* bounty of the Lord

CADFRAWD (*Welsh*), battle-judgment

CADIFOR (*Welsh*), battle-lord

CADLYW (*Welsh*), battle-chief

CADMA(W)R (*Welsh*), battle-great

CADMUS (*Greek-Phoenician*), Eastern

CADOGAN (*Welsh*), little battle

CADOR (*Welsh*), shield; *or* warrior

CALEB (*Hebrew*), dog

CALVERT (*Anglo-Saxon*), keeper of a calf-herd

CAMERON (*Gaelic*), crooked nose

CAMILLO, CAMILLUS } (*Latin*), attendant at a sacrifice

CAMPBELL (*Gaelic*), crooked mouth

CANUTE (*Germanic*), kind, race; *or* knot

CAREY (*Latin*), dear

CARNEY, a variant of *Corney*

CARLETON, CARLTON } (*Anglo-Saxon*), peasants' farm

CARLYLE (*Celtic*), fortress of Luel (Lugh, the Celtic sun-god)

CARMICHAEL (*Celtic*), Michael's fortress

CARTER (*English*), cart-driver

CASEY (*Celtic*), valorous

CASIMIR (*Polish*), proclamation of peace

CASSIAN, CASSIUS } (*Latin*), plant-name (cassia)

CASSIDY (*Celtic*), ingenious

CASTOR (*Latin*), beaver

CATILINE (*Latin*), pure
CATO (*Latin*), cub
CAVAN
CATO (*Greek*), downy
CELESTINE (*Latin*), heavenly
CELYNEN (*Welsh*), holly
CENEU (*Welsh*), cub
CERI (*Welsh*), loved one
CERWYN (*Welsh*), fair love
CEURED (*Welsh*), giant (?)
CHEIRO (*Greek*), hand
CHENEY (*French*), oak-grove
CHERRY (*English*), grower or seller of cherries
CHESNEY (*French*), oak-grove
CHESTER (*English-Latin*), fort
CHRYSANDER (*Greek*), golden man
CHRYSOGONUS (*Greek*), gold-born
CHRYSOSTOM (*Greek*), golden mouth
CINCINNATUS (*Latin*), curly-haired
CLAIRMOND (*Latin+Germanic*), famous protection
CLARK (*English-Latin*), clerk, cleric
CLAY (*Anglo-Saxon*), dweller on the clay-site; worker in a clay-pit
CLAYTON (*Anglo-Saxon*), dweller in the clay town

CLEDWYN (*Welsh*), blessed sword; *or* river-name (in Denbighshire)
CLIFTON (*Anglo-Saxon*), settlement on the cliff
CLINT, CLINTON (*Anglo-Saxon*), headland farm
CLYDAI (*Welsh*), fame
CLYDE (*Scottish*), river-name
CLYDRI (*Welsh*), fame ruler
COEL (*Welsh*), trust
COLLEY (*Anglo-Saxon*), swarthy; black-haired
COMYN (*Irish*), crooked
CONCHUBHAR, CONNOR, CONOR (*Irish*), high desire
CONROY (*Irish*), hound of the plain
CORBET(T), CORBIE (*Old French*), raven; crow
CORCORAN (*Celtic*), ruddy
CORDELL (*English-French*), rope-maker
COR(E)Y (*Germanic*), the chosen one
CORMAC (*Irish*), charioteer
CORNELIUS (*Latin*), Roman family name
CORNELL (*English-Latin*), a form of *Cornelius*; (*American*) from the famous university
CORNEY, a (mainly Irish) pet form of *Cornelius*

CORYDON (*Greek*), lark; *or* helmet

COSIMO, COSMO (*Greek*), order, pattern

COURTENAY, COURTNEY (*French*), place-name

COVENTRY (*English*), place-name

CRAIG (*Gaelic*), crag

CRANOG (*Welsh*), heron

CULVER (*Anglo-Saxon*), dove

CURRAN (*Celtic*), hero

CURTIS (*Old French*), courteous

CYNAN (*Welsh*), chief

CYNDDELW (*Welsh*), chief image

CYNFAEL (*Welsh*), chief metal

CYNFOR (*Welsh*), chief-great

CYNFRAN (*Welsh*), chief raven

CYNFRIG (*Welsh*), chief offshoot

CYNGEN (*Welsh*), chief son

CYNIDR (*Welsh*), chief serpent

CYNLLO (*Welsh*), chief calf

CYNYR (*Welsh*), chief hero

DACRE, from Acre (Palestinian town)

DAGOBERT (*Anglo-Saxon*), day-bright

DALE (*Anglo-Saxon*), valley

DALLAS (*Anglo-Saxon*), dweller in the dale; (*American*) place-name

DALTON (*Anglo-Saxon*), dweller in the valley near the village

DAMIAN, DAMON (*Greek*), tamed *or* tamer

DANA (*Anglo-Saxon*), Dane

DANTE (*Italian*), enduring

DAPHNIS (*Greek*), laurel

DARCY, from Arcy (French place-name)

DARIUS (*Persian*), possessing wealth

DARRAGH

DARREL(L), DAR(R)YL(L) (*Anglo-Saxon*), beloved

DEAN(E) (*Anglo-Saxon*), valley

DEDWYDD (*Welsh*), happy

DELANO (*French-Latin*), alder-grove

DEMETRIO, DEMETRIUS (*Latin-Greek*), belonging to Demeter (goddess of fruits and crops)

DEMOSTHENES (*Greek*), strength of the people

DENHAM (*Anglo-Saxon*), home in the valley

DENHOLM (*Anglo-Saxon*), island valley

DENMAN (*Anglo-Saxon*), valley dweller

DEODATUS (*Latin*), God-given

DERFAEL (*Welsh*), stubborn metal

DERWENT (*English*), river-name

Derwin (*Anglo-Saxon*), dear friend

Desideratus } (*Latin*), desire
Desiderius }

Despard

Devin (*Irish*), swarthy poet; (*Old French*), outstandingly superior

Dexter (*Latin*), right hand; adroit

Digby (*Anglo-Saxon*), settlement by the ditch or dike

Diggory (*Old French*), lost, gone astray

Dillon (*Celtic*), faithful (?)

Dilwyn (*Welsh*), place-name

Diocles (*Greek*), divine glory

Diomede (*Greek*), divine ruler

Doan(e) (*Anglo-Saxon*), man from the hills

Donat }
Donatus } (*Latin*), given
Donnet }

Donovan (*Irish*), dark-brown

Doran (*Irish*), stranger; exile

Dorian (*Latin-Greek*), man from Doris, in ancient Greece

Doyle (*Irish*), dark stranger

Drogo (*Germanic*), bearer

Drummond

Duan(e) (*Gaelic*), poem, song

Duarte, the Portuguese form of *Edward* (p. 102)

Duff (*Gaelic*), black(-haired)

Durward (*Anglo-Saxon*), door-keeper

Dusty, nickname used with surname Miller

Dyfan (*Welsh*), tribe ruler

Dyfrig (*Welsh*), princely hero

Dynawd (*Welsh*), given

Eben (*Hebrew*), stone

Ebenezer (*Hebrew*), stone of help

Edan (*Celtic*), fire

Edbert (*Anglo-Saxon*), rich-famous

Eden (*Hebrew*), delight

Edlin, diminutive of an Ed- name

Edmead (*Anglo-Saxon*), noble reward

Ednyfed (*Welsh*), bird-bold

Edric (*Anglo-Saxon*), noble rule

Edryd (*Welsh*), restoration

Edsel (*Anglo-Saxon*), rich self

Edwald (*Anglo-Saxon*), rich power

Edwy (*Anglo-Saxon*), rich-beloved

Egerton (*Anglo-Saxon*), fringe of a settlement

Egmont (*Anglo-Saxon*), sword protection

Einar (*Scandinavian*), warrior chief

Eirig (*Welsh*), gay

EIROS (*Welsh*), bright
ELAETH (*Welsh*), intellect
ELDAD (*Hebrew*), beloved of God
ELDON (*Anglo-Saxon*), elf-mound
ELDRED }
ELDRID } (*Anglo-Saxon*), old counsel
ELDWIN (*Anglo-Saxon*), old friend
ELFED (*Welsh*), autumn
ELFYN (*Welsh*), brow-hill
ELGAR (*Anglo-Saxon*), noble spear
ELIAB (*Hebrew*), God is my father
ELIAN (*Latin*), bright
ELIDR (*Welsh*), brass
ELIEZER (*Hebrew*), God is help
ELIPHALET (*Hebrew*), God is deliverance
ELKANAH (*Hebrew*), God has created
ELLARD (*Anglo-Saxon*), noble-hard
ELLERY (*English-Greek*), sweetly-speaking
ELMO (*Italian-Greek*), amiable
ELON (*Hebrew*), terebinth
ELPHIN (*Welsh*), brow-hill
ELRED (*Anglo-Saxon*), noble counsel
ELROY (*Latin*), regal
ELSON (*English-Hebrew*), Eli's son (see p. 105)
ELTON (*Anglo-Saxon*), old settlement
ELVIS (*Scandinavian*), all-wise
EMANUEL: see *Emmanuel*, below
EMBERT (*Germanic*), work-famous
EMIL (*German-Latin*), striver
EMLYN (*Welsh*), either from *Latin* 'Aemilianus,' 'striver,' or *Welsh* 'border(-dweller)'
EMMANUEL (*Hebrew*), God with us
EM(M)ERY }
EMORY } (*Germanic*), work rule
EMYR (*Welsh*), honour
ENAN (*Welsh*), anvil; stability
ENOS (*Hebrew*), man
EPHRAIM (*Hebrew*), very fruitful
ERSKINE
ERWIN (*Anglo-Saxon*), bear-friend
ESDRAS (*Hebrew*), help
ESLAND (*Germanic*), foreign
ETHAN (*Hebrew*), firmness, constancy
ETHELRED (*Anglo-Saxon*), noble advice
ETHELWIN }
ETHELWYN } (*Anglo-Saxon*), noble friend
EUBULE (*Greek*), good counsellor
EUCLID (*Greek*), true glory
EUDES }
EUDO } (*Germanic-Scandinavian*), child
EURFYL (*Welsh*), 'gold'+diminutive
EURWYN (*Welsh*), gold-fair

EUSEBIUS (*Greek*), honourable; pious
EUTYCHES (*Greek*), fortunate
EVANDER (*Greek*), benefactor of men
EVARISTUS (*Greek*), most excellent
EYNON (*Welsh*), anvil; stability
EZEKIEL (*Hebrew*), God strengthens
EZRA (*Hebrew*), help

FARAMOND (*Germanic*), journey protection
FARLEY (*Anglo-Saxon*), fair meadow
FARMAN (*Germanic*), a form of *Faramond*
FARQUHAR (*Gaelic*), friendly man
FARREL(L) (*Celtic*), valorous
FAXON (*Germanic*), long-haired
FAYETTE (*French*), beech-grove
FIDEL (*Latin*), faithful
FILMER
FINLAY (*Gaelic*), fair hero
FIRMIN (*Latin*), strong, steadfast
FITZROY (*English-French*), king's son
FLAVIAN, FLAVIUS (*Latin*), tawny(-haired)
FLETCHER (*Old French*), maker of arrows
FLINT (*English—mainly American*), flint; hard, unyielding
FLOBERT (*Germanic*), glory-famous
FLORENCE, FLORENTIUS, FLORIAN, FLORY, FLURRY (*Latin*), flourishing
FOLKO (*Germanic*), people
FORBES (*Scottish*), place-name
FORD (*English*), ford
FORTUNATUS (*Latin*), prosperous
FOSTER (*Old English*), forester
FRANCHOT, a French diminutive of *Francis* (p. 116)
FREEMAN (*English*), free man
FREER (*Old French*), friar
FRITH (*Anglo-Saxon*), woodland dweller
FULBERT (*Germanic*), very bright
FULCHER, FULCO, FULK(E) (*Germanic*), people
FULVIAN, FULVIUS (*Latin*), tawny

GAD (*Hebrew*), luck, fortune
GALE (*Anglo-Saxon*), pleasant, merry
GAMALIEL (*Hebrew*), benefit of God

GAMBLE
GAMEL } (*Scandinavian*), old

GANYMEDE (*Greek*), rejoicing in manhood

GARBETT (*Germanic*), spear-bold

GARCIA (*Spanish*), fox

GARDNER (*English*), gardener

GARFIELD (*Anglo-Saxon*), spear field

GARLAND (*English-French*), crown; wreath

GARMON (*Welsh-Latin*), German

GAROLD (*Germanic*), spear strength

GARRET(T), an old form of *Gerard* (p. 125)

GARRICK (*Anglo-Saxon*), spear rule

GARTH (*Scandinavian*), enclosure

GASTON (*French-Germanic*), guest

GAYLORD (*French*), merry, jolly (from 'gaillard')

GEMMEL (*Scandinavian*), old

GERAINT (*Welsh-Latin*), old

GERBERT (*Germanic*), spear-bright

GERBOLD (*Germanic*), spear-bold

GERONTIUS (*Latin*), old

GERSHOM (*Hebrew*), bell

GERWYN (*Welsh*), fair love

GETHIN (*Welsh*), dark-skinned

GILDAS (*Latin-Gaelic*), servant of God

GILEAD (*Hebrew*), dweller in Gilead

GILLIAN, a (mainly American) form of *Julian* (p. 165)

GILMOUR (*Gaelic*), servant of (the Virgin) Mary

GILROY (*Gaelic*), servant of the red-haired man

GLANMOR (*Welsh*), seashore

GLAUCUS (*Latin-Greek*), grey-eyed

GLEN(N)
GLYN(NE) } (*Celtic*), valley

GOFANNON (*Welsh*), smith

GOLDWIN
GOLDWYN } (*Anglo-Saxon*), gold-friend

GOMEZ (*Spanish-Germanic*), man

GORONWY (*Welsh*), hero

GOWER (*Welsh*), a district in Wales

GRAEME
GRAHAM
GRAHAME } from Grantham (Lincs.), found in Domesday Book as both *Grantham* and *Graham*; in Scotland it occurs as *Grame* in 1411 and *Graym* in 1467

GRANT (*Old French*), great

GRANVILLE
GRENVILLE } (*Old French*), great town

GRIFFITH (*English-Welsh*), strong warrior

GRISMOND (*Germanic*), Christ's protection

GRISWOLD (*Germanic*), Christ's power

GROVER (*Anglo-Saxon*), grove-dweller

GRUFFYDD (*Welsh*), srrong warrior

GRUGWYN (*Welsh*), white heather

GUNT(H)ER (*Germanic*), bold in battle

GUSTAVE, GUSTAVUS (*Germanic*), counsel (?) staff

GUTHRIE (*Anglo-Saxon*), good rule

GWAEDNERTH (*Welsh*), blood strength

GWERN (*Welsh*), alder-tree

GWESYN (*Welsh*), little lad

GWION (*Welsh*), elf

GWYDDON (*Welsh*), seer

GWYLFAI (*Welsh*), May festival

GWYNFOR (*Welsh*), fair place

GWYNLLYW (*Welsh*), blessed leader

HAAKON (*Scandinavian*), high race

HABAKKUK (*Hebrew*), embrace

HACON (*Scandinavian*), high race

HADLEY (*Anglo-Saxon*), heath meadow

HADWIN (*Anglo-Saxon*), family friend

HAFIZ (*Arabic*), he who remembers

HAGGAI (*Hebrew*), festive

HALBERT, a North Country form of *Albert* (p. 40)

HALDANE, HALDEN (*Anglo-Scandinavian*), half-Dane

HALMAR (*Scandinavian*), helmet glory

HAM (*Hebrew*), warm, hot

HAMAN (*Hebrew*), gracious

HAMILCAR (*Phoenician*), favour of Melkarth (a god)

HAMILTON (*Scottish*), place-name

HAMLET (*English-Germanic*), a form of *Hamon*, 'home'

HAMLIN, HAMLYN (*Germanic*), small homestead

HAMMOND (*Germanic*), home protection

HAMO, HAMON (*Germanic*), home

HANANIAH (*Hebrew*), grace of the Lord

HANNO (*Phoenician*), grace

HARCOURT (*French*), place-name

HARDING, HARDWIN (*Germanic*), intrepid friend

HARDY (*Old French*), brave

HARLAN(D) (*Germanic*), army country

Harley (*Anglo-Saxon*), hare-meadow

Haroun, an Arabic form of the Egyptian name *Aaron*, 'high mountain'

Hartley (*Anglo-Saxon*), hard meadow

Hassan (*Arabic*), handsome

Hayden, Haydn, Haydon (*Celtic*), fire

Haymon (*Germanic*), home

Hazael (*Hebrew*), (whom) God sees

Heath (*English*), heath

Heathcoat (*Anglo-Saxon*), cottage on the heath

Heber (*Hebrew*), associate

Heddle

Heddwyn (*Welsh*), blessed peace

Hedley (*Anglo-Saxon*), grassy meadow

Hefin (*Welsh*), June

Heilyn (*Welsh*), cup-bearer

Helmut (*Germanic*), famous courage

Hengest, Hengist (*Germanic*), stallion

Heracles (*Greek*), glory of Hera (a goddess)

Herbrand (*Germanic*), army sword

Hercules (*Latin-Greek*), glory of Hera (a goddess)

Herman(n) (*Germanic*), army man

Herod (*Middle English*), herald

Herrick (*Germanic*), army rule

Hezekiah (*Hebrew*), strength of the Lord

Hiawatha (*American Indian*), maker of rivers

Hil(de)bert (*Anglo-Saxon*), battle-famous

Hildebrand (*Anglo-Saxon*), battle-sword

Hildred, Hildreth (*Anglo-Saxon*), battle-counsel

Hilkiah (*Hebrew*), my portion is the Lord

Hiram (*Hebrew*), exalted brother

Hobart (*Old English*), a form of *Hubert* (p. 140)

Holden (*Germanic*), gracious

Holger (*Scandinavian*), noble spear

Holly (*English*), plant-name

Holman (*Dutch*), man of the hollow

Homer (*Greek*), pledge (hostage); *or* (*Old French*) maker of helmets; *or* (*Anglo-Saxon*) pool in a hollow

Hope (*English*), hope

HOWELL (*Welsh*), eminent

HUMBERT (*Germanic*), Hun-famous

HYACINTH(US) (*Latin-Greek*), flower-name (in Greek=iris, larkspur, *not* hyacinth)

HYMAN (*Anglo-Saxon*), tall man

HYWEL (*Welsh*), eminent

ICARUS (*Greek*), dedicated to the moon

ICHABOD (*Hebrew*), the glory is departed

IESTIN } (*Welsh*), from *Justinus*
IESTYN } (*Latin* 'justus,' 'just')

IEUAN, a Welsh form of *John* (p. 158)

IGNATIUS (*Latin*), fiery

ILBERT (*Germanic*), battle-famous

ILLTYD (*Welsh*), ruler of a district

IMMANUEL (*Hebrew*), God with us

INIGO (*Welsh-Latin*), a form of *Ignatius*

INIR (*Welsh*), honour

IONWYN (*Welsh*), fair lord

IRA (*Hebrew*), watchful

IRFON (*Welsh*), anointed one

IRVING } (*Anglo-Saxon*),
IRWIN } boar-friend

ISEMBARD (*Germanic*), iron+the folk-name *Bard*

ISHMAEL (*Hebrew*), heard by God

ISIDORE (*Egyptian+Greek*), gift of Isis

ISLWYN (*Welsh*), the bardic name of William Thomas; also a place-name

ISSACHAR (*Hebrew*), hired labourer

ISUMBRAS (*Frankish*), iron arm

ITHAMAR (*Hebrew*), isle of palms (oasis)

ITHEL (*Welsh*), lord-generous

JABEZ (*Hebrew*), causing pain, sorrow

JAIR(US) (*Hebrew*), he will enlighten

JANUS, a Dutch short form of *Adrianus* (p. 36); *or* (*Latin*) opener

JAPHET(H) (*Hebrew*), enlargement

JARED }
JARETH } (*Hebrew*), rose
JARRATH }

JASON (*Greek*), healer

JAY (*English-Old French*), chatterer

JEDIDIAH (*Hebrew*), beloved of the Lord

JEHOSHAPHAT (*Hebrew*), the Lord judges

JEHU (*Hebrew*), he shall live

JENICO, a form of *Ignatius*, 'fiery'

JEPHTHAH (*Hebrew*), he opens

JERMYN (*Old French-Latin*), German
JEROBOAM (*Hebrew*), the people increases
JETHRO (*Hebrew*), pre-eminence
JOAB (*Hebrew*), the Lord is father
JOACHIM (*Hebrew*), the Lord will establish
JOB (*Hebrew*), persecuted
JOEL (*Hebrew*), the Lord is God
JONAH, JONAS (*Hebrew*), dove
JORAH (*Hebrew*), early rain
JORAM (*Hebrew*), the Lord is exalted
JORDAN (*Hebrew*), torrent
JORIS, a Dutch form of *George* (p. 122)
JOSAPHAT (*Hebrew*), the Lord judges
JOSIAH, JOSIAS (*Hebrew*), may the Lord heal
JOTHAM (*Hebrew*), the Lord is perfect
JOVIAN (*Latin*), of Jupiter
JUNIOR (*Latin*), younger
JUNIUS (*Latin*), born in June
JUSTIN, JUSTINIAN, JUSTINUS, JUSTUS (*Latin*), just

KAMPER (*Germanic*), fighter
KANE (*Welsh*), beautiful; *or* (*Manx*) warrior
KEAN(E) (*Manx*), warrior
KEGAN (*Manx*), son of the little poet
KELVIN, KELWIN (*Anglo-Saxon*), ship friend
KENDAL(L) (*Celtic*), chief of the valley
KEN(D)RICK (*Anglo-Saxon*), valiant ruler
KENELM (*Anglo-Saxon*), valiant helmet
KENNARD (*Anglo-Saxon*), valiant protection
KENT (*Celtic*), chief
KENWARD (*Anglo-Saxon*), valiant protection
KENYON
KERRY
KIERAN (*Irish*), black(-haired)
KIM, short for *Kimball*
KIMBALL (*Anglo-Saxon*), kin-bold; *or* (*Welsh*) war-chief
KINGSLEY (*Anglo-Saxon*), king's meadow
KIRBY (*English*), place-name
KITTO, a pet form of *Christopher* (p. 76)
KNUD (*Scandinavian*): see *Canute* (p. 281)

LABAN (*Hebrew*), white
LACHLAN (*Gaelic*), warlike
LADISLAS (*Slavonic*), glory of power
LAIRD (*Scottish*), landed proprietor
LAMECH (*Hebrew*), strong youth
LANDRIC / LANDRY (*Germanic*), land rule
LANGLEY (*Anglo-Saxon*), long meadow
LATIMER (*Old French*), interpreter (literally, Latin-speaker)
LAZARUS (*Greek-Hebrew*), God is help
LEANDER (*Greek*), lion-man
LEAR (*Irish*), calf-keeper
LEGER (*French-German*), people's spear
LEIGH (*Anglo-Saxon*), meadow
LELAND (*Anglo-Saxon*), meadow-land
LEMUEL (*Hebrew*), dedicated to God
LENNOX (*Celtic*), chieftain
LEOFRIC (*Anglo-Saxon*), beloved ruler
LEOFWIN (*Anglo-Saxon*), dear friend
LEONIDAS (*Greek*), son of the lion
LEONTYNE (*Greek*), lion-like
LEROY (*Old French*), the king
LESTER (*Anglo-Saxon*), dyer; *or* place-name (Leicester)
LEVIN (*Anglo-Saxon*), dear friend
LINCOLN (*English*), place-name *or* surname
LINDO (*Germanic*), lime-tree; *or* gentle
LINDSAY / LINDSEY (*English*), place-name
LINWOOD (*English*), lime-wood
LLEUFER (*Welsh*), splendid
LLYWARCH (*Welsh*), ruler-horse
LOFTY, nickname for a tall man
LOGAN
LON, a short form of *Alonso* (p. 276)
LOVE (*English*), love; *or* (*Old French*) wolf
LOVELL (*Old French*), little wolf
LOWELL (*English-French*), wolf-cub
LUBIN (*Anglo-Saxon*), dear friend (=*Leofwin*)
LUCRETIUS (*Latin*), Roman family name
LUDOLF (*Germanic*), famous wolf
LUPIN, a variant of *Lubin* (above)
LYCIDAS (*Greek*), wolf-son
LYCURGUS (*Greek*), work of light
LYLE (*Old French*), island
LYMAN (*Anglo-Saxon*), splendour

LYNDON (*Anglo-Saxon*), lime-grove

LYNFA (*Welsh*), place of the lake

LYNWOOD (*English*), lime-wood

LYSANDER (*Greek*), liberator of men

LYULF, LYULPH (*Anglo-Saxon*), flaming wolf

MABON (*Welsh*), youth

MACARIUS (*Latin-Greek*), blessed

MACHUTUS

MAELGWYN (*Welsh*), metal-chief

MAELRYS (*Welsh*), metal-impetuous

MALACHI, MALACHY (*Hebrew*), messenger

MALCHUS (*Hebrew*), king

MALDWYN (*Welsh*), place-name (=Montgomery)

MALISE (*Gaelic*), servant of Jesus

MAL(L)ORY (*Old French*), unfortunate

MALVIN (*Gaelic*), smooth brow

MANASSEH, MANASSES (*Hebrew*), causing forgetfulness

MANDEL (*Germanic*), almond

MANDER (*Old French*), stable-lad

MANFRED (*Germanic*), man peace

MANLEY (*Old English*), manly

MANOAH (*Hebrew*), repose

MANSEL(L) (*Welsh*), Norman place-name

MANUEL (*Hebrew*), a form of *Emmanuel*, 'God with us'

MANVILLE (*French*), place-name

MARCH (*English*), boundary; *or* born in March

MARIO(N), MARIUS (*Latin*), dedicated to Mary, the Blessed Virgin

MARLON

MARLOW

MARLY (*French*), place-name

MARMION (*Anglo-Saxon*), lake-dweller

MARSHAL(L) (*Old French-Germanic*), farrier

MARTIAL (*Latin*), warlike

MATH (*Welsh*), treasure

MAUGER (*Old French-Germanic*), work-spear

MAYNARD (*Germanic*), strong-valiant

MEDWIN (*Anglo-Saxon*), worthy friend

MEILYR (*Welsh*), man of iron

MEIRION (*Welsh*), place-name

MELMOTH (*Celtic*), servant of Math (a Celtic demi-god)

MELVILLE, MELVIN (*Scottish and French*) place-names

MERRELL, MERRILL (*Welsh and Irish*), son of Muriel

MERTON (*Anglo-Saxon*), sea-dweller; lake-dweller

MERWIN, MERWYN (*Anglo-Saxon*), famous friend

MESHULLAM (*Hebrew*), reward

MEYER (*Germanic*), steward

MILBURN (*Anglo-Saxon*), mill-stream

MILITIADES (*Greek*), bright complexion

MILLARD (*Anglo-Saxon*), miller; mill-keeper

MILTON (*Anglo-Saxon*), mill enclosure

MITCHELL, a form of *Michael* (p. 195)

MODRED (*Anglo-Saxon*), brave adviser

MOELWYN (*Welsh*), fair-head

MONRO(E) (*Gaelic*), man from the river Roe, in Derry, Ireland

MORDECAI (*Babylonian*), worshipper of Marduk (a god of Babylon)

MORDEYRN (*Welsh*), great monarch

MORSE (*English*), a form of *Maurice* (p. 191)

MORTON (*Anglo-Saxon*), moor village

MORYS (*Welsh*), a form of *Maurice* (p. 191)

MOSTYN (*Welsh*), field fortress

MUNRO(E): see *Monro(e)*

MURPHY (*Irish*), sea-warrior

MYRON (*Greek*), fragrant

NAAMAN (*Hebrew*), pleasantness; darling

NAHUM (*Hebrew*), comforter; compassionate

NAPOLEON (*Greek*), of the new city

NARCISSUS (*Greek*), daffodil

NEHEMIAH (*Hebrew*), consolation of the Lord

NENNOG (*Welsh*), heavenly one

NEOT (*Low Latin*), novice

NESTOR (*Greek*), remembrancer; wise old man

NETIS (*American Indian*), trusted friend

NEWEL(L), a form of *Noel* (p. 207)

NEWTON (*Anglo-Saxon*), new town

NICANDER (*Greek*), victory man

NICANOR (*Greek*), victorious man

NICO (*Greek*), victory

NICOMEDE (*Greek*), victorious ruler

NIGER (*Latin*), black

Nils (*Scandinavian*), a form of *Niel* (p. 206)

Ninian (*Celtic-Latin*), a corruption of *Vivian* (p. 264)

Noah (*Hebrew*), repose

Nobby, nickname associated with surname Clark (from 'noble')

Nolan(d) (*Irish*), noble, famous

Norbert (*Germanic*), famous in the North

Norris (*Anglo-French*), northerner

Norval (*Old French*), northern valley

Norwood (*Anglo-Saxon*), north wood

Oakley (*Anglo-Saxon*), oak-meadow

Obadiah (*Hebrew*), servant of the Lord

Obed (*Hebrew*), servant; serving

Odell (*Anglo-Saxon*), valley-dweller

Odo (*Germanic*), wealth

Offa

Ogden (*Anglo-Saxon*), oak-valley

Ogier (*Old French-Germanic*), wealth-spear

Oman (*Scandinavian*), high protector

Omar (*Arabic*), eloquent

Onesimus (*Greek*), useful, beneficial

Onllwyn (*Welsh*), ash-grove

Oran (*Irish*), wren (often used in Ireland for *Adrian*, p. 36)

Original (*English-Latin*), first-born

Orsino (*Latin*), little bear

Orval, Orvil(le) (*French*), place-names

Oswin (*Anglo-Saxon*), divine friend

Othniel

Otho, Otto (*Germanic*), wealth

Otis (*Greek*), keen of hearing

Otway

Padarn (*Welsh*), fatherly

Palmer (*English*), pilgrim

Pancras (*Greek*), all strength

Parker (*English*), dweller near the enclosed woodland

Parry (*Welsh*), son of *Harry* (p. 135)

Patroclus (*Greek*), glory of his father

Payton (*Anglo-Saxon*), (St) Patrick's town

Pelham (*Anglo-Saxon*), Pella's settlement

Penrod (*Welsh*), top of the ford

PENROSE (*English*), place-name
PENWYN (*Welsh*), fair-head
PEREGRINE (*Latin*), pilgrim
PERSEUS (*Greek*), destroyer
PETROCK
PHANUEL (*Hebrew*), countenance of God
PHARAMOND (*Germanic*), journey protection
PHELAN (*Irish*), wolf
PHILANDER (*Greek*), lover of men
PHILARET (*Greek*), lover of virtue
PHILEMON (*Greek*), kiss
PHILETAS, PHILETUS (*Greek*), beloved
PHILIBERT (*Germanic*), very bright
PHILOPATER (*Greek*), lover of his father
PHINEAS (*Hebrew*), mouth of brass
PHOEBUS (*Greek*), the shining one
PILGRIM (*English*), pilgrim
PIRAN, a variant of *Kieran* (p. 291)
PIUS (*Latin*), dutiful
PLANTAGENET (*French*), the broom plant (emblem of Geoffrey of Anjou)
PLATO (*Greek*), broad
POLYCARP (*Greek*), fruitful
POMEROY (*Old French*), apple-orchard
POMPEY (*Latin*), of Pompeii
POST(H)UMUS (*Latin*), born after his father's death
POWYS (*Welsh*), man from Powis, an ancient Welsh region
PRENTICE, PRENTISS (*English*), apprentice
PRESCOTT (*Anglo-Saxon*), priest's home
PRESTON (*Anglo-Saxon*), priest's village
PROBUS (*Latin*), honest
PROSPER, PROSPERO (*Latin*), prosperous
PUNCH, an English diminutive of the Italian *Punchinello*
PWYLL (*Welsh*), prudence

QUERON
QUILLION (*Old French*), sword-hilt
QUINCY (*French*), place-name
QUINN (*Irish*), counsel

RADCLIFF(E) (*Anglo-Saxon*), red cliff
RADFORD (*Anglo-Saxon*), reedy ford
RALEIGH
RALSTON
RAMSAY, RAMSEY (*Scandinavian*), rams' island

RANGER (*English*), rover; forest officer
RAYNER (*Germanic*), counsel army
REDWALD (*Anglo-Saxon*), counsel power
REMI(GIUS) } (*Latin*), oarsman
REMY }
RENATUS (*Latin*), born again
RENÉ (*French-Latin*), born again
RENFRED (*Germanic*), might peace
REUBEN (*Hebrew*), behold, a son
RHAIN (*Welsh*), lance
RHIDIAN (*Welsh*), dweller by the ford
RHONWEN (*Welsh*), tall, slender and fair
RHUN (*Welsh*), grand
RHYDWYN (*Welsh*), dweller by the white ford
ROCH(US) (*Germanic*), repose
ROMEO (*Latin*), Roman
ROMUALD (*Germanic*), fame power
ROMULUS (*Latin*), Roman
ROMWALD (*Germanic*), fame power
RONAN
ROSCOE (*Germanic*), deer-park
ROSS (*Germanic*), fame
ROWAN
ROYAL (*English*), royal
RUBE, a pet form of *Reuben* (*Hebrew*), 'behold, a son'
RUDYARD (*English*), place-name
RUSS (*Anglo-French*), red, russet
RUTHERFORD (*English*), place-name

SABINE (*Latin*), a tribal name
SACHEVERELL (*Old French*), place-name (='kid's leap')
SADOC (*Hebrew*), sacred
SALADIN (*Arabic*), goodness of the faith
SALOMON (*Hebrew*), peaceful
SALVATOR (*Latin*), saviour
SAMSON (*Hebrew*), sun-like
SANDFORD (*Anglo-Saxon*), sandy ford
SAWYER (*English*), woodcutter
SAXON (*Anglo-Saxon*), short-sword warrior
SCHOLEM (*Hebrew*), peace
SCHUYLER (*Dutch*), shelterer
SCOTT (*Anglo-Saxon*), a Scot
SEARLE (*Germanic*), armour
SEBA (*Greek*), venerable
SEBAG
SEBALD (*Anglo-Saxon*), victory-bold
SEBERT (*Anglo-Saxon*), victory-famous
SEDGWICK (*Anglo-Saxon*), sedgy (reedy) village
SEFTON (*English*), place-name

SELBY (*English*), place-name (= 'seal-town')

SELWYN (*Anglo-Saxon*), blessed friend

SENIOR (*Latin*), older

SERLE (*Germanic*), armour

SETH (*Hebrew*), compensation

SETON (*English*), place-name

SEWARD (*Anglo-Saxon*), victory protection

SEWELL (*Anglo-Saxon*), victory rule

SHALLUM (*Hebrew*), perfect

SHEM (*Hebrew*), name; renown

SHERLOCK (*Middle English*), cropped head

SHERMAN (*Middle English*), shearer

SHERWIN (*Middle English*), cut-wind (*i.e.*, a fast runner)

SHOLTO (*Gaelic*), sower

SIEGFRIED (*Germanic*), victory peace

SIG(E)BERT (*Germanic*), victory-famous

SIGFRID, a form of *Siegfried*

SIGHELM (*Germanic*), victory helmet

SIGISMUND, SIGMUND (*Germanic*), victory protection

SIGURD (*Germanic*), victory defence

SIGWALD (*Germanic*), victory power

SIWARD (*Anglo-Saxon*), victory defence

SOCRATES (*Greek*), self-restrained

SOLOMON (*Hebrew*), peaceful

SOLON (*Greek*), grave

SOMERSET (*English*), place-name

SOPHOCLES (*Greek*), glory of wisdom

SPIKE, SPIK(E)Y: nicknames for a tall, thin man or one with close-cropped hair

SPUD, nickname used with surname Murphy

STAFFORD (*English*), place-name

STANFIELD (*Anglo-Saxon*), stony field

STANFORD (*Anglo-Saxon*), stony ford

STANTON (*Anglo-Saxon*), stone village

STIRLING (*Scottish*), place-name (='easterling'—*i.e.*, man from the Baltic [East Sea])

STRUAN

SULGWYN (*Welsh*), Whitsun

SULIEN (*Welsh*), sun-born

SULWYN (*Welsh*), sun-fair

SUMNER, SUMNOR (*English*), summoner, court-officer

SWEYN (*Anglo-Saxon*), servant; swineherd

SWITHIN, SWITHUN (*Anglo-Saxon*), strong

SYLGWYN (*Welsh*), Whitsun

TALBOT (*Old French*), cleave-faggot

TALFRYN (*Welsh*), brow of the hill

TALIESIN (*Welsh*), radiant brow

TAMAR (*Hebrew*), palm-tree

TANCRED (*Germanic*), thought advice

TANGWYN (*Welsh*), blessed peace

TAYLOR (*English*), cutter of cloth

TEAGUE (*Irish*), poet

TECWYN (*Welsh*), fair and white

TEGYD (*Welsh*), beautiful

THANE (*Anglo-Saxon*), follower, courtier

THEODOSIUS (*Greek*), God-given

THERON (*Greek*), hunter

THORGEIR (*Scandinavian*), Thor's hawk

THORKIL (*Scandinavian*), Thor's cauldron

THORNTON (*Anglo-Saxon*), thorny enclosure

THOROLD, THORWALD (*Scandinavian*), might of Thor

THORP(E) (*Anglo-Saxon*), village

TITCH, nickname for a small man (from surname of a dwarf comedian, 'Little Titch')

TITUS (*Latin-Greek*), honoured

TORQUIL (*Scandinavian*), Thor's cauldron

TOSTIG (*Welsh*), sharp, severe

TRAC(E)Y (*French*), place-name

TRAHAIARN, TRAHERN(E) (*Welsh*), as long-lived as iron

TRAVERS, TRAVIS (*French*), crossroads

TRELAWN(E)Y (*Cornish*), place-name (='church town')

TUDWAL (*Welsh*), tribe-wall

TULLIUS, TULLY (*Latin*), Roman family name

TUNSTAN (*Anglo-Saxon*), town stone

TUNSTELL (*Anglo-Saxon*), town place

UCHTRED (*Anglo-Saxon*), twilight counsel

UFFA

UGHTRED, a form of *Uchtred*

ULRIC(K) (*Anglo-Saxon*), wolf ruler

UPTON (*Anglo-Saxon*), town on the heights

URBAN (*Latin*), townsman

URIAH (*Hebrew*), fire of the Lord
URIEL (*Hebrew*), fire of God
URIEN (*Welsh*), town-born
UZZIAH (*Hebrew*), the Lord is strong

VALERIAN / VALERIUS } (*Latin*), healthy
VALMOND (*Germanic*), power protection
VAUGHAN (*English-Welsh*), little
VERE (*French*), place-name
VERNON (*French*), place-name
VIBERT (*Anglo-Saxon*), battle-famous
VIRGIL (*Latin*), flourishing
VITAL(IS) (*Latin*), lively
VLADIMIR (*Russian*), ruling the world
VYCHAN (*Welsh*), little

WADE (*Anglo-Saxon*), dweller by the ford
WADSWORTH (*English*), place-name
WALCOT(T) (*Anglo-Saxon*), walled cottage
WALDEMAR (*Germanic*), power glory
WALDEVE (*Anglo-Saxon*), rule thief
WALDO (*Germanic*), power
WALFORD (*Old English*), place-name (= ford by the bank)
WALMAR / WALMER } (*Germanic*), power glory
WALMUND (*Germanic*), power protection
WALSTAN (*Anglo-Saxon*), wall-stone, corner-stone
WALTHEOF (*Anglo-Saxon*), rule thief
WARD (*Germanic*), protection
WARE (*Anglo-Saxon*), prudent; *or* (*Scandinavian*) born in spring-time
WARWICK (*English*), place-name
WAYLAND, the Saxon smith-god
WAYNE (*Old English*), wain-wright; dweller at the sign of the wain (waggon)
WELLAND, a variant of *Wayland* (above)
WENDELL
WERN(H)ER, German form of *Warren* (p. 267)
WESLEY (*Anglo-Saxon*), west meadow
WHITNEY (*English*), place-name
WIGRAM (*Anglo-Saxon*), battle raven
WILBERT (*Germanic*), will-bright
WILDFORD / WILFORD } (*Anglo-Saxon*), wild ford

WILDON (*Anglo-Saxon*), curving valley

WILLIS (*English*), son of Will(iam) (p. 270)

WILLOUGHBY (*English*), place-name

WILMAR, WILMER (*Germanic*), will-fame

WILPERT (*Germanic*), will-bright

WIMUND (*Anglo-Saxon*), battle protection

WINDSOR (*English*), place-name

WINFRED, WINFRID (*Anglo-Saxon*), friend peace

WINTHROP (*Anglo-Saxon*), friend village

WINWOOD (*Anglo-Saxon*), friend wood

WOLDEMAR (*Germanic*), power fame

WOODROW (*Anglo-Saxon*), dweller in the house in the row by the wood

WORTH (*English*), esteem

WULFRIC (*Anglo-Saxon*), wolf rule

WULFSTAN (*Anglo-Saxon*), wolf stone

WYATT (*Middle English*), son of *Guy* (p. 131)

WYBERT (*Anglo-Saxon*), battle-famous

WYNDHAM (*Anglo-Saxon*), windy settlement

WYNFORD (*Old English*), place-name

WYSTAN (*Anglo-Saxon*), battle stone

XENOPHON (*Greek*), strange-sounding

YARDLEY (*Anglo-Saxon*), owner of a thirty-acre meadow

YEO

YESTIN (*Welsh*), from *Justinus* (*Latin* 'justus,' 'just')

YNYR (*Welsh*), honour

ZADOC, ZADOK (*Hebrew*), just

ZEBADIAH, ZEBEDEE (*Hebrew*), gift of the Lord

ZEDEKIAH (*Hebrew*), the Lord is righteous

ZEKE (*Hebrew*), pet form of *Ezekiel*, 'God strengthens,' or of *Hezekiah*, 'strength of the Lord'

ZENO (*Greek*), stranger

ZEPHANIAH (*Hebrew*), whom the Lord has hidden

LIST OF REFERENCE BOOKS USED

BARING-GOULD, S.: *The Lives of the Saints* (London, 1897).
BENET, W. R.: *The Reader's Encyclopedia* (London, 3rd ed., 1956).
BLAKENEY, E. H. (ed.): *A Smaller Classical Dictionary* (London, 1920).
BUTLER, A.: *Lives of the Saints* (1756–59; rev. ed. by H. Thurston and D. Attwater, London, 1956).
CAMDEN, W.: *Remains Concerning Britain* (London, 7th ed., 1674).
CAMPBELL THOMSON, C.: *Names for Every Child* (London, 1947).
DAUZAT, A.: *Les Noms de Personnes* (Paris, 1956).
DAVIES, T. R.: *A Book of Welsh Names* (London, 1952).
GRAVES, R.: *The Greek Myths* (Penguin Books, 1955).
HARVEY, SIR P.: *Oxford Companion to English Literature* (Oxford, 1946).
HASTINGS, J. (ed.): *A Dictionary of the Bible* (Edinburgh, 1900).
LANGER, W. L.: *An Encyclopedia of World History* (London, 1956).
MENCKEN, H. L.: *The American Language* (New York, 1936).
MOODY, S.: *What is Your Name?* (London, 1863).
PARTRIDGE, E.: *Name This Child* (London, 2nd ed., 1938).
VORAGINE, JACOBUS DE: *The Golden Legend* (London, 1934).
WEEKLEY, E.: *Jack and Jill* (London, 1939).
WELLS, E.: *What to name the Baby* (*A Treasury of Names*) (Garden City Books, New York, 1953).
WITHYCOMBE, E. G.: *The Oxford Dictionary of English Christian Names* (Oxford, 2nd ed., 1959).
WOULFE, P.: *Irish Names and Surnames* (Dublin, 1923).
YONGE, C. M.: *History of Christian Names* (London, 2nd ed., 1884).
The Bible: Authorized Version.
The Book of Common Prayer, Deposited Book (1928).
Chambers's Biographical Dictionary (Edinburgh, 1953).
The Dictionary of National Biography.
The Larousse Encyclopedia of Mythology (London, 1959).
Missale Romanum (Authorized edition, 1951).
Notes and Queries, passim.
Who's Who.